Feeling Better

Feeling Better

BEAT DEPRESSION and IMPROVE YOUR
RELATIONSHIPS with INTERPERSONAL
PSYCHOTHERAPY

CINDY GOODMAN STULBERG, DCS, CPsych,
and RONALD J. FREY, PhD, CPsych,
with JENNIFER DAWSON

New World Library
Novato, California

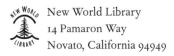 New World Library
14 Pamaron Way
Novato, California 94949

Text design by Tona Pearce Myers

Library of Congress Cataloging-in-Publication Data
Names: Stulberg, Cindy Goodman, date, author.
Title: Feeling better : beat depression and improve your relationships with interpersonal
    psychotherapy / Cindy Goodman Stulberg, DCS, CPsych, and Ronald J. Frey,
    PhD, CPsych.
Description: Novato, California : New World Library, [2018] | Includes index.
Identifiers: LCCN 2018023097 (print) | LCCN 2018036476 (ebook) | ISBN
    9781608685691 (ebook) | ISBN 9781608685684 (alk. paper) | ISBN
    978160868569-1 (ebook)
Subjects: LCSH: Interpersonal psychotherapy. | Interpersonal relations. | Self-esteem.
Classification: LCC RC489.I55 (ebook) | LCC RC489.I55 S88 2018 (print) | DDC
    616.89/14—dc23
LC record available at https://lccn.loc.gov/2018023097

First printing, November 2018
ISBN 978-1-60868-568-4
Ebook ISBN 978-1-60868-569-1

Printed in the USA on 30% postconsumer-waste recycled paper

 New World Library is proud to be a Gold Certified Environmentally Responsible Publisher. Publisher certification awarded by Green Press Initiative.
www.greenpressinitiative.org

10   9   8   7   6   5   4   3   2   1

Contents

Get Ready to Feel Better

Cindy's true confession: I'm one of those people who skips introductions. I'm busy. Just get me to the good stuff. This is your journey, so skip to Week 1 if you like. But if you're interested in knowing more about Ron and me, the approach that we use, and the four main individuals we'll follow over the next twelve weeks, read on.

We want to let you in on a secret. Your relationships hold the key to your happiness.

Yup, your relationships. Not your bank account, your job, a Caribbean vacation, having a baby, not having a baby, getting a promotion, building your dream kitchen, or losing ten pounds. Those things may give you a momentary boost. But it's your relationships with your friends, family, spouse, girlfriend, boyfriend, coworkers, and neighbors — even your hairdresser — that will determine whether you're happy for the long term.

The flip side is also true. Your relationships hold the key to your unhappiness. It's not your inflexible thinking, negative self-talk, perfectionism, inability to bounce back, or wonky brain chemistry. These may contribute to the fact that you feel lousy and depressed. But take a look at the important people in your life — the ones you spend the most time with and the ones who have the greatest influence on you. I bet there are one or two relationships that make you feel stressed, worried, frustrated, inadequate, angry, and basically like crap.

We're going to give you the tools and techniques to get the most from your supportive relationships, improve your challenging ones, and, if necessary, make the tough decision to end a relationship that's holding you back from feeling better.

By the end of this book, you'll know how to communicate effectively; recognize and modify your interpersonal style; set and achieve goals; make constructive decisions; deal with the difficult people in your life; identify your strongest allies and supporters; explore, clarify, and understand expectations; and determine who you want to connect with — and who you don't.

You can apply your new skills to prevent divorce, raise healthy children, deal with overeating, cope with a breakup, stop choosing the wrong partner, earn employee of the month, avoid stress-related illnesses, talk with your teenager, "consciously uncouple" from your spouse, survive holiday dinners with your in-laws, and more.

PEP TALK: *Connect with people, share feelings, embrace change, and put less pressure on yourself — we'll help you do all four, starting now!*

It works fast — people have made real improvements in their lives in as little as eight weeks. And you don't need to be diagnosed with depression to benefit.

So what's the secret?

It's a research-proven approach called *interpersonal psychotherapy*, or *IPT*. IPT is an action-oriented treatment that teaches skills, step by step, to improve relationships and alleviate depression.

IPT was developed by Dr. Myrna Weissman and her husband, Dr. Gerald Klerman, in the 1970s. More than 250 studies have shown that IPT is an effective way to treat a number of mood disorders, used with medication or on its own. Today, IPT is recognized as a gold-standard, evidence-based psychotherapy by the American and Canadian Psychiatric Associations, the American and Canadian Psychological Associations, the

UK's National Institute for Health and Care Excellence, and the international organization Cochrane. IPT has been chosen by the World Health Organization as one of only two psychotherapies to be shared worldwide.

We want you to give IPT a try. And we want to be your coaches and cheerleaders, sharing helpful advice and words of encouragement every step of the way.

Meet Your Coaches

Imagine a grandma who watches *Orange Is the New Black*, and you've got me, Cindy Stulberg. Ron says I'm the bossy one. I'm also the one who gets stuff done — which is why I'm the one who does most of the talking in this book! I believe that friends and family are the most important things in life, so it's not surprising that I liked IPT's emphasis on relationships right from the start. I became a real fan when I completed my training and started using it with clients — because it works. Fast. I've been using IPT for more than twenty years, specializing in helping adults and teens cope with depression and eating disorders. When the clinicians we train want to take their IPT skills even further, I'm the one who supervises their work.

I like to say Ron is the younger, cuter one. His work has taken him into prisons, above the Arctic Circle, and even to Hollywood. He discovered IPT when he was a grad student. Everyone was training in cognitive behavioral therapy (you might know it as CBT), but Ron thought focusing on a client's bad thoughts and inflexible thinking was a lot like blaming the victim. IPT was a refreshing change. Instead of keeping tedious thought journals, IPT encourages people to look outward and engage with others as a way to feel better. IPT made sense to Ron. After all, who wouldn't rather hang out than do homework?

Together, we founded an institute dedicated exclusively to IPT. We had been looking for a good book to recommend to clients for a long time, but there was nothing on the shelves. So we decided to write it ourselves.

Twelve Weeks to Feeling Better — the Natural Way

For years, the first line of defense for depression has been pharmaceuticals, but we believe people can be taught the skills to help themselves feel better — no pills required.

That's a good thing, since more and more people are looking for ways to feel better without using antidepressants; they want to deal with the issues contributing to their unhappiness, not just rely on drugs to alleviate the symptoms. Some don't like the side effects of prescriptions. If women are pregnant or nursing, they may worry about the impact of pharmaceuticals on their babies. For others it's a point of pride: they want to feel better on their own.

Some people have tried antidepressants, but have noticed they aren't working as well as they used to. Or they may be sleeping and eating better on the pills, but are still fighting with the important people in their lives. Perhaps they were feeling better using medication, but then relapsed.

If you're suffering from depression, we can help you recover without a trip to the drugstore. And if you're currently taking antidepressants, we can help you get the most from your prescription, using tools and techniques that will help you feel better because they improve your relationships. The good news? You just might not need that next refill.

We've divided the book into weeks, rather than chapters, so we're being true to IPT, which is a short-term therapy that asks people to work on particular tasks in a particular order over eight to twelve sessions. Think of it as making an appointment with yourself every week to work on feeling better — like therapy, only cheaper! Ultimately, though, the pacing is up to you.

Each week we introduce a new topic, teach new skills, and offer tools and resources to help you practice. Look for the "Try This" and "Pep Talk" callouts if you need quick words of wisdom, friendly reminders, and on-the-go encouragement. Brief anecdotes about "clients" will help you apply the approaches to real life (though the anecdotes and the names we've given the "clients" have been made up). To-do lists will help you stay on track. The "Guy Talk" sidebars, written by Ron, address issues unique to men (which we think women will like to read too).

In Week 1, we help you understand that depression is an illness as legitimate as any physical ailment and give you permission to take time off from some of your regular responsibilities to get better.

In Week 2 you'll draw your social circle — identifying the relationships that help and the ones that hurt — and then explore a few of the stressful ones in detail.

Week 3 is all about feelings and their connection to our relationships and our behavior. You'll get information and tools to help you express and manage your feelings in ways that will improve your relationships and your mood.

TRY THIS: *Want to know what you're getting yourself into? Skim the book once; then read it week by week and complete the exercises the second time through.*

Week 4 is where we talk about the four problem areas that people experience when they feel down, depressed, and lousy and help you pick one to focus on.

In Week 5 we offer step-by-step instructions for setting a "smart" goal. Case examples help you make your goal the smartest it can be.

You can feel free to vent in Week 6. What situation or encounter bothered you the most last week? How did you feel about it? How did you handle it? By the end of the chapter, you'll be thinking about what you might like to change.

In Week 7, it's time to go back to the relationship inventory you created in Week 2. We help you identify your "whos" — the people you can count on when times get tough — and coach you to use these people effectively.

PEP TALK: *People of all ages and backgrounds use these strategies to feel better, regardless of their challenges. Let's do this — together!*

In Week 8, we help you choose something to change, offering suggestions specific to your particular problem area and helping you cope with the fear of the unknown.

Week 9 is all about expectations — how to uncover yours and understand someone else's — so you can close the expectation gap that often contributes to depression. We teach you a helpful exercise for couples that Ron brilliantly calls the Matrix (Keanu Reeves impression not required).

Week 10 gives you tips and examples for practicing an important conversation or encounter. What's the best outcome? The worst? The most realistic? We'll help you rehearse all three.

In Week 11, we cheer you on from the sidelines while you have a conversation or experience that's important to achieving your goal.

Week 12 is the happy ending. We help you celebrate your successes, share them with others, and apply what you've learned to other areas of your life.

Introducing Kate, Ana, John, and Becky

The star of this book is you, and we've invented a supporting cast of four characters, drawn from more than three decades of work with clients, to help you shine. Our hope is that you'll identify with one individual character, but see aspects of your struggles in all of them, learning each week as they grapple with the concepts, try out the tools, experience setbacks, and celebrate accomplishments.

Meet Kate, a forty-seven-year-old school administrator whose increasingly clingy and controlling husband is making her wonder whose life she's leading — hers or his. He had been so excited about his retirement from the police force, but six months into his freedom Kate feels as though she's in prison. She's exhausted from her husband's attempts to program her time and embarrassed by his stalker-like behavior when she goes out on her own. "I married you in sickness and health," she tells him one night. "But not for breakfast, lunch, and dinner."

Ana is a new mom. She's having a hard time accepting that having a baby isn't like the posts she reads on Facebook, and she misses her old life: the career she worked so hard to build, her prepregnancy body, time with her husband, going out for Sunday brunch with her girlfriends, and eight hours of uninterrupted sleep. She's ashamed of her feelings — Ana and her husband tried for more than a year to get pregnant, and she feels she should be so happy and grateful to have a healthy, beautiful baby girl. But the reality is that Ana spends every day waffling between resentment and guilt, crying about how much she's lost and then crying about her inadequacy as a mother. Her husband comes home from work every day — late — and all she wants to do is hand her daughter to him and hide.

John has lived his whole life as the black sheep of his family. He's the one who, at forty, still lives at home with his mom and dad, doesn't have friends, and works as a delivery guy for a Chinese restaurant. All John wants is a little respect, but people are such jackasses, judging him, treating him badly, and refusing to play by the rules. He'd like to have a girlfriend, a buddy to hang out with, and civil relationships with his co-workers. But everyone turns out to be a disappointment. Why bother?

When her brother died from cancer a year ago, twenty-three-year-old Becky was devastated. She had put her life on hold to be his only caregiver and in the process lost touch with her friends and fell out of step with her peers. Her days as an art student seem so long ago that it feels as if it was someone else's work that was nominated for an award last year. And was that really her, that person who loved shopping, turned her hair every color of the rainbow, and never missed a chance to hit the clubs? Becky hasn't had her hair cut for ages. And her computer might as well be her best friend; they spend so much time together.

Spoiler alert: We helped Kate and her husband see each other's side. We helped Ana embrace a new role in life. We helped John see in shades of gray. We helped Becky find life after death. We helped all four deal with their depression. And we can't wait to help you too. Get ready to feel better.

GUY TALK: THE F-WORD

Hi, guys (and gals). I'm Dr. Ron Frey, and Guy Talk is the place where I help men — and the women who love them — make sense of the steps and strategies we present on these pages.

Here's a friendly heads-up. A lot of what we'll do together comes down to the F-word.

You know. *Feelings.*

For many guys, feelings are a foreign language. We'd rather drink, smoke, punch, run, shoot hoops, or yell than say we're scared, lonely, angry, jealous, frustrated, disappointed, or hurt. We're doers, not talkers. And those of us who like to talk usually steer clear of the personal stuff. But to feel better, men need to be able to recognize and talk about their feelings.

Many of my clients are male police officers and soldiers. They're trained to deal with other people's problems, not their own, and they work in very hierarchical, structured, controlled environments. Orders are issued. Rules are followed. Situations — and people — are either right or wrong. Bad days are choked down. So it's no wonder that when a cop's marriage is falling apart, his drinking is getting out of hand, or he's arguing with his kids, he's at a loss.

One police officer laid it on the line during our first session. "Dr. Frey," he said, breaking a silence that was clearly awkward for him. "I don't normally talk about myself. When I'm supposed to say something, you'll have to tell me."

Not only did he not know how to talk about emotions; he needed a commanding officer to give the order. Call me Captain Feelings.

Another of my clients had spent his last twelve years drinking and getting high every weekend, sometimes at the bar his band was playing at, other times on his back deck with friends. One morning he woke up in a strange hotel room with absolutely no memory of how he got there. It scared the heck out of him. "I've been using booze and coke to numb my feelings for too long, Dr. Frey," he told me. "There's a lot of stuff I don't know how to talk about. It's time I learned how."

Look for me in every chapter. I'll help guys learn this new language of feelings. And I'll help gals understand what the men in their lives are going through — and how they can help.

WEEK

1

What If You Had a
Broken Leg Instead?

*Our first step is to discover what depression is — and what it isn't.
(You might be surprised!) You'll learn why you may need to take a
temporary break from some of your activities and how to talk to the
important people in your life about what you're going through.*

A woman's life had been turned upside down by a car accident. She
was coping with a lot of pain, had given up her successful business,
and was struggling with depression.

"Who have you talked to about what you're going through?" Ron
asked her.

"No one," she answered. "I don't want to burden my friends. If they
saw me like this, they'd be shocked. And I'd be embarrassed. I'll just wait
until I feel better, and then I'll talk to them."

"What if you broke your leg instead?" Ron asked. "Would you still go
out for coffee with them?"

"Sure," she said.

"How would it make you feel if you went out for coffee with them
even though you had a broken leg?"

"It would feel awkward and like a hassle and a little painful, but I'd
probably feel better for having seen my friends," she said.

"And how would you feel if you didn't go out?" Ron asked.

"If I stopped socializing, I'd feel isolated and lonely," she said. "It'd be depressing."

Bingo. If we don't see our friends and family, we feel worse. If we do see them, we feel better.

But Ron wasn't done. "And what if you did go out? How do you think your friends would feel if they saw you with a broken leg?" he asked.

"They'd probably be happy to see me," she answered. "It wouldn't bother them that I had a broken leg."

"So how is that different from going to see your friends when you're feeling depressed?" Ron asked. "They'll be happy to see you, and you'll feel better — so everybody wins. But if you don't go out to see your friends, you'll feel socially isolated and they'll miss you. Everybody loses."

TRY THIS: *Use questions to explore how you're feeling. Ask them of yourself, or get a friend to help you!*

That's why we need to look at our mood difficulties as if we had a broken leg — so everybody wins.

It's hard to do. When we have a broken leg, people line up to sign our cast, but when we're depressed, there's no cast to sign — so we sign out of our social lives, ashamed and embarrassed by our invisible illness. It's way better to take a risk, reach out, and break the silence. And we'll show you how.

Diagnosis: Depression

You don't have to be diagnosed with depression to benefit from the strategies we'll teach you. If you feel bad or down or stressed, we can help you feel better.

Understanding what depression is — and what it isn't — is important, though. Depression is a highly treatable medical illness that negatively impacts how we feel, think, and act. It comes in all different shapes and sizes. Sometimes it's short-lived (though according to most authorities on mental health, it always lasts more than two weeks). Sometimes it's mild. Other times it's severe.

Sadness is part of being depressed. So is losing interest in things that used to get you jazzed. But there's also a whole list of symptoms that people don't usually associate with depression: trouble concentrating, indecision, loss of appetite, irritability, difficulty sleep-ing, and even body aches and pains with no apparent physical cause.

One in six people will experience depression at some point, and the numbers are even higher for women. In fact, some studies show that one-third of women will experience a major depressive episode during their lifetime. So even if you feel alone, you definitely aren't. Half of those who have one episode of depression will have another if they don't get treatment. Eighty percent of those who've had two episodes without treatment will have a third.

PEP TALK: *Depression is a highly treatable medical illness. Yes, highly treatable.*

Those last two stats aren't meant to make you feel worse. Quite the op-posite. Studies have shown that the techniques we'll teach you, which are based on the treatment model called interpersonal psychotherapy (IPT), can help you avoid experiencing this soul-crushing ill-ness again.

Depression goes by many labels: disruptive mood dysregulation disorder, major depressive disorder, dys-thymia, premenstrual dysphoric disorder, persistent depressive disorder, clinical depression, postpartum depression, perinatal depression, seasonal affective disorder, and even unspecified depressive disorder.

PEP TALK: *If you find it hard to believe you'll ever feel better, that's probably the depression talking. It's common to feel negative and pessimistic when you're depressed —but stick with us.*

Some labels you may have heard. Other labels you may have been given. It doesn't matter whether your depression is chronic and mild, related to your hormones, tied to the low light of winter, or anything else. We can help you with them all.

Only a trained health professional can diagnose depression, but as far as trusted, validated self-administered assessments go, we like the World Health Organization's Major Depression Inventory (MDI). It only has twelve questions, and you can access it online for free. Just remember, a questionnaire can't diagnose depression. If a diagnosis is important to you or your score on the quiz has you concerned, see your doctor.

Depression Debunked

Depression is not a sign of weakness, proof that you're a bad person, or a form of punishment. You don't deserve to be depressed. And you didn't bring it on yourself. No matter how many times your mom tells you to buck up, your buddy tells you to get off your butt, or that little voice inside you says, "Suck it up, buttercup," it's not a matter of simply trying harder and — poof — bye-bye depression.

You aren't selfish, lazy, self-centered, a whiner, or to blame — which is hard for a lot of depressed people to believe, since feeling ashamed and worthless are key symptoms of depression. Depression isn't a curse. And it isn't a blessing either (even if a well-meaning person tells you it'll make you stronger). But it is a very treatable illness.

PEP TALK: *Depression is not something you deserve. Don't let anyone — most of all you — tell you it's your fault!*

Depression can affect anyone — even therapists. During the weeks after my first child was born I was a mess of emotions. Even now, decades later, it's still hard to admit. I remember pacing the hallway in my apartment, wishing I wasn't so tired, wishing my husband understood how I was feeling, wishing I knew what I was doing. I'm not sure who was crying harder, me or my daughter. I was a therapist. Wasn't I supposed to have all the answers? My feelings of incompetence were overwhelming.

When my mother-in-law was in palliative care, I experienced mood difficulties again. It was probably while eating my twentieth bag of cookies that I realized it wasn't just my mother-in-law I was grieving — it was my mom.

You'd think I'd have figured it out sooner. My mother-in-law was in the same hospital that my mom had been in twenty years earlier, and every time I visited I had to walk past the room where my mom had been so ill. Back then, I was too busy being the strong one, the capable one, and the one everyone admired to really grieve my mom's passing.

Trust me, this is a journey. I'm still learning that experiencing feelings is okay. And I still sometimes turn to the bag of cookies.

PEP TALK: *It takes guts to acknowledge you have a problem and work on making things better. You are one brave, smart, and courageous person!*

Depression may not be the only thing on your plate. If you have anxiety, a concussion, a learning disability, an eating disorder, or any other physical condition or mental illness as well as depression, you may find it takes longer to feel better. You may also need some extra help from your family doctor, a therapist, or a support group. Think of it as having two broken legs instead of just one. You'll need some extra time to heal, and a wheelchair, not just crutches. Be patient and you'll make progress!

Depression definitely has a cultural component. Some languages don't have a word for depression as we use the term in English; if that's true of the language you learned to speak first, there's a greater likelihood that you'll express your depression physically, as pain, digestive problems, headaches, and more. There may be a strong taboo against talking about mental illness in your culture. It may be seen as bringing shame on your family, as evidence that you've sinned, proof you've been cursed, or simply that you're British — stiff upper lip and all that. Be aware that these forces will influence your attitude toward depression and affect who you can feel safe talking to about it.

Depression can be so severe that you feel like harming yourself. First, you need to tell someone how you're feeling. Then you need to see a doctor. You may worry that you'll scare the person you tell. You may feel as though there's nothing a doctor can do for you. But I'm telling you, help is available. Depression is very treatable. Don't do something you can't undo. Ask someone for help. Your safety is more important than anything else.

THIRTEEN SIGNS YOU MAY BE DEPRESSED

If you find you've been experiencing a number of the symptoms on this list for at least two weeks and they've been affecting your relationships and your day-to-day functioning, you could be depressed:

1. I feel sad a lot of the time.
2. I just don't care about things anymore.
3. I'm overcome with feelings of guilt.
4. I feel worthless.
5. I can't concentrate.
6. I've gained or lost weight (without dieting).
7. I'm having trouble sleeping, or I sleep all the time.
8. My performance at work or school is suffering.
9. Making decisions seems harder than it used to.
10. I'm experiencing physical symptoms that don't have a physical cause.
11. I avoid seeing my friends.
12. I think about hurting myself.
13. I just can't seem to see the positive side of anything.

Asking Why

It's not common, but mood difficulties can have a physical cause, such as a vitamin deficiency, Addison's disease, multiple sclerosis, pancreatic cancer, traumatic brain injury, or Lyme disease. Depression can even be a side effect of some medications. Ron is still embarrassed to admit that one of his clients, who had been working hard in therapy but wasn't making any progress, ended up having hypothyroidism. As soon as her doctor started her on medication, all of the skills she'd been practicing with Ron worked like a charm. Visit your doctor to rule out any physical illness or condition that could be causing your depression.

Outside of a biological cause like a disease, deficiency, or medication side effect, no one knows exactly what causes depression. Is it a biochemical imbalance? Is it about serotonin levels? Genetics? Is it something we pick up from our parents growing up? Is it our personality? The reasons for depression are controversial and complex. This is one way depression differs from a broken leg — in most cases there's no defining moment or single event we can point to as the cause of our emotional pain and malaise.

But that doesn't stop us from asking why. Many people look at their lives — their family, their health, their partner, their job — and say, "I've got it so good. So why do I feel so bad?"

Ana, whom we met in the introduction, wonders why she isn't over the moon when she has such a healthy, beautiful baby girl. So many couples struggle for years to conceive, with so much heartache and expense. So many babies are born with health challenges. "What's wrong with me?" Ana wonders.

Kate, the second of the four individuals we'll follow through this book, is shocked when her doctor suggests she might be depressed. "I know I've been feeling sad and low since my husband retired, but I'm so lucky that we can afford to live on one income," she says. "It's my friends who worry they'll never be able to retire who should be depressed, not me."

Becky, whose brother died of cancer, knows how fleeting life is. "I should be making every second count," she thinks. "So why can't I get out of bed?"

It's also tempting to point a finger at the past. John, the fourth person we'll regularly check in with on these pages, has spent his whole life feeling inadequate and incapable because of the way his parents and siblings treat him — so it makes sense to him that his depression is their fault.

Do you think your mood difficulties are linked to your childhood, your first romantic relationship, your choice to study one subject in college rather than another, the city you settled in, or your career path? Spending time in the past may help you to answer the question why, but it won't give you the tools to feel better in the present.

TRY THIS: *We won't spend too much time dwelling on the past to find answers. Instead, we'll look at what's going on in your life right now.*

The founders of interpersonal psychotherapy saw a pattern among the people they helped with mood difficulties. Their patients, they discovered, were all experiencing problems in at least one of four different areas in their lives at the time they became depressed: *life transitions, complicated grief, social isolation,* or *interpersonal conflict.* These four problem areas aren't causes, but they *are* contributing factors to why people feel sad, blue, down, and depressed. At least one of them can almost always be linked to a recent depressive episode.

Your problem area (or areas) — whether it's conflict with another person, grief that won't go away, a life change, or lack of supportive relationships — may be connected to what happened years ago, but we'll be keeping the focus on what you're experiencing in the present and what you can do in the here and now to feel better. In Week 4, we'll describe each of the problem areas in detail and help you pick one to work on. (To be true to interpersonal psychotherapy, which is a short-term approach that helps people feel better in eight to twelve weeks, we talk about "weeks" throughout the book. Ultimately, the pacing is up to you. Read as quickly or slowly as you like!)

You Deserve a Break Today

You may need to take a temporary break from some of your day-to-day responsibilities and commitments to work on feeling better.

It's another good reason to think of your depression as if it were a broken leg. When we have a broken leg, our priorities have to shift. Recovery becomes our most important job, so we go to medical appointments, do the exercises the physical therapist prescribes, and put our feet up (literally) when we're tired. We won't be taking the kids to the park, hitting the dance club, spring-cleaning the house, or hosting the big family dinner. It's obvious that we can't do what we'd normally do, so we don't try. And we might even accept the help that others offer us.

Depression is a medical illness as legitimate as that broken leg. We need to give ourselves permission to take the time we need to figure out what interpersonal problem is contributing to our unhappiness and learn new skills to cope. Taking time off isn't forever. It's just until we're back on our feet.

Depression is hidden — often even to ourselves — so we think we have to power through it. We beat ourselves up for having a short fuse, not being able to concentrate, feeling tired, lacking drive, missing deadlines, or being indecisive.

The temptation to suck it up and keep going will be very powerful if you feel you're the only one keeping your family's boat afloat. You might be working three jobs and still struggling to make ends meet; have an ill parent, a child with a disability, a partner who can't manage without you, a demanding job, or an unsympathetic boss; or there may be strong cultural expectations for your role.

Sometimes to take care of others, you have to put yourself first. Go for coffee with a friend instead of volunteering at the food bank. Sit down with your spouse to discuss how to divide up the household chores to lighten your load a little. Take your social media accounts down for a while. Ask your sister to take the kids for a weekend. Talk to your boss about next week's deadline. You might discover that some of the things you thought others needed you to do for them are actually your own expectations of yourself. Think of taking care of yourself as a job. Make a list of self-care tasks and schedule them on your calendar.

PEP TALK: *The world isn't on your shoulders alone. Sometimes when you step back, it makes room for others to step forward.*

Work is often the last place we want to lighten our load. We worry that the boss may not be willing to mod-ify workloads or change deadlines or that asking for time off or light duties may affect our next promotion — or worse, we'll be demoted or fired. We may not have any sick days or disability insurance.

If these are your concerns, here are some ideas. Check with your human resources department in case there are resources available at your workplace that you don't know about. If you can't talk to your boss, maybe you can speak with a coworker or two. They may have some advice or ideas about how to manage, and they may offer to help.

In the end, if you have to keep your depression hidden at work, that's okay. Just make sure your friends and family know that a lot of your energy is going toward keeping your job and that you may need some extra help at home.

Now, not everybody has to give something up in order to feel better. Becky, for example, has no one relying on her now that her brother has died, so she sleeps a lot during the day. She's already stopped going to school, answering emails and texts, picking up the phone, and seeing her friends. She doesn't eat much. Showering is always optional. Becky already has the space in her life to make positive changes — she just needs help taking that first step.

Tell Someone about It

If you've been keeping your depression to yourself, it's time to share the burden with someone else. If we let others know about our temporary limitations, we're more likely to receive support for our efforts and new ideas for how to cope. Opening up also gives others the opportunity to share their struggles with us — experiences we may never have known they had. Suddenly, we don't feel so alone anymore.

It's normal to feel shy, scared, embarrassed, and anxious about telling people. Many of us — me included — have our feelings of self-worth tied up with being seen as one of those people who have their act together. (It's common among people in helping professions. We help others, but we don't always have the skills to help ourselves.) If you're used to being the capable one, it can feel uncomfortable to admit to others that you're struggling. Plus, if you haven't reached out for help before, you don't know it's possible for someone to offer you support and show they care.

The first step is to acknowledge that being strong isn't always a strength. The next is to imagine a different future, one where there's a little more give-and-take in your relationships. Many people will want to help you as much as you want to help them. Let them in.

Don't feel you have to tell everyone about your depression. Start with one or two people who are affected by your illness or who you think will be understanding.

PEP TALK: *When you share your depression with someone you trust, you're admitting that you're human. It can make your relationships stronger!*

It's usually helpful to share the symptoms of depression with the person you're confiding in. That way you both have the same understanding of the many physical and emotional impacts of the illness and can speak a common language. Let the person know that you're working hard to feel better. Explain that you need to take a break from some of the things you usually do to give yourself the time and energy to make positive changes. Reassure them that the situation is temporary. Listen to their concerns, and be open to their suggestions.

Some people will really understand. Some may offer to help. (Don't refuse the casserole.) Some might not get it; you can sense they're trying, but they're struggling to empathize. If that person is close to you or you need their help with some of your responsibilities, try sharing this chapter of the book with them. Of course, you won't want to assign reading homework to a person who isn't a reader. Instead, show them the book and talk them through the important information, as in a highlight reel or postgame recap. They'll get the point that your information comes from a credible source — the book — but they won't have to read it themselves.

Unfortunately, some people might not be supportive at all. You can't change that. But at least you'll know who you can turn to the next time you need advice or assistance. Try not to blame those who don't understand. They may show their support through actions, not words, by doing things like fixing the car or spending more time with the kids.

Many people who have depression stop socializing, and their isolation may be compounded by other circumstances, for example, a move to a new city, the arrival of a new baby, a spouse who travels a lot, or the lack of a strong support system. John, for example, never felt he had kind, caring friends or family. Admitting to himself that he was depressed has been hard enough, because it feels like one more way he's failed. How is he supposed to share that with the very people who are responsible for his feelings of inadequacy?

PEP TALK: *There's always someone you can talk to — it could be you just haven't found them yet.*

If, like John, you feel there's no one you can talk to about your depression, we encourage you to open up to one person anyway. John swallows his pride and tells his brother (the most supportive of his unsupportive siblings) about how he's feeling. First, he explains the symptoms. Then he says that he's working on getting better. His brother expected John to say the things he's said so many times before: "I'd feel better if I had a girlfriend," "The problem is my job," "I just need more money," "If I'd stayed in school, this wouldn't be happening," "It's because I'm living with Mom and Dad." When John's brother doesn't hear John singing the same old tune, he's pleasantly surprised. He praises John for making an effort — a first in their relationship.

Often our words are received poorly not because of what we want to say, but because of how we say it. It takes a little self-reflection to recognize the patterns in the way we communicate with the people in our lives, but it's worth taking a look. John's go-to style has been to make excuses and blame others. You may find, like John, that making a change in the way you communicate helps you feel you have someone to talk to. It's not something you can accomplish overnight, but now's as good a time as any to start — and we'll continue working on this together over the weeks ahead.

PEP TALK: *Sometimes it's not what we say that makes us feel unsupported. It's how we say it.*

You may feel there's no one you can talk to about your depression because, in your family and community, talk of mental illness is shameful and therefore off-limits. You may worry that if it gets out that you're depressed, it could affect your future. Rest assured, there will be someone you can talk to. That person may be outside your immediate family or cultural community. They may be more of an acquaintance than a friend, or they may be a professional.

Here are some things you could say to your spouse, family, friends, or boss to start the conversation about your depression and your need to temporarily take some commitments off your plate:

TO YOUR SPOUSE:

"I know I've been really negative lately, and it's not about you. I think I'm struggling with depression, and I'm trying to learn more about it and get better. It may be hard to understand, and I know that you're doing a lot as it is, but I want you to know I'm trying my best."

"I know I'm the one who usually cleans up after dinner and takes the kids to their lessons, but I'm so tired after work. This depression thing just sucks my energy, and I want to be able to focus on feeling better. Can we figure out a way to make evenings work for both of us?"

"I don't have the energy to keep the house clean, but I know a clean house would have a positive effect on my mood. Can we hire someone to do it for a couple of months?"

TO YOUR FRIEND:

"I'm sorry that I haven't been up to going out on a regular basis like I normally do, and I want you to know it's nothing you've said. My mood has been low lately, and I've been struggling with it. It's not that I'm mad at you or don't want to spend time with you. I'm hoping to be feeling better soon, and I'll keep you in the loop as best as I can."

TO YOUR FAMILY:

"I know you guys seem worried about me, and I really appreciate your concern. I've been feeling stressed at work and kind of down in the dumps lately. I don't want to get into a lengthy conversation, but if you can take the kids this Sunday afternoon for a few hours that would be so helpful."

"I know you guys are busy, but I really miss spending time with you. It's a highlight of my week when we arrange a dinner together or you bring a meal over. If you could do that sometime soon, I would really appreciate it."

TO YOUR TEENAGER:

"You might be surprised to hear me say this, but I really don't like nagging you, and I know sometimes I can get a little crazy about minor things. I just want to tell you I love you, and I get that you're just being a normal teenager. Sometimes I struggle with my mood, and I want you to know I'm really working on feeling more positive, and I'm going to try to be less picky and argumentative with you."

TO YOUR BOSS:

"I've been to see my doctor, and she told me I have depression. I'm making some important changes in my life, so that I can get better as fast as possible. She said I should talk to you about taking some time off or cutting back one day a week until I feel better."

Hello? Is Anybody Listening?

These conversations don't always go as well as we hope. Ana, for instance, decides to write her husband, Peter, a letter one morning while the baby is napping. It seems smarter to write something while she's feeling fresh than to wait until Peter gets home from work, when she'll be too tired and cranky for a constructive conversation. Plus, writing things down helps her collect her thoughts. This way, she won't forget anything.

She starts the letter by telling Peter she loves him and acknowledging that she's been having a hard time since the baby was born. She tells him how she's been feeling — sad, unworthy, guilty, incompetent, distracted, irritable — and tells him those are actually symptoms of depression. She writes that she knows he's tired too, but that she hopes he can help her with some of her responsibilities for a little while so she can work on feeling better.

Peter reads the letter that night, and although he gives Ana a big hug and says he's happy she told him how she feels, he doesn't actually address her request for help. Ana decides not to make a big deal of it. Maybe he just didn't know what to do or say next.

Over the next week, she notices that it's business as usual as far as Peter is concerned. He still wants dinner on the table within minutes of his arrival home and buries his nose in the newspaper instead of holding his daughter. He doesn't even load the dishwasher. Ana can feel her resentment rising. Didn't she hold up her end of the bargain? Didn't she share the symptoms of depression, talk about her efforts to get better, ask for help, and say it would only be temporary?

Yes, Ana did everything right. But when we're talking about spouses (and other family members, for that matter), it may take more than one letter or conversation to cover all the issues and work out all the kinks. Relationships are works in progress, and intimate partnerships have well-established patterns. You're asking to shake up the status quo, and it's not likely to happen right away.

PEP TALK: *It may take several conversations with someone — especially a spouse — to work out how they can help you best. Be patient, stay open-minded, and maybe show them this chapter!*

Ana will need to continue the conversation with her husband. Not in a "You're such a jerk; why didn't you start helping out more like I asked you to" way (even if that's what she's feeling), but using a more constructive approach. "Peter," she could say, "I appreciate that you care how I'm feeling. If I'm going to get better, we need to share the work when you get home." No apologies. No aggression. Just a civil, respectful request for what she needs.

Be patient, be constructive, and keep trying. If you don't seem to be making progress on your own, you can always suggest that your spouse come to a doctor's appointment with you. Hearing about depression from a medical professional may help give your request for support some credibility. You can also talk to an understanding friend or family member. What are their ideas?

Taking Off the Training Wheels

It's completely natural for us to feel anxious and even afraid when we're asked to try something new. What if this doesn't work? What if I don't start to feel better? What if my family can't manage without me doing everything I've always done? What if my boss doesn't understand? What if my friends judge me? Asking "what if" is a common way for depressed people to express anxiety. (Stick with us. We're going to help you turn your "what ifs" into "whos": Who can I talk to? Who has gone through something similar?)

You've been functioning a certain way with your depression and, even if you feel bad, at least it's a feeling you're familiar with. Depression often runs in families, so the way you cope may be similar to the way you saw your mom or dad (or both) deal with their mood difficulties.

It's like learning to ride a bike. When someone says, "Let's take the training wheels off," it feels unsafe. What if you fall? There's fear and uncertainty. But think about the joy and freedom you'll experience when you ride without those extra wheels slowing you down.

GUY TALK: HOUSTON, WE HAVE A PROBLEM

Ron here, with some quick words about guys and depression.

Men don't usually recognize depression, even when it is staring us right in the face. Sure, that tired guy in the mirror has insomnia, can't concentrate, and is always angry, but that's normal, right? We just need to power through, suck it up, distract ourselves, or pour another beer.

Often it's our partner who gives us the wake-up call that something's not right. They want us to talk to someone — our doctor, a therapist, a friend. But chances are we resist. I'm as bad as the next guy about going to the doctor. When I went for a checkup last year, it'd been well over twenty years (and it was my wife who made it happen). Most guys don't want to know if we've got high blood pressure or bad cholesterol or skin cancer or depression. If we don't go, we don't have to know.

Feeling crappy for more than two weeks isn't normal. That short fuse and constant low-level irritation are probably sadness, hurt, disappointment, and other feelings that many guys aren't comfortable expressing. Our instinct is to stick our head in the sand. It takes a brave man to recognize that, Houston, we have a problem.

Fortunately, depression is a problem we can solve. First, we have to admit that it's not normal to feel like crap. Then we have to stop pretending to be superhuman. If you've been powering through, that means temporarily cutting back on some of your day-to-day activities.

Now this isn't a free pass to watch the game every night instead of going for dinner with your mother-in-law or putting the kids to bed. You'll need to let the people who are affected by your choices know why you're cutting back.

It can feel awkward. For example, what do you say to your boss to save face, now that you're going to stop working all that overtime? If you can't answer that question yourself, I bet you know someone who's been through something similar whom you could ask.

Your spouse may already have her hands full. How can you make sure she stays supportive? An open conversation in which you talk about what you're doing to cope with your depression and you strategize together on the best ways to cut back can go a long way to keeping your partner on your side. Most women love it when we're open and talk about ourselves. It doesn't make us wimps.

Acknowledge there's a problem, and take steps to fix it. Your family and friends will thank you — and you'll start to feel better.

This Week's To-Do List

Show the "Thirteen Signs You May Be Depressed" list to someone. Could be your spouse, your girlfriend, your cousin — break the silence about depression and help clear up some myths!

Pay attention to the way you usually communicate when you're feeling bad or upset. This awareness is the first step to modifying your communication style.

Talk to someone about temporarily reducing the number of things you're responsible for. A friend or family member can help you brainstorm things to let go of and may have ideas for approaching a difficult conversation with someone whose help you need. Remember to share the symptoms of depression, tell the person you're working hard to feel better, and reassure them that your reduced responsibilities are only temporary.

Draw Your
Social Circle

This week we play detective, investigating the kind of relationships
you have and identifying what you wish were different about them.
These relationships (and how you handle them) hold the key to your
mood. This week's work will help open the door to a new world of
possibilities with the people in your life.

It was almost Passover. The day before the big dinner, I was driving my
grandson home from school.

"Who's coming tomorrow, Bubbe?" he asked.

I resisted the urge to rattle off all the family members who'd be sitting
around the seder table and instead looked at him in the rearview mirror
and waited for part two of the question.

"Wasn't there someone who used to bring us toys and candy?"

I smiled. Yes, there was someone — my sister.

"Is she coming this year?" my grandson asked.

"No," I replied.

"Is she ever going to come again?" he continued.

"I don't know," I said.

There had been a number of conflicts over the years between my sister
and me and between my sister and my immediate family, and each one had

taken its toll. To make my grandson happy, all we had to do was hit the candy store before tomorrow, but it was more complicated for me. I hold out hope that the fences will be mended someday, and I bring my box of tools to help out whenever I can. But my sister wasn't on the guest list. Not this year anyway.

My situation probably isn't so different from yours. Every family has its rifts, reunions, and reminders of the way things were, brought into sharp focus by chance encounters, special dates on the calendar, and in my case a little boy with a sweet tooth.

PEP TALK: *This week is all about exploring the important people in your life — however you define "important."*

The model that Ron and I practice is called "interpersonal" psychotherapy for a reason. All of us are part of a web of relationships. The size of the web differs from person to person — my web is way bigger than Ron's, for example — but it's a web nonetheless. Some relationships are held close with a short, strong thread. Others are distant, the spider silk stretched so thin you can hardly see it. Sometimes, the thread's been broken.

We're social beings, and our web of relationships is important to our happiness. Supportive relationships help us survive life's storms and celebrate its successes. Stressful and dissatisfying relationships — ones that leave us feeling angry, hurt, or disappointed — contribute to our feelings of sadness and depression. There's an expression that really brings that point home: "A mother can only be as happy as her least happy child." Our relationships with others affect our mood. Our kids, our partners, our coworkers, our parents, our siblings, heck, even our neighbors — they can all help us feel better. Or worse.

PEP TALK: *The "whos" in our lives are closely tied to how we feel.*

Let's take a closer look at the "whos" in your life — how often you see them, what you do together, and what you like and don't like about the relationships. We'll start by drawing your social circle, and then we'll complete an exercise we call Four Questions.

ACQUAINTANCE OR FRIEND?

People sometimes struggle with telling the difference between an acquaintance and a friend. Does it matter? Yes. And not because of a judgy belief that only friends are important. We need both in our lives. We can practice new coping strategies and communication styles with acquaintances. And they can be a low-risk sounding board and source of advice.

You can tell the difference between acquaintances and friends by thinking about what you talk about and the way you communicate with each other. Have you ever talked with them about personal things? Asked them for advice? Had them come to you for help? If the answers are no, they're probably an acquaintance. Friendship requires vulnerability and intimacy — you know stuff about each other that an acquaintance just doesn't. Open up to the right acquaintance, and you just might make a new friend.

Step 1: Time to Draw

Now let's draw your social circle. Grab a pencil and a sheet of paper. Plain 8½ × 11-inch paper is fine. Markers, colored pencils, and glitter are optional. You don't need to get fancy, but you'll be referring to your circle for reminders of your relationships as you work through the next ten weeks. You might even change your circle over time, as relationships grow, wane, or are resuscitated.

Draw a small circle about an inch wide in the middle of your paper and write your name (or simply "me") in it. Then draw another circle around that one, about an inch from it, and a third one around the second. (You can add more circles if you need to as you go along.) You're drawing your social universe, and everything revolves around you.

Next, think of the names of the people who are important to you and jot them down in the circles around "you." Those closest to you go in the first circle; more distant relationships go in the outer circles, depending on how close you consider the relationship to be. Your friend, your mom's friend, your husband, your wife, your kids, your hairdresser, your bartender, your work colleague, your therapist, your doctor — they all may have a place on your social circle. Who did you see the most last week? Who drove you crazy? Put 'em both on the circle. (Or maybe they're the same person!) You can include names from the past as well as the present.

Just because a relationship is close doesn't mean it's positive. Some of our closest relationships are our most stressful ones, and these are exactly the relationships we want to explore this week. Another tip? Just because she's your sister or your mom doesn't mean she has to be in your inner circle. Moms and daughters and sisters (and dads and sons and brothers) are sometimes on the periphery of our lives or not in our lives at all, and no one (including you) should make you feel guilty about that. It might be just the way you like it. If it's not, we'll figure out if it's something you'd like to change.

Some people will immediately jump to mind, and you'll know exactly where to put them on your drawing. If you get stuck, take a look at your texts, your email inbox, and your Facebook account for reminders. You can also answer these questions:

Who did you spend time with on the weekend?
Who do you work with?
Who aggravated you the most last week?
Which professionals do you see on a regular basis?

If someone who was close to you died, put them on your social circle as well — and don't worry about getting it "right" if you aren't sure where to put them. It can sometimes help to place them where you would if they were still alive. Similarly, if you were close to someone in the past but aren't now, you can decide whether you want to put that person in an inner or outer ring. This is your circle, and you get to decide where things go — there's no right or wrong here.

Focus on documenting who is in your life, not on whether you can (or should) make changes to those relationships. Remember, one step at a time!

ARE FACEBOOK FRIENDS REAL FRIENDS?

There is a paradox of the internet: so many friends, and at the same time no friends at all. Face-to-face friendships are rich, multidimensional experiences that are enhanced by being together in the same place, seeing body language, sharing good and bad experiences, and more. An online encounter doesn't offer the same depth. It's just too easy to control our virtual personas and turn off the computer when we've had enough. The investment and accountability just aren't there if we've never breathed the same air in the same room.

By all means, build your online circle of friends, connections, and followers, especially if face-to-face interactions are stressful or challenging for you. It *is* possible to experience genuine care and intimacy with people online, and they can be a great resource when you want to try out new communication styles or coping strategies. But there is a difference.

Our verdict? Online friends are real. But they aren't a replacement for face-to-face friends. If you feel your circle has too few friends of the face-to-face variety, we can work on that together.

Step 2: Let's Play Four Questions

Putting everyone on the social circle is step 1. The next step is to choose a few of the most important relationships and explore them in more detail.

Officially, this step is called "exploring the interpersonal inventory." But it's more fun to think of it as playing Four Questions.

Remember, these relationships don't need to be the ones that make you feel good. In fact, it's the stressful, hurtful, and disappointing relationships that are often the most important to explore, because they're the ones that are most likely connected to your depression.

Here are the four questions you'll ask yourself about each of the most important relationships in your life right now:

1. How would I describe the relationship? Review your relationship a little. Think of what you do together, how you communicate (face-to-face, by text, email, or phone), how often you see each other, and what you usually talk about (and don't talk about). How have things changed over time? How do you feel when you think about seeing that person? After you've seen them? Who initiates contact? How do encounters start? End?

2. What do I like about the relationship? Think about what works and what you'd miss if you didn't have that person in your life anymore. This can be hard to answer if your relationship is full of conflict or you've been really hurt or disappointed by the person. Try to remember what made you connect in the first place. Try imagining what others might say they like about the person, even if you can't feel those things yourself.

3. What don't I like about the relationship? Think about when it makes you feel sad, hurt, angry, or disappointed. If you can't come up with anything you don't like, pay attention. Nobody's perfect, so why the imbalanced view? You won't work on it now, but it's something you may want to revisit later.

4. What would I like to be different about the relationship? Think about what you'd change to make the relationship better for you and what you wish bothered you less, even if you can't imagine anything will change.

Ana's Circle: Things Just Aren't the Same

Ana has drawn her circle and is ready to add some names. First there's Peter, Ana's husband. Five months ago, she would've put him so close to her on the circle that they would've been sharing the middle. Today, things are a little different. If anyone should be in the middle with Ana, it's Ruby.

Should Ana put Ruby on the circle at all? Ruby is only a baby, but to be honest, Ana's connection to Ruby is just about the most intense one she's ever had. She adds Ruby to the first circle along with Peter.

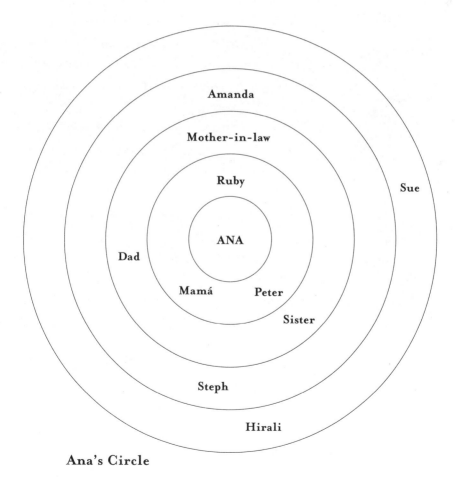

Ana's Circle

Ana's mom lives in Texas, but they FaceTime frequently, so she writes "Mamá" near the center. Her dad is a little farther out. They've never been really close, and after his Alzheimer's diagnosis she's finding it harder to connect with him. Her mother-in-law, who has perfected the art of the poorly timed surprise visit, is closer to the center than Ana would like. Ana's older sister lives in the same city, but they aren't really as close as they had been — an emotional distance that seems to have become greater since Ruby's birth.

After that, Ana finds it a little hard to fill in the rest of her circle; so much has changed since the baby was born. She never sees her work friends now that she's on maternity leave, and her nonwork friends, who were so attentive during the first few weeks after baby Ruby arrived, have all but disappeared. She's stopped going to the gym (and yes, that makes her feel crappy), so she doesn't see her gym buddies either. Her circle has shrunk. A lot.

PEP TALK: *The people in your circle aren't good or bad — your expectations of each other may just be different, and that's what's causing a rocky relationship.*

She puts her closest work friends, Sue and Hirali, and her closest girlfriends, Amanda and Steph, on the circle — but a lot farther from the center than she would've, say, five months ago.

Ana decides to play Four Questions with her relationship with Peter, her mom, her sister, and Peter's mom. She wonders if she should play Four Questions with Ruby too, but decides against it. It's the changes in Ana's life that are causing Ana stress, not Ruby.

Here's how it turns out when she examines her relationship with Peter:

1. How would I describe the relationship? Peter and I met at college when we both joined a recreational baseball league. We love playing and watching sports together, inviting friends over for a beer or a barbecue, and listening to live music, but since Ruby's birth we're cocooning a lot more — planning a night out or inviting people over seems too overwhelming. All we can manage after Ruby falls asleep is to collapse on the couch and watch TV.

2. What do I like about the relationship? I love Peter's optimistic personality. He always sees the bright side of things and is a very reliable, trustworthy guy.

3. What don't I like about the relationship? Peter isn't a big talker, and it really bugs me when I say, "Let's talk," and he gets this glazed look in his eyes. Also, he's pretty traditional when it comes to who does what at home. Sometimes I need his help, and he just doesn't seem to think it's his job. He's been coming home late from work a lot recently, which is really hard for me.

4. What would I like to be different about the relationship? I really want Peter to understand me better. When I'm feeling stressed about his mother or having trouble with my sister or worrying that I'm not a good mom, I want him to listen and "get it" rather than dismiss my concerns. I've been feeling pretty tired and lonely lately, and the feeling that Peter just isn't there for me has gotten stronger. It would be great if he saw himself more as a partner in our home life, including taking care of Ruby.

Ana writes her responses to the four questions on sheets of paper, then staples them to her social circle, and puts them in her desk drawer for future reference.

CAN YOU PLAY FOUR QUESTIONS WITH YOUR KIDS?

Ana decides not to play Four Questions with her baby, Ruby, because it's not the relationship with her baby that's causing trouble; it's the new role Ana is now playing as first-time mother.

But how about older children? If your relationship with your five-year-old is causing you grief because he's become withdrawn and combative or your eleven-year-old comes home from school every day with enough attitude to sink a ship, okay, yes, you can ask yourself the four questions about them. Identifying what you don't like and what you'd like to be different about the relationship will help you figure out how to move forward. But remember, the responsibility for making the relationship better will lie squarely with you as the mom or dad, and you'll need to go to others in your circle for help.

Of course, once your kids are teenagers and adults, the parent-child relationship changes, and your son or daughter can play a more active role in improving the relationship between you.

Kate's Circle: Handcuffed to Hubby

Kate's inner circles include her husband, Don, a recently retired police officer, and their two grown children, Dominic and Heather, who has a new baby. Kate's parents passed away a few years ago, and she hasn't spoken with her younger sister in almost a year — she just can't take her sister's endless bragging about her perfect life. Kate also adds the principal at her school, Brad, to the outer ring of her circle — he may be her boss but they've worked closely together for years.

When it comes time to add her three closest girlfriends (Leslie, Diane, and Mona) and her yoga classmates (Suzanne, Alex, and Andrea), Kate feels sad. Since Don's retirement, she's found it harder to make time to see her friends and has stopped going to yoga altogether, since Don says it's a waste of money and they need to be careful with their finances now. She wants to put them closer to her on the circle, but that's just not the way things are right now.

Kate writes Don's name right below hers in the middle of the circle. She can't make a move without his being there. It's almost like he's suffocating her.

TRY THIS: *If there's a relationship that you know is making you feel bad, that's one you should definitely play Four Questions with!*

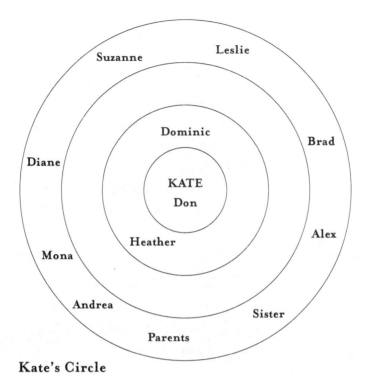

Kate's Circle

Kate knows that her depression is linked to the simmering conflict and outright arguments between her and Don. This isn't the life she imagined when Don retired, and it's definitely affecting her mood.

Here's how she plays Four Questions with her relationship with Don:

1. How would I describe the relationship? We've been married for twenty-seven years, moving around the country in the earlier years as Don built his career. Most of it's been great. We did all the typical couple things: bought houses, raised kids, went on holidays, and enjoyed hobbies. Each of us had our own career, and for most of the marriage we each had a lot of independence. Since Don retired, though, he's become more and more involved in my day-to-day life. I never really questioned marrying an older man until now. It's only been since Don retired that I've felt we're out of step with each other.

2. What do I like about the relationship? Don is a good father and faithful partner. When he was working, he had an interesting life outside of the one we shared together.

3. What don't I like about the relationship? I feel handcuffed to Don — everywhere I am, he's there too, asking what we're doing together that day, texting me endlessly at work, interrogating me about how I'm spending my time, offering his two cents on what I should buy, and complaining about things that before his retirement he never even knew I did. Yes, I married a police officer, but I certainly never expected to feel under investigation myself.

4. What would I like to be different about the relationship? I want things to go back to the way they were B.R. — before retirement. I want my independence back. I want the judgment and micromanaging to stop.

John's Circle: "People Just Piss Me Off"

John finds it pretty easy to draw his circle. Near his name he puts his older brother, Tom, and his mom and dad. Tom is definitely the sibling John gets along with best. Tom's wife, Greta, and their son, Riley, are also close to the center. Lisa, Karen, and Kim — John's three sisters — say and do such stupid and unfair things that John is forever arguing with them or giving them the cold shoulder. So Tom is close to the middle, and the rest of his siblings? To hell with 'em.

John's dad mostly ignores him. His mom can't seem to do anything but nag and criticize. He realizes they're old and have helped him out by letting him live with them, but they could include him on occasion when they go out for dinner or let him know that his siblings are coming over, so he doesn't make other plans.

John has one buddy, Mark, whom he used to work with, but they haven't spoken in a while. His ex-girlfriend, Isabelle, has been married

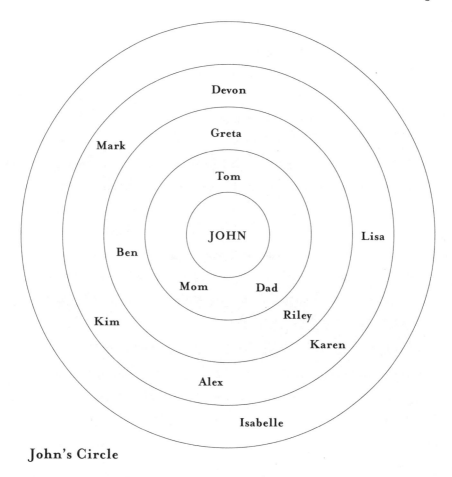

John's Circle

for years now. John would love to have a girlfriend but lacks confidence around women. It's been so long since he dated, he wouldn't even know where to start.

John works at a local Chinese restaurant doing deliveries, so he puts his manager, Devon, and coworkers Ben and Alex on the circle too. Alex makes John's life really difficult. The rule at work is that drivers take turns claiming deliveries, so that they each have an equal opportunity for tips. But Alex will often call out that it's his order when John is up next. And that's just one example of Alex's bad behavior. John could go on and on.

John has confronted his manager about Alex many times, but Devon is just about as much trouble as Alex. John is grateful he was hired, and

TRY THIS: *When no one can do right by you, sometimes the best thing you can do is to let them be wrong and work on having it bother you less. Keep reading to find out how!*

Devon was nice at the start, but now he dismisses John's complaints and routinely tells him to "give it up" and "just do the job." It goes against everything John believes in. Rules are meant to be enforced, and all employees should be treated fairly.

John's biggest problem is definitely with Alex, so he decides to play Four Questions with that relationship first. Next in line will be Tom, his mom, his dad, and his manager.

I. How would I describe the relationship? I usually see Alex three or four days a week when we work the same shifts. And that's about all we have in common. Alex is in his twenties, and I'm forty. Alex talks about cars and sports and porn — and I'm not interested in any of those things. Alex lives with his girlfriend, and I live with my parents. See? Nothing in common.

2. What do I like about the relationship? I don't like anything about Alex on his own. If I'm forced to answer this, I guess there are times when Alex, Ben, and I joke around when the restaurant isn't too busy, and it's fun. But not because of Alex.

3. What don't I like about the relationship? How about everything. I hate that Alex is so disrespectful and treats me like I'm not even there. His arrogance and rudeness make me so mad. He's a lot younger than me, but acts like he knows everything. He's a show-off and a bully and never follows the rules. He's turned bugging me into another one of his sports. Sometimes I get so mad I could punch him.

4. What would I like to be different about the relationship? I want Alex to do what he's supposed to and not be such a smartass. I'd be happy if he just left me alone — we don't have to be friends.

Becky's Circle: When Someone You Love Has Died

At first, Becky feels energized by the social-circle project — she's all but abandoned her art since Brian died, and this seems like a perfect opportunity for some creative expression. But now that it's time to start, she can only stare at the pile of magazines, paint tubes, markers, string, and the blank white piece of bristol board in front of her. Why did she think she could do this? What if her work sucks? How is this going to make things better anyway?

She sweeps her supplies onto the floor, and the tears start flowing. After five minutes of hard crying, she's exhausted.

So now what? No one says she has to do this — at least not today. She can just leave the crap on the floor and go for a nap.

But what if she gives it a go?

She takes a deep breath, grabs a piece of paper and a pencil, and quickly draws three barely round circles, one inside the other. Forget the paint and string. This is her circle, unplugged.

She puts Brian on the circle first, right above her in the center. Before he died, she ate, drank, slept, and breathed her brother and his illness. But the rest of the circle is hard. Names come easily. Writing them down hurts. She hasn't spoken to her parents since she moved out at seventeen. And it's been more than a year since she's seen her three best friends, Amber, June, and Sheree. Wow. They used to be inseparable. What happened? The tears start coming again. Everything feels broken. Maybe she should take that nap. Or watch some Netflix and eat a big bag of salt and vinegar chips. That never makes her feel better for long, though. Stuff may be broken, but you don't have to fix it today, she reminds herself.

Becky quickly writes Amber, June, and Sheree — her best friends since forever — on the circle, three rings from the center. Her parents she banishes to outer space — two small names written on the outer edge of the page.

There are no names of people she actually sees on Becky's circle. That can't be right, can it? Sure, she hasn't gone out much since Brian got sick,

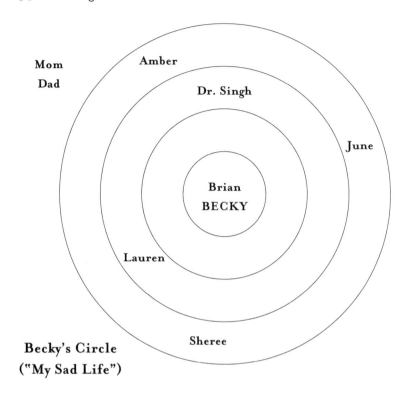

Mom
Dad

Amber

Dr. Singh

June

Brian
BECKY

Lauren

Sheree

Becky's Circle
("My Sad Life")

but she isn't a total hermit. She runs through the past week in her head: a trip to the market, one to the corner store for snacks, a bunch of time spent lurking on Facebook, an appointment with her doctor.

Her doctor. There's someone. She writes Dr. Singh on the second circle from the center. She also remembers saying hi to Lauren, her hairstylist, a couple of times last week. Lauren's salon is below Becky's apartment, and they sometimes run into each other on their way in or out. She writes "Lauren" on the same circle as her doctor, puts down her pencil, and, taking her paper with her, goes to the kitchen for the bag of chips. On her way to the cupboard she sticks her social circle on the fridge as a reminder to play Four Questions tomorrow. She's done enough for one day.

Next morning, coffee in one hand and smartphone in the other, Becky is ready to play Four Questions with her relationships with Brian, Amber, June, and Sheree. She decides to record her thoughts on her phone to keep it real. She explores her relationship with Brian first, putting questions 2, 3, and 4 in the past tense, so that it doesn't seem so strange to answer them:

1. How would I describe the relationship? Brian was five years older than me, and I guess we had a typical big brother–little sister relationship. He didn't get along with Mom and Dad either, so when he got cancer, it was up to me. That's when we actually started to get close — to put aside all the dysfunctional crap we'd learned growing up. I asked him to move in with me when he really started to go downhill. That was a very intense period in our relationship. I really didn't do much other than take care of him.

2. What did I like about the relationship? I'm really grateful for the year we lived together, that opportunity we had to get to know each other for who we really were. Brian was a fighter, and I admired him so much — his spirit, his courage, his willpower. He fought the disease every step of the way.

3. What didn't I like about the relationship? Nothing. There's nothing I didn't like about Brian. Next question?

4. What would I have liked to have been different about the relationship? I wouldn't change anything. Except maybe I wish we'd been closer earlier in our lives. And I wish I could've done more for him when he was sick.

Becky stops recording. She's emotionally exhausted and a little pissed that two of the questions asked her to think badly of Brian. Isn't it bad luck to speak ill of the dead? Plus, there just isn't anything to complain about where Brian is concerned.

TRY THIS: *When you try something new, pat yourself on the back. Completing this exercise is worth feeling good about!*

Gaining New Awareness

When you draw your social circle and play Four Questions, you'll learn some interesting things about your relationships — and maybe about yourself — that you can build on in the weeks ahead.

A new awareness may come as you draw your circle. Maybe the circle is almost empty. Or it's full — but of acquaintances, not friends. If a few relationships are causing you stress or sadness, that's probably not going to come as a shock. But how any one of those relationships is impacting your circle may be a surprise, as when Kate realizes that her husband's controlling behavior is keeping her girlfriends on the periphery.

You might gain new awareness from exploring relationships in greater detail. One of Ron's clients whom we'll call Drea was a fashion model. She found it hard to have close relationships throughout her life — as she put it, people were always a disappointment. She was used to not being able to count on family and friends, but when she started to have problems getting modeling gigs because clients said she was too difficult to work with, she made an appointment with Ron. Maybe interpersonal relationships weren't important to Drea, but paying her rent was.

When she drew her circle, the only two people on it were her boyfriend and her agent. Ron asked her who was missing. Her parents — they never supported her choices. Her sister — she was a know-it-all and was never there when Drea needed her. Her clients — like that jerk who gave her a broken umbrella at the shoot the other week, just so the photographer could get her reaction when the "rain" poured right onto her head. No one played by the rules.

By drawing her circle and playing Four Questions, Drea learned how much always being right was hurting her. No one solves their problems after one week of work, but Drea's new awareness of the connection between her behavior and her relationships set the stage for her to focus her efforts on something that would make a big difference.

Garrett, a firefighter, was feeling depressed after the high-profile deaths of two of his men. When Garrett drew his circle, there was nothing remarkable about it. It wasn't in flux, he had supportive relationships, and there wasn't much in the way of conflict. When he and Ron played Four Questions with the people on his circle, though, he had the same things to say about everybody, from his wife to his colleagues to the

TRY THIS: *Be open to the "aha" moments that happen as you complete your circle. What is your circle telling you about your relationships?*

widows of the two men, whom he saw on a regular basis. "All we do is talk about the guys who died," Garrett said. "Maybe it seems like the right thing for us to do, but I can't move on."

Garrett was becoming a professional mourner — and it was having a negative impact on his mood and functioning. Playing Four Questions helped Garrett realize that he was going to have to figure out a way to rewrite his role and manage people's expectations of him if he was going to feel better.

Now It's Your Turn

We only included one four-question example each for Ana, Becky, John, and Kate, but you'll be completing the Four Questions exercise with four or five of the people who are part of your circle. Depending on how "into" the exercise you get and how much your depression is affecting your emotions and energy level, you may get tired. Take breaks. Do it over a few days. Better to give yourself the time and space to play Four Questions with all of your most important relationships than to get exhausted after one and stop there.

If it feels strange to ask yourself the four questions, try recording your answers, either on paper or on your phone. Or have a friend ask you the questions. Maybe they'd be willing to take notes for you too. The more you put into these exercises, the more you'll get out of them!

If you're having trouble identifying the first (or second, third, or fourth) relationship to examine, here are some questions that can help:

Who did you add to your social circle first? Second? The relationships that jump to mind immediately are often the important ones.

What relationship is the most challenging? What relationship do you wish was different? The tough relationships — the ones that cause you pain and are full of conflict — are good ones to look at more closely.

What relationship helps you the most? It's useful to look at a relationship that already makes you feel better.

Did you leave your mother, father, sibling, or old friend off your circle initially? The fact that you left them off your circle may indicate there is some painful history here, and it's worth taking a closer look.

Has anyone close to you died? It may be hard to add a person who's died to your circle, but that death may be related to your feelings of sadness or depression.

Some relationships are so painful that you don't want to think about them. Of course, you don't have to. But if you keep doing what you've always done, which is not thinking about the relationship that bothers you, you aren't going to feel any differently than you do now. And if you do think about the relationship, you might feel better. Eventually you'll figure out what you want to do: reconnect with the person or really let it go.

GUY TALK: LESSONS I LEARNED MOVING A COUCH

Hi, it's Ron here, and I've got a few thoughts on guys and social circles.

As a general rule, us guys don't invest much time in creating or maintaining our circles. We connect with others, but it's not a conscious thing. It happens informally: on the ice, at a wedding, or watching the game. Even moving a couch.

One of the most profound moments I ever shared with my best friend was when he was helping me move out of my apartment after my girlfriend broke up with me. My friend was at one end of the couch, and I was at the other. Out of the blue and in less time than it takes to grab a beer, open it, and take a swig, he told me exactly why she broke up with me.

I had done everything for my girlfriend, including her university homework. My intentions were good, but to some people — including my girlfriend and my best friend — my behavior was controlling. At the time I didn't recognize it. I needed someone more objective to see it and speak up.

That couch confession was a watershed moment — the right person at the right time with the right message — and I carried it into my next relationship (which ended up being with my wife). But my friend didn't phone me up and arrange to meet over coffee to have a heart-to-heart. We were just two guys moving a couch.

Most men can identify our key relationships with no problem. But describing the positives and negatives about the relationships and stating what we'd like to be different? We may be able to do that with our intimate partners, but no one else.

There are probably some people in your circle whom you could rely on in times of need. And some people who piss you off. And some who are hard to read, and some who are awkward. My neighbor is an example. He's a great guy but he reminds me of Spock — he has a hard time reading social cues.

All of those people should be on your circle — the good, the bad, and the awkward. By playing Four Questions with them, you'll be able to identify what you like and what bugs you about the relationships. It's information you can use later to help yourself feel better.

This Week's To-Do List

Draw your social circle. Include both helpful and stressful relationships. Don't forget people who used to be very important to you, but whom you don't see anymore. There's no right or wrong here — just a drawing with some names on it.

Play Four Questions. Choose four or five of the most important (and most stressful) relationships on your circle and answer the four questions. Remember, this is just about describing your relationships, not making changes to them. Write down your answers, record them on your phone, or ask a friend to help you.

Put your circle in a safe place. You'll want to be able to come back to your circle in later weeks, so don't toss it yet! If you live with others, choose a place that's private, but that you can easily access. If you live alone, you can hang it up.

Name That Feeling

This week we help you make connections between your feelings and the interactions you have with others. With practice, you'll become better at naming your feelings, understanding where they come from, and choosing how you want to handle them — with the end result of feeling better.

Let's say you get home from work, and there are exactly eight pairs of your kids' shoes cluttering up the hallway. Do you yell? Hide in your room feeling ashamed at your failure to instill personal responsibility in your children? Sigh, put the shoes away, and try to forget about it? Whichever reaction you have, how do you feel?

Imagine that you get a group text from a friend about a party everyone went to last night that you weren't invited to. Do you text back something catty? Cry? Vent to someone? Depending on your response, how do you feel?

Your coworker invites you out for lunch and out of the blue tells you he doesn't like the way you act in staff meetings. Do you listen quietly? Angrily defend your behavior? Say nothing and feel nauseous? Tell your spouse about it later? Whichever you do, how does it feel?

Your spouse calls to tell you that, for the third time this week, she can't take the kids to soccer, because she has to stay late at work. Do you get mad and end the call quickly? Laugh and tell her she owes you dinner out this weekend? Tell her it's okay, but inside you're seething? How does your response make you feel?

There are no right or wrong answers to these questions. The point of our scenarios is simply to show that many of our feelings (and our resulting behavior) have an interpersonal component — they're a direct result of the interactions we have with people every day. These interactions, either immediately or over time, affect our mood.

Making that connection between interactions, feelings, behavior, and mood is important for people who have depression. That's because depression is a feeling illness. When we're depressed, we feel sad, lonely, disappointed, angry, frustrated, hopeless, guilty, discouraged, ashamed, and pessimistic. The feelings add up, interaction after interaction, day after day, until we can't imagine what it would be like to feel good again.

PEP TALK: *When you can see connections between your relationships, feelings, and behavior, you'll be able to make choices that help you feel better.*

This week, we'll help you identify the feelings that you experience as a result of your interactions with others and give you tools to express and manage them in ways that will improve your relationships and help you feel better. Let's get started.

Feelings and Moods: What's the Difference?

Feelings are the emotional reactions we have to experiences. When you put a number of similar feelings together, you have a mood.

A fight with your sister will trigger a feeling (or a few). That fight, plus the fact that you dropped your iPhone in the toilet, canceled a coffee date with a friend because you weren't feeling up to it, skipped lunch, and ate a tub of ice cream, *plus* the fact that it's raining for the fourth day in a row — all lead to a low mood. That mood might last for a couple of hours, lifting when your friend calls to check in, your kids come home from a sleepover, or the sun comes out. But it might continue into the next day if, for example, you don't sleep well that night, stay inside the next day, and let the conflict with your sister simmer.

The Six F-words

The first step to managing our feelings is being able to name them — in the moment. It can be tough. When you see your mother-in-law's number pop up on your phone, you aren't asking, "How am I feeling?" You're probably debating whether to answer the call. When your boss calls you into her office, you skip right past "How am I feeling?" You're too busy grabbing last month's sales reports and figuring out how to explain the results. When you've just told your friend something personal, you don't ask, "How am I feeling?" Instead, you're probably running through the conversation in your head again. "Did I say too much? Does he think I'm weird?"

It's time to stop, take a breath, and ask yourself: *How am I feeling?* That's because when you can name your feelings while you're in the heat of battle or the throes of despair or anticipating a conversation with your mother-in-law, you'll make better choices about how — and even whether — to act on them.

There may be dozens of emoticons on your phone, but there are only six main feelings — what we affectionately call the six F-words — *sadness, fear, anger, surprise, happiness*, and *disgust*.

These six emotions are hardwired into humans. Fear, for example, prompts the adrenaline-fueled "fight or flight" response. Disgust probably evolved to keep us safe from rotten food and contagious diseases. Anger helps protect us from threats.

Each of the six feelings triggers behavior. Four of them — disgust, fear, sadness, and surprise — cause us to back away from the situation (and the people) that prompted the feeling. Anger and happiness, in contrast, prompt us to engage with people. Anger, when expressed outwardly, usually leads to confrontation. Happiness makes us want to stick around and keep the feeling alive.

PEP TALK: *We're going to ask you to name your feelings a lot. So you might as well make it your new mantra: "How am I feeling? How am I feeling? How am I feeling?"*

Naming Feelings

Naming feelings can be a challenge. It's easier to describe the event or situation as if we were recounting the plot of a movie or giving the play-by-play of a game — "We were in the car, he said this, then I said that" — but that's telling the story of what happened, not how we were feeling about it.

It's also common to answer the question "How do you feel?" with words like, "Okay" or "Fine." (Think of the last time someone asked, "How are you?" You probably said, "Fine." That response is culturally programmed!) "Okay" and "fine" aren't real feelings. They're statements of degree. If you're okay or fine, you're saying your feelings aren't bothering you that much, but you aren't saying what those feelings are.

Sometimes people will say, "I don't know how I feel." That's understandable. Feelings can be messy, confusing, and changeable, and naming them isn't a skill that we're taught very often. In fact, naming feelings is sometimes actively discouraged in some families and communities.

One of Ron's clients grew up in an abusive family where he wasn't allowed to express any feelings. When Ron asked him what happiness was, he said he knew what it was intellectually. "I can pretend to be happy, Dr. Frey," he admitted. "I can play the role. But I don't actually know what it feels like." Not many of us will be starting from square one, like Ron's client. But almost all of us need to practice identifying how we're feeling.

PEP TALK: *Naming feelings is a skill we can learn. Be patient, and don't forget to practice.*

If you're having a hard time naming your feelings, it can help to pinpoint where in your body you experience different emotions. Disgust is often felt in the belly or the throat. Many people feel fear as a tightness in the chest. Does your face feel hot when you're angry? Do you feel a heaviness across your shoulders when you're sad? Do you get headaches after arguing with your husband? Or feel tired after talking about the death of your sister? Maybe your back stops hurting when you're going to see your grandchildren. All of these are physical expressions of emotions. Tune in to these physical signs, and you may unlock your body's unique language of feelings.

Sometimes the problem isn't naming the feelings; it's knowing which ones, from the overwhelming jumble, are contributing to your depression.

Ana, for example, is resentful that her husband, Peter, gets to go to work and envies his adult conversations and his free time. When he has to work late, she misses him and feels tired and frustrated. She's lonely most days and feels disappointment that her mom can't come from Texas to visit because of Ana's dad's illness. She's annoyed and humiliated by her know-it-all mother-in-law's judgmental surprise visits. She's anxious about whether she's taking care of Ruby properly. In a single day, Ana feels happy, uncertain, inadequate, puzzled, confused, scared, excited, loving, and angry. The emotional roller coaster is exhausting.

Our advice to those struggling to name their feelings is to keep it simple. There are only six F-words. Are you feeling angry? Sad? Happy? Surprised? Disgusted? Afraid? After a while you may be able to say you feel furious, jealous, or frustrated instead of just "angry" or anxious, worried or alarmed instead of simply "afraid." But for now, just choose one of the six. In Ana's case, focusing on an overriding, general feeling that is affecting her mood (anger, perhaps) rather than on the minute-by-minute changes she experiences will help her figure out what she can do to help herself feel better.

TRY THIS: *Keep your feeling list simple at the start. You don't have to say you feel furious or frustrated or jealous — just say you're angry.*

There are hundreds of words in English to describe feelings. This diversity, which makes for interesting conversations and evocative writing, can make it a challenge to identify an overall feeling when we're looking for a starting point to feel better.

A few of the words in the chart on the next page fit in more than one category. "Offended" could go under "angry" as well as "disgusted." "Disillusioned" belongs just as much under "sad" as it does under "surprised." What matters more than where we list the feeling is what's causing it. Or, even better, who's contributing to it.

FEELING WORDS

ANGRY

Aggravated
Agitated
Annoyed
Bitter
Cheated
Displeased
Dissatisfied
Enraged
Envious
Exasperated
Frustrated
Furious
Grumpy
Impatient
Incensed
Indignant
Irate
Irritated
Jealous
Offended
Outraged
Provoked
Resentful
Wrathful

SAD

Alienated
Apathetic
Ashamed
Bored
Defeated
Dejected
Depressed
Despairing
Disappointed
Discontented
Disillusioned
Gloomy
Glum
Grieving
Homesick
Hopeless
Hurt
Ignored
Indifferent
Isolated
Left out
Listless
Lonely
Melancholy
Neglected
Pitiful
Rejected
Remorseful
Sorrowful
Unhappy
Unloved
Weary
Worthless

SURPRISED

Amazed
Astonished
Astounded
Bewildered
Disbelieving
Disillusioned
Dumbfounded
In awe
Shocked
Startled

DISGUSTED

Abhorring
Averse
Contemptuous
Disliking
Hateful
Hostile
Loathing
Nauseous
Offended
Revolted
Scornful
Sickened

HAPPY

Admired
Appreciated
Blissful
Capable
Cared for
Cheerful
Competent
Confident
Connected
Contented
Courageous
Delighted
Determined
Ecstatic
Enthusiastic
Euphoric
Excited
Glad
Gleeful
Hopeful
Joyful
Loved
Optimistic
Peaceful
Proud
Respected
Satisfied
Serene
Thrilled
Triumphant

SCARED

Afraid
Alarmed
Anxious
Apprehensive
Cautious
Dreading
Dubious
Edgy
Fearful
Insecure
Jumpy
Nervous
Overwhelmed
Panicked
Reluctant
Reserved
Shy
Suspicious
Tense
Terrified
Trapped
Uneasy
Wary
Worried

What Does It Mean to Feel Happy?

Every one of us has a need to feel loved, cared for, and connected to others, but there isn't a single person on earth who wakes up every day feeling happy — not even Oprah. Life isn't a chick flick, where the girl always gets the guy and everyone lives happily ever after. In real life, we experience triumph and also defeat, joy and also sorrow, delight and also disappointment. If we never felt sad, how would we know how great happiness feels?

It's important to have realistic expectations of our feelings and mood. Sometimes we'll feel grouchy. Sometimes we'll feel angry. Sometimes we'll feel unloved. And sometimes we'll feel capable, proud, satisfied, and appreciated. When we're feeling down and depressed, it's easy to focus on the feelings we consider "bad," creating a spiral of negativity that makes it harder for us to recognize the moments when we feel better.

Feelings, in themselves, aren't good or bad, positive or negative. Don't judge yourself harshly because you have a moment of insecurity, anxiousness, or displeasure. It's okay to feel hurt, sad, and angry. Feeling low and blue sometimes is normal. We just need to make sure we have effective tools in place to help lift our spirits when the inevitable down times happen.

PEP TALK: *Feelings aren't good or bad. We need both anger and joy in our lives. It's what we do with those feelings that makes all the difference.*

It might help to think of life as an ever-changing river. Sometimes the water flows gently, sometimes it goes over the rapids, and occasionally there's a waterfall. From a distance, that waterfall can look beautiful — there's even a rainbow. But when you're going over the edge, all you feel is fear for the future and longing for the times when the river was calm and predictable. Most parts of the river of life are normal. What we need to learn is to go with the flow.

MAKE TIME FOR POSITIVE EXPERIENCES

Try to do something that makes you feel good every day, preferably with another person. Play a game (not Solitaire!), go to a yoga class, volunteer, invite a friend for a walk, buy a gift for someone special, text a friend, write a letter, or do something else that you enjoy.

Understanding Anger

Remember when I said feelings aren't good or bad? That's hard for many of us to believe when it comes to anger. We see the destructive, wild, and potentially violent side of the emotion and don't see its helpful side.

When anger is constructively expressed, it allows us to stand up for ourselves, assert our needs, and release tension. But many of us — particularly women — would rather accommodate others than ask for what we need, if it requires raising our voices or being direct. We don't want to risk fanning the flames of conflict, feeling out of control, or driving other people away.

Keeping the peace by avoiding and denying anger isn't healthy. We *are* feeling it. It *will* come out. And when it does, it can be ugly. We might direct it at ourselves, explode at the person we're mad at, take it out on innocent bystanders, or transform it into another feeling, such as self-loathing.

PEP TALK: *When anger is expressed in a way that's respectful, it can be a helpful emotion.*

Kate, for example, was raised to believe that good girls don't get angry. She prefers to put her daily irritations, disappointments, and frustrations away in their respective boxes in her anger closet and close the door. She avoids the inevitable conflict between teachers at her school whenever possible and plays peacemaker when conflict lands on her desk — a role she performs well, having practiced the art of diffusing, redirecting, and hiding angry feelings all her life. She's having a hard time keeping the door of the anger closet closed when it comes to Don, though, and it's making her feel like a failure.

On the opposite end of the spectrum are those of us who are always angry. It's our go-to feeling. We rage. We blame. We stew. We slam doors. We yell. We may even break things. We go from zero to a hundred in a millisecond, muttering under our breath or screaming long before we've even figured out what's bothering us.

Ask John what he feels about the people in his life, and the anger surfaces immediately. He's bitter about his parents. He's disgusted by his siblings (except his brother, Tom, who simply disappoints him). His co-workers, particularly Alex, are at best irritating and at worst infuriating. There is open conflict in every one of his relationships.

Angry people do experience other feelings — they just don't recognize them. These other feelings may be painful to think about or may make them sad. So they skip right over them and get mad. If they can uncover the unexpressed feeling — which is actually an indication of an unmet need — they can handle things more constructively.

Acknowledging emotions other than anger would be going against years of conditioning and decades of practice for John. If he's honest with himself, though, John feels sad and lonely a lot of the time. He wishes people were kinder to him. He feels he's a nice guy. Why don't people see it? John's anger is like a protective shield. He feels he has to stand up for himself, because no one else will.

If you're an anger-first person like John, ask yourself, "What else am I feeling besides anger?" "What do I really want?" "What am I missing?" Maybe you're angry because you feel someone isn't listening to you, or because you feel excluded by your friends, or because you feel misunderstood by your boss. What you're missing is feeling validated and respected. What you want is to be included and acknowledged. You're feeling sadness as well as anger. Recognizing that will help you cope.

ALL THAT AND A BAG OF CHIPS

Many people cope with their feelings of sadness, anxiety, and depression by using alcohol, drugs, or food. I'm an emotional eater, so I know exactly how, in the short term, these strategies can help us calm ourselves and ease painful and uncomfortable feelings. But over the longer term, these coping styles may negatively affect our relationships and health. If you're game to give other approaches a try, we're here to help.

Next time you want to pour a drink, open a bag of cookies, or light a joint, ask yourself what's going on right now. Did you just get off the phone with your judgy mother? Did you hear a song that reminded you of someone who isn't in your life anymore? Are you T minus two hours to leaving for a big party? Once you've put your finger on the interpersonal trigger for your desire to self-medicate, ask yourself how you're feeling. Are you angry? Sad? Afraid? Is there another way you could handle that feeling? Is there someone supportive you could talk to?

It won't be easy to substitute other coping strategies for self-medication, but stick with it. Over the next few weeks you'll be learning and practicing skills that will help you feel better — without the bag of chips.

Feelings, Behavior, and Relationships

Working through feelings is a lot like sorting through the stuff you've stored in a messy basement. Every item has a story. Every item had value for you at some point. Some items are recent. Some are very old. Some aren't even yours. It's hard work figuring out what to keep and what to sell, give away, or toss in the trash. It's a pain following through on the plan. The whole experience can even be a little embarrassing, depending on what you're storing down there. But when it's all done, it feels darn good.

When I was younger, everything made me cry. I cried on the golf course, on the couch, in bed, in the car, at work. I cried when my husband didn't hit the tennis ball near me, so I had to run to return it. I cried in my bowl of Kraft Macaroni and Cheese, because I thought I was a terrible wife who didn't know how to cook. I cried when my friend didn't call me. I cried when she did call me and said something that hurt my feelings. When I was angry, I cried. When I was sad, I cried. When I was afraid, I cried. When something unexpected happened, I cried. I even cried tears of joy.

It took me a long time, with a lot of help from my husband, to learn how to name my feelings, talk about them, and express them in a way that wasn't uncontrolled weeping. I needed to develop the skills to regulate my emotions — to bring down their intensity without denying or suppressing them.

Feelings are only a problem if they negatively impact you or your important relationships. My constant crying was hard for my husband, who wasn't sure how to interpret the tears or offer support. It was also hard on me when I wanted to have a constructive conversation. If you're constantly angry, it may make it difficult for you to keep a job. It may put stress on your marriage. And you may develop high blood pressure. If you keep all your emotions inside, your stoicism might make it hard for you to open up to people and ask for (or accept) help. It may also create conflict with your partner, if he or she needs and expects emotional connection.

TRY THIS: *Your feelings are never "wrong" or "bad," but learning to express them differently can improve your relationships and your health.*

If your relationships are full of conflict, stress, disappointment, and sadness, you may want to find ways to manage your feelings differently, so you can maintain a job, a marriage, relationships with family and friends, and your health. Either that, or you can find new friends, a new partner, and a new job. (Sadly, we only get one body, although parts of us do get replaced as we age!)

What's Your Interpersonal Style?

People usually have well-established ways of interacting with others that impact their relationships. These relationships result in feelings. These feelings influence mood.

We call these go-to ways of interacting with others an "interpersonal style." Each style has short-term and long-term costs and benefits for us. Sometimes we'll apply the same style to pretty much all of our relationships. Other times we pick and choose, depending on the situation. We might be quiet and deferent at work, but loud and angry with our kids. Or we always want to be right with our spouse, but don't engage in direct conflict with our friends.

The first step to seeing if your interpersonal style is helping or hindering your mood is to identify which of the three types is your dominant style:

PASSIVE STYLE

I say yes when I don't really want to.

I don't want to disappoint others.

I'm worried about being rejected if I say what I really feel.

People take advantage of me.

Short-term gain: You don't have to worry about disappointing people and being rejected.

Long-term pain: Your own needs don't get met, which leads to resentment, sadness, frustration, anger, and possibly depression.

AGGRESSIVE STYLE

I like to be right.

I enjoy being in control.

I interrupt and talk over others.

I like to have the last word.

Short-term gain: You win the battle — with the accompanying adrenaline rush and feeling of power. You rarely feel ignored or vulnerable.

Long-term pain: You lose the war. People distance themselves from you, or they let you dominate them, which results in one-sided relationships. Isolation and conflict may lead to feelings of sadness, loneliness, and symptoms of depression.

ASSERTIVE STYLE

I care about others' feelings, but not more than my own.

I don't like conflict, but I know sometimes it's necessary.

What others think of me matters, but not so much that I'd do something I don't want to.

I will listen to the other person's side as long as they will listen to mine.

I realize that I won't always get my way.

I'll risk disappointing people to ask for what I want or need.

Short-term pain: Not knowing how others will respond to your direct expression of needs, values, or expectations can feel scary.

Long-term gain: People respect you because you respect both them and yourself, and they want to maintain a relationship with you. You get your key needs met, but not in a way that alienates or hurts others.

THE BOY IN THE CORNER

Ron here. Sometimes an aggressive style comes in disguise, and in the case of a teenage boy I was counseling the disguise was black baggy pants, a black hoodie, and a baseball cap pulled right down over his eyes.

The boy never said a word in our early sessions together, just slouched in a chair in the corner of my office. Eventually I figured out the benefits of his passive-aggressive interpersonal style. In the short term, he avoided conflict and could completely control the situation. But long-term, this style was responsible for his social isolation and the anger of his parents and teachers. It also meant he had to come to therapy every week and sit — in silence — with me.

I asked him how it would feel if he didn't have to see me anymore.

He looked up from under his baseball cap and smiled.

"Okay," I said. "Let's work on that." I told him I could meet his expectation of no longer seeing me if he agreed to use a different interpersonal style — one that used words.

Our first conversation started slowly and awkwardly. Eventually I asked him what it was like to communicate without words. How did it make him feel? How did it benefit him? How did it affect other people? How did they feel? What effect did their feelings have on him?

By the end of our time together, he was able to recognize the benefits and costs of communicating more assertively. In the short term, he was risking rejection and loss of control, but in the long term connecting with others and expressing his needs made him feel better. And the icing on the interpersonal cake? He didn't have to see me anymore.

How's That Working for You?

Our feelings may come to us automatically, but our behavior is a choice.

It's possible to consciously change your interpersonal style to suit certain situations or relationships. It's even possible to change your interpersonal style altogether. But it's darn hard. It takes a lot of courage, commitment, and practice, and it's not something anyone can do in one week.

Modifying your interpersonal style is an experiment, not a personality overhaul. It's like trying on a new outfit that's not your usual look. You're going to feel uncomfortable at first. Your instinct may be to take it off as fast as possible and throw it on the "What was I thinking?" pile. You can do that — but the outfit you've always worn probably doesn't make you feel so great either. So what do you have to lose? Wear the new outfit once, in front of a person you trust. What happens? How does the person react? How does that make you feel? If it doesn't make you feel better, you can always go back to your old wardrobe.

Remember Drea, the fashion model who lashed out when people didn't play by the rules? After working with Ron for a few weeks, she recognized that her aggressive interpersonal style was impacting her career, so she bravely decided to try a different style on for size.

TRY THIS: *Trying on a new interpersonal style is like experimenting with a new look. Show it to one person, and see how you feel.*

She got the opportunity at a shoot where she was supposed to jump into a pool. She hit the water, and it was absolutely freezing — the latest example of a client tricking her in order to capture a spontaneous reaction on camera. Drea had a split second before she surfaced to make a choice. Should she use her old style (burn them with anger) or try a new style (play it cool)? She opted to coolly let the people on the shoot know that the freezing pool wasn't something she had agreed to and that she was very unhappy.

At her next appointment, Ron asked Drea how it felt to use the new interpersonal style.

"It felt weird," she admitted. "I didn't get the immediate rush I usually get. I had to wait until the shoot was over to get my feelings out, and even then I had to stay calm."

Ron asked how she felt later.

"I felt pretty good," she said. "Usually people get really defensive with me, which makes me even madder. But this time, they apologized and explained why they did it. Their excuses didn't make things okay, but I was able to tell them that without yelling. And get this — they've already called me for another gig."

Turns out they'd expected her to throw a hissy fit over the cool pool. When she didn't, she earned a new level of respect — from others and from herself.

TRY THIS: *Whether you're thinking about how you usually handle a situation or trying something new, the most important question is, "How do I feel?"*

If you're ready to try a different interpersonal style, you'll need to put your interactions under the microscope. Choose a situation and break it down, moment by moment, feeling by feeling. Then imagine a different outcome. How could you handle a similar situation differently next time, so you — and the other person or people involved — feel better? A handy way to do this is to work through ten questions that we lovingly call "Ten Questions for Emotional Enlightenment."

As an example, let's use the opening scenario from this week's chapter: the eight pairs of kids' shoes in the hallway. You walk in the door and see the shoes. Maybe you even trip over one. The first step is to ask yourself: *How am I feeling?* Are you angry? Disappointed? Ashamed? Frustrated? Hurt? Don't say, "Okay" or "Fine." If you're stuck, pick one of the six F-words. If there are several feelings mixed together, focus on the feeling that's most intense.

The next step is to ask: *What's making me feel this way?* Is it the fact that you've told the kids a million times before that their shoes go in the closet? Are most of the shoes your eldest son's, and he should know better? Did you just talk to them about this yesterday? Is it just one more example of how they ignore what matters to you?

Next, ask: *How do I usually handle this?* Do you squash the feeling down and remove the evidence — in this case, by cleaning up the shoes yourself? Do you try to address it with the kids right then and there? Eat a big bowl of last night's dessert? Go somewhere private and close the world out? Or do you take some deep breaths, calm down, and make a plan to deal with the issue when the time is right?

Step four is to ask: *What happens when I handle things that way?* Let's say you usually call the kids down and yell at them. Does it start a screaming match? Do you say things you later regret? Do you end up doling out punishments that you have a hard time enforcing later? How do the kids react? Do they withdraw? Say things that hurt your feelings? Fight with each other the rest of the night? How's that working for you? Does it change anything — and is it for the better or the worse?

Next, we go back to feelings. Ask: *How does that make me feel?* Let's say you handle a situation like the shoes by withdrawing. Do you feel better after your self-imposed time-out? Or do you spend your time alone thinking about all the ways your kids fail you or you fail them, which makes you feel sad, inadequate, incompetent, and sorry for yourself?

Then ask: *How do the other people involved feel?* Do your kids feel sad when you yell? Are they angry? Do they feel scared? Do your kids feel ashamed when you withdraw? Powerless? Relieved?

Next, we're going to imagine a different way of handling the situation. If your interpersonal style isn't resulting in feelings you want for yourself or others, ask: *What could I do differently?* Instead of withdrawing, could you text a friend right away to vent and ask for advice? Instead of yelling, could you try writing out what you'd like to say to your kids, so you can share your feelings and expectations more calmly? Instead of eating, drinking, or smoking, could you do an emotional reset by going for a walk or taking a shower? Instead of denying your feelings, could you role-play a scenario with someone you trust in which you express your feelings to your kids directly?

TRY THIS: *Ask others how they feel in certain situations, and you may discover they feel the same as you. Plus, their way of handling their feelings might give you some ideas!*

Then ask the last three questions: *What effect might that have? How might that make me feel? And how might other people feel?* Let's say you decide to text a friend right away for advice. If you've never done it before, you probably don't know what might happen and what feelings it might evoke. But you can give an educated guess. Chances are your friend will have at least one good idea you can try, which will make you feel optimistic and your friend feel special because you value her opinion. Even if she doesn't have an idea that you think will work, you'll have calmed down and will maybe have a couple of ideas of your own. You may also have discovered that your friend feels similarly about her kids' behavior.

TEN QUESTIONS FOR EMOTIONAL ENLIGHTENMENT

Ask yourself these questions to understand where your feelings are coming from, how you handle them, what you could do differently, and how that might feel. The end result of this en-lighten-ment? Feeling a little lighter, of course.

1. How am I feeling?
2. What's making me feel this way?
3. How do I usually handle this?
4. What happens when I handle things that way?
5. How does that make me feel?
6. How do other people involved feel?
7. What could I do differently?
8. What effect might that have?
9. How might that make me feel?
10. How might other people feel?

One Small, Brave Step at a Time

It's one thing to try on your new interpersonal outfit in a changing room and another thing entirely to wear it in public. How will it feel? How will people react? What if the first few times you wear it, people like it, but one time they don't? What if you forget to wear it one day and put on your old clothes instead?

Human interactions and the relationships that grow from them can't be reduced to mathematical equations: if I always do *X*, the end result will always be *Y*. If we try something and it doesn't work once, it's not game over. If we intend to try something new and things go sideways, it's not a forever failure. If it worked yesterday but it didn't work today, it doesn't mean it won't ever work again.

If you're normally passive, and you try a new tool like assertiveness, you'll disappoint some people sometimes. They'll wonder, "Who is this new person who stands up for herself?" And you'll wonder, "Will they still want to be my friend if I don't say yes?" It takes some time to become more comfortable with that short-term feeling and to see the long-term benefits.

Try the strategies. Use the tools. And have realistic expectations of yourself and others. You won't change overnight. And neither will your relationships. But it's worth taking small steps if they make you feel better.

Taking Your Emotional Temperature

I know a successful tennis player who always checks his heart rate before he serves. He knows that if his pulse is too high, he's much more likely to fault on the serve and risk losing a point. Consistently (and discreetly) checking his heart rate is his way of optimizing his physical performance.

You can optimize your interpersonal performance by doing something similar: taking your emotional temperature. You probably won't be looking at your smart watch — unless you've made a connection between your heart rate and your emotional state. Instead, you'll be taking your emotional temperature by asking yourself that all-important question: *How am I feeling?* Your answer will determine what you do next.

It'll be easier to optimize your interpersonal performance if you don't wait until something throws you off

TRY THIS: *Take your emotional temperature at regular times of the day and when an interaction brings up intense feelings. Ask yourself, "How am I feeling?" and "What could I do to feel better?"*

your game to check how you're feeling. Take your emotional temperature at regular times of the day: when you wake up, when you arrive at work, at lunch, before you leave work, before you pick up the kids from day care, before your spouse walks in the door, before bed. You can also do it whenever something happens that messes with your emotional mojo. And then take it again after you've taken action to bring things back into balance.

There are some great ways to moderate your emotional temperature — to cool things down if they've become too heated or warm things up if they've become too icy. We've included a few to try.

Ways to Cool Things Down

Give yourself some space. Count to 50 (10 usually won't cut it). Take some deep breaths. Do some push-ups. Tell the other person you need some time to cool down.

Create helpful mental pictures. Visualize turning the volume down. Imagine a thermometer and put ice around the base. Think of a traffic signal and turn the emotional red light to yellow. Think of yourself as a sieve, and let hurtful words or emotions that aren't helping you run through the holes.

Keep it respectful. Think about how your words will be received by the other person before you say them. When sharing what has made you angry or hurt, focus on the person's behavior rather than making statements about the person. For example, instead of saying, "You're rude," say, "When you say that, it feels rude to me." Help the other person understand where you're coming from without belittling them or making them feel ashamed.

Clarify. Repeat what you heard the other person say: "So you're saying..." Ask for clarification if you're confused. This will make the other person feel listened to and clear up misunderstandings; it'll also give both of you a chance to take a breather.

Ways to Warm Things Up

Ask people how they feel about the way you're acting. If you're feeling lonely or left out and want to increase your feeling of connection to others, practice assertiveness by asking someone you trust how your behavior makes them feel. Is your anger making them pull away? Is your "poor me" attitude making them feel as though nothing they do or say helps you, so why bother? Is your negativity causing you to misinterpret their words and behavior? It'll take courage on both sides — yours to ask directly and theirs to answer honestly — but you may learn something and have the opportunity to clarify, which could make you feel better.

Put yourself in the other person's shoes. Imagine how you'd feel if the roles were reversed. What could you do or say to make the interaction more successful? You can also ask them straight out what they need.

Stay open to possibilities. Don't assume you know how someone else is feeling and why. Ask the person directly, and then accept what they say. Your boyfriend may want to see you less, but that doesn't necessarily mean he's stopped loving you. Maybe his expectations of a romantic relationship are different from yours. Maybe he misses his friends. Or maybe he needs some alone time to recharge. If he says he still loves you, try believing him. It's enough to take care of yourself without taking on everyone else's feelings too. Respect the people in your life enough to believe what they're telling you.

Pick a good time. Approach someone for a discussion when there aren't a lot of distractions, when you're both feeling well rested and well fed, and when you have the time to talk. Agree to a time that works well for both of you.

Don't forget to ask yourself, "How am I feeling?" again after you've tried something to warm up or cool down your emotional temperature. If you're feeling better, fantastic. Remember what you did and try that approach again another time! If you're still feeling angry, sad, lonely, disappointed, left out, or afraid and it's affecting your mood or your relationship, you might need to take other steps to feel better.

GUY TALK: ONE SIZE DOESN'T FIT ALL

Men may be able to connect feelings to golf shots ("I feel great about the way I sunk that punt"), but most of us don't connect feelings to relationships. The end result is that we may continue to act in a way that's served us well in the past or in a particular setting, even when it's negatively affecting relationships that are important to us and making us feel bad.

For example, soldiers and police officers often use an aggressive, command-and-control interpersonal style. It's a necessity on the job, but it doesn't work so well at home when they try to run family life like boot camp. Kids rebel. Spouses withdraw or fight back. And the soldier or police officer ends up feeling angry, powerless, incompetent, and depressed.

The same can be true of executives. Oscar, one of my clients, was a finance director who had recently moved from a hierarchical, eat-or-get-eaten corporate environment to a more collaborative, horizontal organization. After six months on the job he was assigned a coach — me — to help him with workplace conflict. In the past, he'd moved ahead through a very loud, aggressive, win-at-all-costs style. His new team was looking for cooperation and collegiality.

As part of our work together, Oscar had individual conversations with each of his colleagues to find out how they felt about his communication style. Before his first conversation, I asked how he was feeling.

"I'm worried they're going to laugh at me and think I'm weird," he said.

After he'd had a few conversations with his colleagues, we met again. "How are things going?" I asked him.

"I'm surprised," he said. "Almost everyone is supportive. One guy apologized to me before I could even talk to him."

I asked him how he felt.

"I'm happy people are responding to me more positively, but I want my employer to know how hard this is for me."

It *is* hard to use a different interpersonal style, particularly for type A guys who aren't comfortable with vulnerability. Being assertive when your go-to style is aggressive or passive won't feel like getting a hole in one every time. Just know that, shot by shot, you're improving your game. And that's going to feel good.

This Week's To-Do List

Take your emotional temperature. Set regular times each day to check in on how you're feeling and decide if you need to do anything about it. Set alarms on your phone or your smart watch to remind you. Write down your responses if you feel that will help.

Tell others how you're feeling. When someone asks, "How are you?" answer honestly, with one of the six F-words.

Ask others how they're feeling. When a friend tells you what happened with her kids or your husband tells you about his day at work, ask, "How did that make you feel?" It's a great way to practice asking that question, and you may discover that other people feel a lot like you do!

Use your feelings to guide your behavior. Think of an interaction that bothered you, and then ask yourself the Ten Questions for Emotional Enlightenment. What did you do? How did it feel? What could you have done differently? How would that have felt? Remember to do something that feels good most days too — preferably with another person!

Choose Your
Own Adventure

This week, we help you figure out which one of four problem areas you were experiencing around the time you started to feel down or depressed. Choosing a problem area will help you focus your efforts over the next few weeks and give you specific steps to take to feel better. Added bonus: the skills you learn can be applied to any future problem!

You've probably heard the ancient Chinese proverb, "A journey of a thousand miles begins with a single step." Then there's this popular saying: "There are many paths to the top of the mountain, but the view is always the same." Both are relevant to the work we'll do together this week. No matter what "adventure" you choose to go on with us — and you'll have picked yours by the end of this chapter — you'll learn strategies that will make you feel better. And it all starts with a single small step.

I have a friend who gets overwhelmed by a sink of dirty dishes. Leyla is a messy soul trapped in a perfectionist's body, and the smallest household chore can paralyze her. She doesn't just see the dishes. She sees everything else in the kitchen that she thinks needs to be dealt with: the dirty cupboard fronts, the crusty oven, the science experiments in the fridge, the greasy gunk trapping dust bunnies in the fins of the microwave fan. Her floor is dirty. Her compost bucket needs to be washed. Her drawers are full of crumbs.

Leyla doesn't have the time or energy to tackle it all, so she doesn't tackle any of it — and the dishes pile up. (For the record, I think her kitchen looks just fine. Would I eat off her floor? Probably not. But that's why we have tables.)

She's recently started dating a guy whose favorite phrase is "baby steps." When she balks at the sink of dishes, starts listing all the other chores she needs to get done, and throws her hands up in the air (or starts to cry), Dan laughs and lovingly reminds her, "Baby steps, beautiful. Let's start with the dishes."

When we think we have to do everything at once, we get overwhelmed. And we often give up. That's why we're asking you to choose a single area to focus on for the rest of this book — a single adventure — and take some baby steps with us.

Back in Week 1, we talked about the four stressful situations or problem areas that most people who feel down, depressed, and lousy are experiencing around the time their mood changes: *conflict* with another person, a *life transition*, *complicated grief*, and *loneliness and isolation*. This week, you'll pick one of these areas to focus on. The small steps you'll take from now until the end of the book are your adventure. You'll set a concrete goal (or two), work toward it, and, in our last week together, celebrate your success. Then you can use your new skills to tackle all the new adventures that come your way.

PEP TALK: *This week you'll choose something to focus on, so you'll learn some new skills you can apply again and again in the future.*

To help you choose your adventure, we provide an explanation of each problem area, examples, and a questionnaire on which you can check off the statements that apply to you. We've separated the questionnaire into four parts, with one for each problem area. By the end of the chapter, you'll be able to look back over each part and see which one has the most check marks — an indication that it might be the area that's affecting your mood.

You may feel confident that you know which problem area is yours, but we recommend reading the whole chapter to make sure you've considered all the options. At the end of the chapter we'll walk you through how Ana, Kate, John, and Becky choose their problem areas and offer some tips for choosing yours. Is it the area with the most check marks? Or does your gut tell you something different? Let's find out.

Interpersonal Conflict: When Relationships Bring Us Down

There's no one I know who can honestly say they've never had an argument or disagreement with someone. If two people talk about anything more than the weather, one of them is bound to eventually express an opinion or act in a way that the other one doesn't like or agree with.

Conflict is a natural and important part of real, meaningful relationships. It's what happens when we share our true selves with others — because those others won't always think, feel, or behave the way we do, or the way we want them to.

Ideally, conflict points out where there's stress or tension in a relationship, so we can figure out what's going on and work together on solutions. It's like a roadside warning sign, telling us to slow down, stay alert, and take action. But sometimes we ignore the signs. Instead of responding responsibly to the sharp curve, icy bridge, or sheep crossing, we maintain speed and hope for the best. Or maybe we follow the signs, but our efforts don't seem to make a difference. The stress or tension isn't resolved. Instead, it simmers or grows.

PEP TALK: *Conflict is a healthy part of every meaningful relationship. When it's really bringing us down, though, it's no longer healthy.*

Conflict takes many forms. It can be with a spouse about how to discipline the kids, a friend who stops calling, an aging parent who refuses to stop driving, or a sibling who manages to ruin every family gathering. Does your boss keep piling work on your desk at 5 PM, expecting it to be done the next day? Is your teenage son or daughter so belligerent that you yell every day (and cry every night)? Is your neighbor's behavior making you seriously consider putting your house up for sale?

There are three types of conflict. In the first, the conflict is out in the open. Often there's arguing (and maybe yelling and tears too). It's obvious there's an issue, and it occupies a lot of our time. We might talk about it with other people. We might raise it with the person we're in conflict with. We might try — unsuccessfully — to resolve it. We're experiencing intense feelings of disappointment, hurt, anger, frustration, and maybe even worthlessness, and the cause is clear.

The second type of conflict is below the surface. We ignore each other. We live separate lives. We may even fool ourselves into thinking things are okay, but really we've simply given up on resolving the problems in the relationship. We aren't openly fighting with each other, but the conflict may take its toll in other ways. Maybe we can't concentrate at work, have a short fuse with our kids, or have physical symptoms that no gluten-free diet, chiropractor visit, or iron supplement seems to fix.

PEP TALK: *You don't have to be openly fighting with someone to have conflict in a relationship. Conflict that goes underground will come out in other ways!*

Sometimes an incident will bring a simmering conflict to the front burner. Maybe a friend leaves her husband, a coworker quits, your girlfriend unfriends you on Facebook, or your teenager says something profound (but probably snarky) about your marriage. Suddenly you're thinking, "Maybe the future could be different. Maybe I should do something."

In the final type of conflict, we know the relationship is over, but we may struggle for a long time with how to end it.

Is interpersonal conflict the area you should focus on? If you're openly arguing or fighting with someone close to you right now and it's affecting your ability to function, it's probably obvious to you that the dispute is what's bringing you down. But if the conflict has been going on for a long time, you've given up hope of resolving it, and you've transferred its effects to other areas of your life, such as other relationships or your physical health, it'll be less clear.

Who are you most angry at? Who has hurt you and you haven't told them? What relationship has been bothering you for a long time, but you just figure it's not worth fighting about anymore?

If you think there might be something you're overlooking, it can be helpful to go back to the social circle you drew in Week 2.

People who feel depressed, down, and blue have a tendency to blame themselves for the way they feel. It's common to think that the problems in the relationship would go away if we just changed ourselves. We're too pushy, demanding, needy, gossipy, boring, or selfish. We should stay longer at work. We should go out more often. We should keep the house cleaner. We should, we should, we should.

It can help to remember that, in most cases, conflict doesn't happen because anyone involved is a bad person. You both just aren't on the same page. Each of you expects something different of the other, and there's no resolution in sight.

PEP TALK: *Conflict isn't about being good or bad, right or wrong. It's about people who aren't on the same page as far as what they want from the relationship.*

If you choose interpersonal conflict as your problem area, we'll help you develop more constructive communication skills, so you can try to work through these differences in expectations. If the differences are truly irreconcilable, we'll help you figure out what to do next.

WHEN CONFLICT GOES TOO FAR

Sometimes people in conflict act in unhealthy, dangerous, and illegal ways. No one should ever harm you physically; criticize you constantly; humiliate, berate, belittle, or bully you; or try to control your every move.

If you worry that your physical safety or emotional well-being is at risk, it's time to get help. Start by telling a professional or someone you trust about the situation. If nothing improves in your relationship, do whatever it takes to get out. Talk to a person who has been through something similar and made a change; they'll listen to your feelings, understand what you're going through, and share what it's like now that they don't live like that anymore. You and your loved ones deserve to live without emotional or physical violence.

Questionnaire, Part 1: Interpersonal Conflict

Check off the statements that are true for you.

When it comes to my relationship with one or more people:

❏ I'm experiencing frequent or intense conflict.

❏ I'm having difficulty identifying or expressing my feelings or needs.

❏ It's hard for me to understand the other person's point of view.

❏ We used to fight, but now we just ignore each other.

❏ I feel the other person doesn't understand or care about my needs or feelings.

❏ I feel like giving up on the relationship.

❏ I feel the other person has given up on me.

❏ I feel like ending the relationship.

❏ I feel things will never change.

❏ I feel if I just tried harder or knew why we were having problems, things would improve.

❏ I say I don't care about the conflict, but if I'm honest, it bothers me.

❏ I feel surprised and disappointed about how the other person has responded to me.

❏ I don't feel I can trust the person any longer.

❏ I'm really surprised by the negative changes in the relationship.

❏ I feel we want different things from the relationship.

❏ I feel the other person isn't trying to deal with the problems.

❏ When I'm with the person, it feels tense and uncomfortable.
❏ I feel worse at the end of a discussion with the person than I did at the beginning.
❏ I feel it's a waste of time to talk about our problems.

Life Transitions: Change Is a Four-Letter Word (with Two Extra Letters)

Spencer West spoke at an event at my grandson's school a few years ago. He's a motivational speaker who lost both his legs when he was five and has accomplished things most of us with two fully functioning lower limbs would never try, including climbing Mount Kilimanjaro.

He took questions at the end of his talk and, kids being kids, one little boy asked Spencer if he ever wanted his legs back. Spencer looked straight at him and without a second thought said, "No." He went on to explain that he was the person he was today because he had lost his legs when he was young, and he wouldn't change that for anything.

Now my knee-jerk response (which I kept to myself, of course!) was, "That's B.S., Spencer. You think your life has been enriched by not having legs, but I don't buy it." But I've thought a lot about his answer since that day, and now I wonder. Legs would change everything in Spencer West's life. It's a strange thing for someone who takes walking for granted to think about, but I had to acknowledge that he might have some difficulty with the transition back to a life with lower limbs.

Transitions are events that occur throughout our lives marking a change from one role or situation to another, often when we move from point to point in the human life cycle. Most of these life changes aren't inherently good or bad, and most have both upsides and downsides — though it's hard for people who have depression to appreciate the upside.

PEP TALK: *Most of life's changes have pluses and minuses.*

A change in our physical abilities (losing our legs — or getting them back after a lifetime without them) is a transition. So is any other major change in our health status, living arrangements, employment, or finances. Marriage is a transition. So is divorce. Getting a new job is a transition, as is getting fired from an old one. Bankruptcy? Transition. Winning the lottery? Yup, transition. Going to college, moving to a new city, having a baby, creating a blended family, recovering from an addiction — they're all transitions.

Transitions aren't always linked to the start of mood difficulties and depression. But if your life change means adapting to a new, unfamiliar role and you miss your old circumstances a lot, it may be associated with your depression.

Do you feel as though your expectations of the new role aren't being met? Is the life change supposed to be a good thing, but actually feels bad? Did the change happen in a way you thought it shouldn't? Do you feel inadequate, unprepared, or as if you're failing in your new role? Have you lost the support people you used to count on as a result of the change? Has your self-esteem taken a hit? These are all telltale signs that the transition may be connected to your mood difficulties.

PEP TALK: *Transitions can be difficult when we choose them, and devastating when they choose us.*

Transitions are harder when we feel we had no say in whether they happened. Think about having children. If you planned to become pregnant, you would probably be excited and a little anxious at the prospect of having a child. If your pregnancy was a surprise, your feelings would likely be a mixture of strong emotions — many of them negative — and you would be full of questions. Should I have the baby? Will I be able to manage? Where will the money come from? Am I ready for the responsibility? Where will I live? What should I tell the father?

A similar situation can occur when you are leaving a job or ending a marriage. If you choose to leave your job, it is one thing; if you are fired, it is quite another. And your decision to end your marriage is vastly different from being told by your partner that it is over. The feelings of loss and uncertainty are magnified when fate deals you a difficult blow.

One of my clients was a woman whose husband had left her for "a younger model," as she put it. She'd begged her husband to stay and offered to go to counseling, but he hadn't wanted to work on the marriage. After she became single, she missed the security and status of being married and worried that she wouldn't be able to manage her home and finances on her own. She felt worthless, angry, frightened, bitter, and resentful. Hers was a classic case of depression connected to a life transition.

Another client, a woman in her late twenties named Emily, came to me because she felt sad all the time. She had stopped seeing her friends, wasn't sleeping well, and hadn't dated in years. She was no longer happy living at home, even though her family was very close. Emily was tired of being her mother's confidante and supporter, but felt that she couldn't move out because her mother needed her too much. Together we worked on her transition from being her mother's caretaker to being an adult child who was free to live her own life.

Sometimes your transition will actually be brought on by a change in someone else's life. One of my clients came to see me after her husband was in a car accident. He had a traumatic brain injury that was affecting his memory and mood, and he wasn't able to work. She was frustrated and tired from carrying all the financial responsibility and being her husband's primary caregiver, and she missed their old relationship and lifestyle. She knew his situation was impacting her mood, but she resisted seeing her problem area as transitions. Wasn't it her husband, after all, who was suffering from the injuries and disability? Our work together helped her acknowledge the impact of the accident on her life and role, so she could get the care and support she needed to manage difficult circumstances and feel better.

PEP TALK: *A change in a loved one's life can sometimes mean a transition for you too.*

Questionnaire, Part 2: Life Transitions

Check off the statements that are true for you.

When it comes to one or more changes in my life:

❏ I feel angry.
❏ I feel confused.

- ❏ I feel powerless to do anything about the situation.
- ❏ I feel a sense of loss.
- ❏ I miss the way things used to be.
- ❏ I feel I had no say in what happened.
- ❏ I feel I've lost my supports because of it.
- ❏ I don't know what's expected of me anymore.
- ❏ I feel incompetent in my new role.
- ❏ I feel I'll never be happy in my new role or situation.
- ❏ I feel overwhelmed.
- ❏ I feel I made the change to make someone else happy.
- ❏ I'm surprised and disappointed that things haven't worked out better.
- ❏ It's hard to get used to the way things are now.
- ❏ I can't imagine what my life will be like in the future.
- ❏ The change is causing conflict or disagreements with people who are important to me.
- ❏ I feel my life has been taken over by the change.
- ❏ It's hard to see the upside of my new situation.

INTERPERSONAL CONFLICT OR TRANSITION?

Life transitions and interpersonal conflicts often go hand in hand. One of my clients had been involved in a difficult dispute with his business partner and ended up taking early retirement after he sold his share of the business to the partner. It wasn't immediately clear where we should focus our time together — the dispute with the partner or the transition to retirement. We decided to focus on the transition. Had he come to me earlier, before his share of the business was sold, we might've worked on the conflict.

Another client was a new mom whose best friend — who also

had a young child — had recently returned to work full-time. They'd grown very close while they were both at home on maternity leave, sharing the ups and downs of motherhood in the comfort of an understanding, supportive relationship. Now they rarely saw each other. My client felt lonely and hurt that her friend was too busy to hang out, and it was affecting her mood. We could have focused on the transition to being a first-time mom, but repairing the relationship with her best friend was so important to my client that we spent our remaining weeks together examining her expectations of that friendship.

If you can make a connection between your depression and both a life transition and a conflict, it may not matter which one you choose to focus on first. Pick one, learn the skills, and then return to the other if you want.

When Grief Gets Complicated

I didn't grieve my mom's death in the most effective way. I didn't want to experience such intense feelings of loss, so I ate cookies, ice cream, and chocolate bars instead. I avoided visiting her grave and rationalized it with a shrug, saying, "I'm just not a cemetery person." Years later, when my mother-in-law's illness and death brought on unexpectedly powerful feelings of sadness, it took a wise friend to put two and two together for me. My mood difficulties were actually about my mom's death, and I needed to address that.

PEP TALK: *The skills you learn while working on one problem area can easily be applied to another area in the future.*

Grief is considered a problem area when we can link our depression to the death of someone we care about. It can be tempting to think we're grieving a job we lost, a friendship that ended, or our children leaving the nest, but these are transitions. We experience complicated grief when someone in our circle has died.

The person we're grieving could be a parent, close friend, sibling, aunt, uncle, cousin, teacher, mentor, colleague, boss, or neighbor. If they're a peripheral person on your social circle, you might want to ask if you're really grieving them or whether their death is reminding you about someone closer to you whom you didn't grieve fully.

PEP TALK:
Complicated grief is always about the death of a person. If you're feeling a sense of loss about something else in your life, it's probably a transition.

The time frame doesn't matter — your depression may have started right after the person died or anytime after, even decades later. What matters more than when the person died is whether you can function. Of course, not functioning is appropriate for a period of time after someone close to you dies. But if you want to begin to resume some of your normal activities but you can't or people who love you are worried that you aren't coping, this might be your problem area.

So go back to your social circle. Was there anyone significant in your life who died?

If the answer is yes, there are some telltale signs that your grief may be complicated. Are your feelings of sadness, guilt, and loss still intense, and even incapacitating, years after the person died? Do you worry that if you let yourself cry, you'll never stop? Do you feel intense or prolonged sadness every year around the anniversary of your loved one's death? Do you avoid talking or thinking about your loved one? Did you feel numb when they died? Instead of expressing your grief, are you transferring your feelings to other people or areas of your life?

Your grief may be complicated because of circumstances at the time of the person's death. For example, if you weren't able to see your loved one before they died, if your last interaction was a fight, or you had to miss the funeral, you may be left with feelings of guilt that won't go away. Guilt is also a common — and very intense — feeling when a loved one takes their own life. You may blame yourself for not doing enough or seeing the signs. Because of the social stigma of suicide, you may also feel that you can't openly mourn the death and receive support for your loss. Lack of support at the time of a loved one's death in general makes it harder to grieve someone's death fully.

Complicated grief is common among parents who have lost a child. Aisha, one of Ron's clients, was waiting at a busy intersection with her daughter and, when they got their signal to cross, the girl skipped off the sidewalk and into the intersection. A taxi driver ran the red light, hit the girl, and killed her instantly.

Aisha felt like she'd lost a part of herself. She was completely overwhelmed by her feelings of sadness, guilt, and despair and was experiencing conflict with her husband because the way he was grieving their daughter's death was so different from the way she was. Aisha withdrew from her social life, made her daughter's bedroom into a shrine, and couldn't imagine ever living a joyful, meaningful life again. To do so, she said, would be like disrespecting her daughter. She worked with Ron to reengage with people in a way that still felt respectful of her daughter's memory — a difficult task.

> **PEP TALK:** *If you didn't (or couldn't) deal with someone's death at the time, you may end up experiencing feelings of sadness or physical symptoms years later.*

Your grief may surface at an unexpected time and be related to a person you have mixed feelings about. For example, Maureen came to see me just before her sixtieth birthday, because she felt sad, couldn't sleep, and had no appetite. When we completed her social circle and I asked her about people in her life who had died, she told me that her mother had died eighteen years ago.

Maureen had had a difficult relationship with her mom, who was a heavy drinker and had relied on Maureen to raise the younger kids. She didn't feel much emotion when her mom died and had a hard time believing that her mood difficulties were because of complicated grief, even when we made the connection with her upcoming sixtieth birthday — the age her mom was when she died.

> **PEP TALK:** *It doesn't always matter why we feel what we feel or whether it makes sense to us. Acknowledge and accept the feelings, and then take steps toward feeling better.*

We explored the three other problem areas to see if any of them fit better. No luck. So we decided to proceed as if her problem area was complicated grief. As she tried some of the strategies we'll teach you, she started to sleep better, eat more, and feel happier.

SOME WORDS ON PETS AND GRIEF

Ron here. Cindy has never had a pet, so she doesn't understand, but the loss of an animal can have a real impact on our mood. I've seen it with police officers in the K-9 unit, blind people who have seeing-eye dogs, elderly people whose pets are their only companions, and childless singles and couples whose pets are what make them a family.

When my cat suddenly died, it was traumatic and difficult to process — harder, I'd say, than when my mom passed away after five years of illness and steady decline. With my mom, I had time to prepare and process. With my cat, I was administering first aid with my hysterical wife and kids standing by. I wouldn't say I had complicated grief over our family pet, but it did mess me up for quite a while.

It would be unusual to have complicated grief because of an animal that died, but I believe it's possible — and you can feel better by following the same steps we'll teach you for grieving the loss of a person.

Questionnaire, Part 3: Complicated Grief

Check off the statements that are true for you.

When it comes to the death of one or more people who were close to me:

- ❏ I'm finding it difficult to accept the loss.
- ❏ I have mixed feelings about the death.

❏ I feel guilty that I didn't do enough to help prolong the person's life or prevent their death.

❏ I feel if I move on with my life, I'm betraying or abandoning them.

❏ I didn't attend traditional rituals (for example, the funeral).

❏ I avoid thinking or speaking about their death.

❏ Two or more deaths happened in close succession.

❏ I feel down or sad around the anniversary of the death.

❏ I don't want to give any of their possessions away.

❏ I feel no one was there to support me at the time of the death.

❏ I felt numb and haven't experienced many sad feelings since their death.

❏ I didn't take any time off work or other responsibilities.

❏ I gave away all their possessions very quickly.

❏ I'm approaching the age when they died.

❏ Someone I know has been diagnosed with the same illness, and it's upsetting me.

❏ I'm experiencing similar physical symptoms, but my doctor can't figure out why.

❏ I seem more upset than expected about the recent death of someone I didn't know very well.

Loneliness and Isolation: No One to Lean On

Ron likes to say that people who experience loneliness and isolation are like Mother Hubbard of nursery rhyme fame: they go to their cupboard and it's bare — not of dog bones, but of meaningful relationships.

If you have had a history of inadequate, unsupportive relationships; difficulty making friends; and challenges maintaining meaningful relationships with family, loneliness and isolation may be your problem area.

Loneliness and isolation is the least commonly experienced problem area. The symptoms of depression may make you feel socially isolated — you don't have the energy to make plans and feel no one would want to spend time with you anyway — but loneliness and isolation isn't likely your problem area unless you've had a lifetime of problems connecting with others.

TRY THIS: *If feeling lonely and isolated is a recent thing for you, your problem area is probably conflict, transitions, or complicated grief.*

Ron was treating a stockbroker who worked thirteen hours a day, six days a week, fifty weeks a year. He had no time for his wife, his sons, or his friends. There were a lot of people on his social circle, but he had almost no meaningful contact with them.

Was his problem area loneliness and isolation?

No. Turns out his lack of close relationships was a relatively recent change. He was sacrificing his whole social circle because he had received a promotion at work and was feeling overwhelmed and inadequate. He felt he needed to give everything to his job in order to keep his new position. As a result, it made more sense for him to choose transitions as his problem area. That way he could develop skills to cope constructively with his new role at work and feel confident that he had the time to emotionally reengage with his loved ones.

Questionnaire, Part 4: Loneliness and Isolation

Check off the statements that are true for you.

When I think about my past and current relationships:

- ❏ I've felt lonely for a lot of my life.
- ❏ I feel I've never had a person I could truly rely on.
- ❏ I have difficulty making friends.
- ❏ I have a hard time keeping relationships going.
- ❏ I'm happier being by myself.
- ❏ Most people disappoint me.
- ❏ There is open conflict or tension in most of my relationships.
- ❏ I feel anxious and uncomfortable when I'm with other people.
- ❏ I feel I don't fit in well with others.

- ❑ I feel other people don't understand me.
- ❑ I feel I don't understand other people.
- ❑ I'm not really interested in what most people have to say.
- ❑ I have a hard time sharing my feelings and thoughts with other people.
- ❑ I worry that other people will think I'm stupid or foolish.
- ❑ I don't enjoy many activities.
- ❑ I feel I have acquaintances, not friends.
- ❑ I get annoyed or frustrated by most people.
- ❑ I have a hard time trusting people.
- ❑ I don't feel that friends and family are worth the effort.

Ana's, Kate's, John's, and Becky's Choices

Ana is pretty sure her problem area is transitions. She wonders briefly whether she should choose interpersonal conflict, given the challenges in her relationship with Peter, but there are definitely more check marks in the transitions section of her questionnaire. Besides, most of the conflict in her relationship with Peter is focused on her feelings about being a mom.

Kate is reluctant to admit it, since having a relatively conflict-free marriage is something she's proud of, but interpersonal conflict seems to be the source of a lot of her challenges right now. Things are tense with her husband, Don. She feels hurt by his behavior. He's been different since retirement, but she doesn't think this is about his transition. It's about what each of them is looking for from the other. When she checks off, "I feel we want different things from the relationship" on the interpersonal conflict part of the questionnaire, it's as if a lightbulb goes on for her.

John's check marks are mostly on the social isolation and interpersonal conflict sections of the questionnaire. So now he has to choose. The conflict is mostly about his coworker Alex. But he's had trouble with relationships of all kinds as far back as he can remember. He's always felt like the outsider — it's hard to find things he likes that other people do too.

When it comes to family, John has always felt left out and misunderstood. He's used to being alone with his computer most of the time. But that doesn't mean he likes it. It would be nice to have a friend. Even better, a girlfriend. So John chooses loneliness and isolation.

Becky knows Brian's death is related to her feelings of sadness. Yes, she's transitioning to living alone, being an only child, and no longer being a caregiver, but it's the sadness she feels about Brian's death that's affecting her the most. Every day she asks herself why he had to die. She feels lost, alone, purposeless. She chooses complicated grief for her problem area — even though she has absolutely no idea what "uncomplicated" grief might look like.

Now It's Your Turn

If one of the parts of this chapter's questionnaire has a lot more check marks than the others, you can feel confident that you should put your efforts there. But if two or more problem areas have almost the same number of boxes checked or the area with the most check marks doesn't feel right to you, answer these questions to refine your choice.

Which problem area is relevant right now? Your problem area should be in the here and now — relevant to today, not something that happened ten or fifteen years ago (unless it's a death that's still affecting you). Ron will often ask his clients, "Out of all the things that were going on in your life around the time you started to feel depressed, which one had the most significant negative impact on your mood?" Link the answer to a problem area, and you'll have your focus for the next few weeks.

Which problem area "feels right"? Our gut reactions tell us a lot. Ask yourself, "Which one of these areas feels right to me?"

Which problem area is doable? Often, people have more than one problem area that they could work on. Our advice? Work on one you think will be less challenging, practice the skills, and then go back and tackle the tougher one.

Who could help you choose? If you're having trouble identifying your problem area, ask a trustworthy friend or family member what they think. Whenever I do group therapy with teens, it's the other kids in the circle that immediately iden- **TRY THIS:** *If you can't* tify what's making one of their fellow group mem- *figure out what problem* bers feel sad or down. For me, it was my friend who *area to focus on, ask a* pointed out that my mother-in-law's illness must be *friend or family member.* bringing back feelings from the time when my mom *It's always a good idea to* was sick and died. *borrow a brain!*

MAKE IT MEANINGFUL

It's possible to use your choice of problem area to accomplish something important to you.

Tiah, one of Ron's clients, had been rapidly promoted at an information technology firm. This didn't go over well with her male coworkers, who figured her rapid rise wasn't deserved; it was because she was a woman. One of the VPs in particular seemed intent on punishing her — and he was the one who would be responsible for her future promotions.

Tiah had a choice. She could pick interpersonal conflict and work on her relationship with the sexist VP — which likely wouldn't end well. Or she could work on making a successful transition from simply doing her new job as a director at the firm to being a crusader for women in IT.

By consciously choosing transitions as her problem area, Tiah started to feel better. Instead of feeling powerless, as she had felt in the face of her interpersonal conflict, she felt empowered.

Remember, choosing your problem area is about becoming more aware of what's contributing to how you feel and giving a focus to the rest of our work together. It's not about picking the *right* area to work on. By getting one task done, you'll feel better and have gained some skills you can use for the next challenge you encounter.

GUY TALK: UNDER PRESSURE

About fifteen years ago, I was newly married, my wife was seven months pregnant with our first child, we'd just bought a house, and I had the job my parents always dreamed of for me — working full-time in a senior government position. Then I found out the position I had given almost two years of my life to was being eliminated. I was losing my job.

Both men and women feel pressure to live up to certain social and cultural expectations. For many guys, these expectations have to do with being the one who brings home the bacon, and when I got laid off, I was feeling that pressure very strongly. Panic set in. Day after day I watched as my wife went off to work while I sat at home. Where was my bright career now? What were my parents thinking of me? How would we pay the mortgage? What about the baby on the way? I felt like a failure as a man, a husband, and a soon-to-be father.

It can be difficult in these situations to choose a problem area. My wife and I didn't argue over the job loss, but my feelings of inadequacy and worry about the future were definitely causing stress in our relationship. Should I choose interpersonal conflict as my focus? I felt lonely — I wasn't seeing my work colleagues anymore and was too ashamed to see my friends and parents — so maybe isolation was my problem area. Then, of course, there was the transition to being jobless.

Rather than get caught up in which problem area was the "right" one, I chose to focus on the transition. I followed the steps we'll share with you, including talking with someone in my circle who had experienced something similar. That someone, who was also a psychologist, helped me set up my private practice. Three months after being laid off, I was seeing my own patients.

Working for myself was way less secure at the start than working for the government, but at least I was helping to support my family. After a few years of networking and building my practice, I had a career with flexibility and freedom — a career that turned out to be a much better fit for my personality.

This Week's To-Do List

Choose your problem area. If you're not sure you've got the right one or want confirmation from an outside source, ask a friend or family member what they think.

Goal Get 'Em

This week, we help you set goals related to your problem area to work on for the rest of the book. By making these goals SMART (specific, measurable, achievable, relevant, and timely) and focusing your efforts on achieving them, you'll build your confidence and prove that you have the power to make yourself feel better.

I was wrapping up some paperwork in my office one day when my next client walked in.

"I'm mad at you," she said.

I was puzzled (though darn proud of her for using an "I" statement and a feeling word), so I asked why.

"Because you didn't fix my relationship with my brother," she said.

She had chosen the interpersonal conflicts problem area, since she felt her depressed mood was connected to the stresses in her relationship with her sibling. The two had even come to see me together to work on their relationship. She'd been practicing using a less aggressive interpersonal style with her brother, but eight weeks into our work together, he told her he wanted to take a break and not speak for a while. She was upset, disillusioned, and standing in my office with her hands on her hips.

"What did I say or do that made you feel I could save your relationship with your brother?" I asked.

"Nothing," she admitted. "I just wanted that to happen."

"Yes, you did," I agreed. "But your brother didn't. So that wasn't an achievable goal for therapy."

Our work continued, helping her deal with her brother's decision.

Goals are necessary to accomplish anything in life. Without them, we drift. Goals give us direction. They help us be selective about what we do and how we do it. And they give us a destination, so when we get there, we can celebrate how far we've come and enjoy the experience.

Setting goals is a skill we have to learn. Our tendency is to focus on a dream we'd like to come true in the future rather than on the small, achievable steps that will help us feel better in the present. A good goal for my client was to work on having calm and respectful exchanges with others, since her aggressive interpersonal style meant she was belligerent and unforgiving in most of her relationships, including with her brother. But saving a particular relationship? That wasn't a good goal — for reasons we'll explore this week.

We start the chapter off with a crash course in SMART goals. Then we go through each problem area. For each problem area, we first share the general goal (or goals) that all people whose depression is connected to that area will be working on. Then we provide examples of smaller, here-and-now SMART goals that have been tailored to individual circumstances. We also check in with Kate and Ana as they choose their goals.

By the end of the week you'll have set a goal or two for your problem area so you can focus, track your progress, increase your feelings of competence, and have something to celebrate at the end of our time together.

Making Your Goal SMART

You may have heard about SMART goals; *S* stands for "specific," *M* is for "measurable," *A* for "achievable," *R* for "relevant," and *T* for "timely." (There's debate about what each of the letters should stand for, but we like those terms.)

Why does it matter if a goal is SMART? Let's say our goal is to go on a trip. With such a general goal, where do we begin? If we make our goal *specific*, say a stay at an all-inclusive resort or backpacking through the wilderness, we can take the next step. Being specific about what we want to achieve helps us decide where to go and how to prepare.

A *measurable* goal lets us know when we've arrived, so we don't turn into that powerless (and annoying) kid in the backseat: "Are we there yet? Are we there yet?"

An *achievable* goal is a realistic goal, one we can expect to attain. If we know we'll never get to the moon, we don't set that as our goal.

A *relevant* goal is consistent with the direction we want to go in. Let's say we decided to go to Iceland — maybe the tickets were cheap — but we really wanted to go to Paris. When we touch down in Reykjavík, we'll have accomplished our goal, but it just won't feel right — because it wasn't relevant.

Timely, for us, means the goal addresses how we're feeling right now, and we can achieve it within a relatively short time frame. It's a trip we want to take today — or in the very near future — not one we think we'll be ready for in a year or two's time.

Here's a story to help you see SMART goal setting in action. My friend Martine was separating from her partner of fifteen years, and I agreed to help her with the transition.

"How are you feeling?" I asked her one day over a glass of wine. She said she was feeling tired, lonely, sad, and anxious.

"What would help you feel better?" I asked.

Martine laughed. "If he wanted me back." That was her dream, even though her laugh told me she knew it wasn't realistic.

"I totally get it," I said. "Do you think that's possible?"

She started to cry. "No. He's moved on. I've done everything I can in that department."

We talked for a bit about her feelings, now that her relationship was over. Then I asked what else might help her feel better.

Martine thought for a bit. "I'd feel better if I wasn't so tired all the time. I don't like feeling lonely. And I wish I felt more confident."

Less tired, less lonely, more confident. None of those were SMART goals — yet. They were relevant because they addressed how she was feeling about her transition. But they weren't specific enough. They weren't measurable. And we needed to get that phrasing worked out before we assessed whether they were achievable or timely.

TRY THIS: *Make your goals specific and measurable before you decide whether you can achieve them.*

I asked Martine more questions. How would she know she felt less tired? If she could get through the day with only one coffee, she said. And how would she know she was feeling less lonely? If she said yes when her friends asked her to go out instead of just going to bed. How about confidence? She wouldn't be afraid to speak with her lawyer. She'd create a profile on an online dating site, and then go on a date.

All of these were specific, measurable, and timely in that they addressed how she was feeling right now. Did she feel she could achieve them in a relatively short time frame?

"Not the dating," Martine admitted. "I'm not ready. And one coffee isn't achievable right now either. I'm currently drinking five a day, sometimes six. I think it'll prove I'm less tired if I can manage on two coffees."

To make the loneliness and confidence goals achievable, Martine needed to quantify them. It wasn't realistic to think she'd say yes to invitations all the time. So what if she phrased her goal as "saying yes more often than saying no"? For the confidence goal, it was regular contact with her lawyer that said would give her the confidence boost. But what was "regular"? How about weekly? Was that achievable? Martine thought so.

TRY THIS: *Start your SMART goal with an action word.*

We made sure each goal started with an action word. After all, goals are something we *do*, not just *think* about doing. So two hours and two glasses of wine later, Martine had three goals to work on:

Goal #1: Drink no more than two coffees every day.

Goal #2: Say yes when a friend asks me to do something more often than I say no.

Goal #3: Communicate at least weekly with my lawyer.

SMART QUESTIONS

For SMART goals, ask SMART questions:

Is my goal specific? What might I be doing and saying when I'm accomplishing this goal? If the goal involves someone else, what might they be doing and saying?

Is my goal measurable? How will I know when I've accomplished it? Have I included numbers or time limits to help me define success?

Is my goal achievable? Is this the most realistic outcome? Does it count as a small step in the right direction?

Is my goal relevant? Does it relate to my problem area?

Is my goal timely? Does it address how I'm feeling right now? Is it something I can accomplish in a month or two?

MISSION POSSIBLE: ACHIEVABLE GOALS

You can set achievable goals by imagining three scenarios: the best outcome, the worst outcome, and the most likely outcome of working on the goal.

If your goal by the end of this book is to feel still connected to your friends after separating from your partner, the best scenario might be that nothing changes. You'll see the same people with the same frequency and do all the same things you always did. The worst outcome would be that all your friends dump you and side with your ex. The most realistic outcome? Probably that the relationships change — you'll see some friends less, other friends more, and you'll spend time talking about and doing different things than before.

That last scenario is the foundation for your achievable goal: that you'll maintain meaningful connections with your friends without expecting all relationships to stay the same. Find the happy medium — the most likely outcome — and you'll have an achievable goal.

Goal Setting When Your Problem Area Is Interpersonal Conflict

The general goal for people experiencing interpersonal conflict is to resolve the conflict — which could mean repairing the relationship, learning to live with it as is, or deciding to dissolve it.

Although your conflict is with a person, you'll want to keep your focus on the problem. That's because the more clearly you see what the conflict is about, the more targeted your goals will be.

For couples, conflict can be about money, sex, the kids, in-laws, time together and apart, who does what around the house, and more. Conflict between friends can be about how often someone calls, who initiates contact, feeling left out of social situations, and feeling taken advantage of. Workplace conflict can stem from many sources, including lack of respect, too much work, lack of recognition, unfair treatment, and workplace culture.

There are four steps to setting goals for the interpersonal conflict problem area. The first is to *name* the conflict. The second is to identify how you're *feeling* about it. Next, ask yourself what would help you *feel better*. (Make sure your feel-better actions involve another person.) In the last step, reword your "feel better" ideas as *SMART goals*.

Remember Oscar, the finance director who needed to adjust to a new collaborative corporate culture? He said he'd feel better if his colleagues saw him as a team player, but he wasn't sure what they considered collaborative and helpful. So that became his SMART goal: to ask the four members of his executive team what they expected of him in the role of team player.

A client of mine was fighting about a lot of things with her teenage son, so it was hard for her to name a single source of conflict. In the past week, though, most of the arguments had been about his iPad. What was she feeling? She was disappointed, angry, and frustrated, but her strongest feeling was fear. She was worried that her son was hiding online. She was afraid that he was

TRY THIS: *To come up with your goal, imagine a situation that hasn't gone well in the past, but this time you're feeling better about it. What are you doing and saying? What makes the difference? If you don't know, maybe that's your goal: to find out.*

avoiding dealing with something that was bothering him. She was concerned that he was isolating himself from people who cared about him. The worst part? She didn't know why.

She decided it would make her feel better if she knew what her son was doing online and if his iPad use had a daily limit. She also wanted to know what other parents were experiencing in this area. She turned these into three SMART goals: to spend at least an hour engaged in an online activity with her son each week, to talk to other parents of teens to see what they were feeling and doing about screen time, and to set a daily limit for her son's iPad use, with input from him. This last goal was a chance for the mom and son to talk about their expectations of each other and for the mom to practice using a different communication style — one that kept the conversation going and cooled things down when they got heated. (If you don't believe it's possible to keep your cool with a teenager, stick with us and we'll show you how!)

SMART GOALS FOR INTERPERSONAL CONFLICT

Here are the steps to follow to set SMART goals if your problem area is interpersonal conflict:

1. Name the conflict.
2. Ask yourself how you're feeling.
3. Ask yourself what would help you feel better.
4. Turn those statements of positive outcomes into specific, measurable, achievable, relevant, and timely goals.

Goal Setting When Your Problem Area Is Complicated Grief

The general goal for all people experiencing complicated grief is to grieve your loved one fully. And how can you tell you've "grieved fully"? You'll be able to talk about your loved one, especially how you feel about the loss, and engage with people and activities again.

To accomplish that general goal, you'll need to set a goal or two of your own, tailored to your circumstances. The first step is to acknowledge that you *haven't grieved* your loved one completely. Next, ask yourself how you're *feeling*. Then come up with some ideas for *feeling better* — ideas that will help you talk about your loved one and get involved with people and activities. Finally, make those "feel better" ideas *SMART*.

One of my clients, Stefani, had lost her mom more than a year earlier to pancreatic cancer. The death was fast and tragic and hard on everyone in the family, but its impact on Stefani was particularly profound. She had stopped seeing her friends, was struggling to pass her college classes, and had dropped out of the rec soccer and softball leagues she'd loved.

Stefani hadn't wanted to talk about her mom when we were drawing her social circle.

"What's stopping you?" I asked.

"What if I start crying, and I can't stop?" she said.

I reassured her that many people had that concern, but in all my years of practice I'd never seen it.

Then the words started tumbling out. Stefani told me about her relationship with her mom before the diagnosis. She recounted what happened during the illness, the death, the funeral, and the devastating days and weeks that followed. She shared what her dad, brother, extended family, and friends were saying and doing. At one point she pulled a beautiful scarf out of her bag. "I brought this back for Mom from a trip I took after her diagnosis. I didn't want to leave her side, but she made me go." I helped Stefani connect every event and interaction to a feeling.

Talking with me was a good first step, but it wasn't enough. "Do you ever talk to your dad about your mom?" I asked her.

"I can't," she said. "It would make my dad too sad."

"What if the situation was reversed?" I asked. "What if your dad wanted to talk to you about your mom, but he was worried it would make you too sad? Would you want him to hold back?"

"Of course not," Stefani said. "I wish we talked about Mom more."

So that became Stefani's first goal: to talk with her dad about her mom — not once, and not for a short time, but as often and for as long as she needed to in order to feel better. Her second goal was to sign up for an indoor soccer league.

Another of Stefani's concerns was her fear that she would forget her mom.

"What if I get busy?" she asked me. "What if I start having fun again and stop thinking about her? I already feel like I can't remember her face."

That fear led to Stefani's last goal: to create at least one way to regularly remember her mom. (She decided to bake her mom's favorite chocolate chip cookies every month.)

It can be very difficult to set a goal of reengaging with people and pastimes if you blame yourself for your loved one's death. The same is true if you feel

TRY THIS: *Sometimes creating a way to remember your loved one can help you feel better.*

guilty that you didn't do enough for them while they were alive. I've never had a client tell me their loved one would want them to lead a lonely, sad life, but guilt and shame have the power to make us feel that's all we deserve.

An example is Aisha, the mom we introduced you to in last week's chapter whose daughter was hit by a taxi. At first, Aisha refused to set a goal that would have her connect with others. How could she enjoy herself when her daughter would never laugh or play again?

Ron suggested she could consciously honor her daughter's memory by volunteering with a nonprofit focused on child safety. This was a connection with others that Aisha could justify. She was doing it for her daughter, not herself, since she was working to prevent such tragedies in the future. She was also doing it for her remaining children, who needed their mom back.

Volunteering with the nonprofit connected Aisha to other people who had similar experiences. She started to feel better. And eventually she was able to return to work and reconnect with her friends and family.

The specific goals you set and work on need to be ones that you believe will help you feel better. Remember Maureen, who was having a hard time believing her depression could be linked to her mother's death eighteen years earlier, given that she hadn't even liked her mom? Maureen set a goal to talk to her husband and adult children about the feelings she had about her mother and her mother's death. It was like opening a door to memories, stories, and events she'd closed off for years — some good, lots not so good — and it helped her feel better.

TRY THIS: *If it feels too hard to connect with other people for yourself, do it in a way that honors your loved one.*

For her, the talking was enough. That, plus she set a goal to donate to an alcohol rehab program every year on her mother's birthday, in the hope that some other mother could get the help her mother never received.

SMART GOALS FOR COMPLICATED GRIEF

Here are the steps to follow to set SMART goals if your problem area is complicated grief:

1. Acknowledge that you haven't grieved your loved one fully.
2. Ask yourself how you're feeling.
3. Ask yourself what would make you feel better. Make sure your ideas involve talking to someone and connecting with others. If there's something else, such as creating a remembrance or ritual, that would help you feel better, include it too.
4. Turn those ideas into specific, measurable, achievable, relevant, and timely goals.

Goal Setting When Your Problem Area Is Transitions

The general goals for transitions are to be more accepting of your new situation and feel more confident in your new role.

It can be hard to move on from the way things were and scary to accept what's facing you now. That's okay. You'll achieve these goals day by day, small step by small step. There's no quick way to say goodbye to your old life and no pill for developing skills for your new one. You probably aren't going to get to the end of this book and shout "I love being divorced!" or "Losing my job was the best thing that could've happened!" But you will have accomplished a couple of small goals that will help you be more comfortable with the change you've gone through — and you'll feel better because of it.

The first step is to *name* the changes you're going

PEP TALK: *Set a goal for your transition and, step by step, you'll come to accept your new situation and feel more confident in your new role.*

through that are linked to your depression. These could be changes that happened a while ago, changes that are ongoing, or changes that you anticipate will happen in the near future. The most important thing is that the changes are affecting you today. Next, identify how you're *feeling*. Then think of actions you could take to help yourself *feel better*. Finally, word these actions as *SMART goals*.

We've already walked through one transition goal-setting example in this chapter: that of my newly separated friend Martine. Her goal to accept her friends' invitations will help her let go of what was and see the positives of what is. Weekly communication with her lawyer will be a confidence booster — she'll be developing the skills to handle the emotional and practical sides of living on her own. And the coffee? Maybe that will be proof that she's coping more effectively.

Here's another transition goal-setting example. Remember Emily, the young woman from last week who wasn't happy living at home, but felt she couldn't move out because her mom needed her too much? She loved her family, but the gossip, lack of privacy, and, most important, her mom's constant complaining about everyone, particularly Emily's father, was bringing her down.

I asked her the standard question to get goal setting started: "How are you feeling?"

"Yesterday was the same as every day," she said. "I came home from work exhausted, and right away Mom asked me to help her make dinner. The whole time she complained about my dad. Work is really hard right now, and I actually wanted to get some support from her for once. I just ended up wishing I'd never come home."

"What would help you feel better?" I asked.

"I'd love to come home from work and go up to my room and relax for a bit before helping with dinner," she said. "But Mom would get mad. Who would she talk to if she didn't have me?"

Those of us who are good at being the "helper" will have a difficult time letting that role go. We like being needed. We feel closer to people who confide in us. We consider caring for our loved ones the mark of a good person, and we like being in the loop. But being the helper, especially when you're the child and the person you're helping is your parent, has its downsides. Emily's depression was proof of that. So I asked her to answer her own question. "Who could your mom talk to if she didn't talk to you?"

She reluctantly considered some options. There was her dad, but he was quiet and hid in the basement in front of the TV. There was her aunt. "How might you feel if your mom started talking to your dad or your aunt?" I asked.

"I might miss some of our conversations," she said. "But it would help me feel better."

In the end, Emily came up with two SMART goals to help her deal with her transition from her mother's helper to an adult child focused on her own life. One was to encourage her mom to talk with her dad at those times when Emily felt she needed some time to herself. The second was to encourage her mom to address issues directly with the person she was complaining about.

PEP TALK: *Letting go of an old, familiar role that you liked will be difficult. Set a goal to get yourself one step closer to your new role!*

SMART GOALS FOR TRANSITIONS

Here are the steps to follow to set SMART goals if your problem area is transitions:

1. Name the changes that are having an impact on you right now.
2. Ask yourself how you're feeling.
3. Ask yourself what would help you feel better.
4. Turn those "feel better" outcomes into specific, measurable, achievable, relevant, and timely goals.

Goal Setting When Your Problem Area
Is Loneliness and Isolation

There's only one general goal if your problem area is loneliness and isola-tion: to become meaningfully connected to other people.

If you've had a hard time making friends or sustaining relationships, you may think you don't need anyone. People are a hassle, right? They can be cruel and untrustworthy. Why open yourself up to disappointment, hurt, and rejection?

The first step in setting your SMART goals for loneliness and iso-lation is to see *value* in connecting with others. Maybe the thought of a roommate scares you, but you want to be able to move out of your par-ents' house and can't afford to live on your own. Maybe someday you'd like to have a family. Maybe your boss has told you to get along better with coworkers and customers, or you'd have to find a new job. Maybe you occasionally catch yourself longing to be part of something bigger than yourself — a community of people who care that you're one of them.

TRY THIS: *If you're socially isolated, look for a reason to connect with other people. What will it help you do? How will it make you feel?*

Once you've thought of at least one good rea-son to connect with other people, it's time to explore how you're *feeling* right now. What would help you *feel better?* Then ask what small step you could take to get closer to that outcome. Make it *SMART* and voilà — a goal.

Your goal might be to strike up a conversation with a stranger at the bus stop, to reach out to an old friend from high school whom you've lost touch with, or to work out a system with your coworker whereby every-one gets a fair share of tips at the end of a work shift. (That last one ended up being one of John's goals. His other one was to come up with three responses he could use with his coworker Alex when he was mad at him and practice using them at least half of the time.)

Volunteering is also an excellent way to connect with people. Help at an animal shelter. Volunteer for the symphony. Neighborhood groups often need help organizing events, putting up posters, and delivering flyers. Churches, mosques, and synagogues are always looking for people to help with their charitable programs, and they're usually very welcoming places.

Dallas, a twenty-something musician, had lost touch with people at every stage of his life; he coped with his feelings of abandonment and rejection by regularly moving. He came for therapy because, after the fourth move, he was seeing a pattern. "Only the environment changes," he told me. "I just end up being lonely in a new town."

Dallas desperately wanted a girlfriend but was intimidated by bars and online dating sites. "I feel like giving up," he said. "I'm constantly looking in on other people's close relationships, but I'm never invited to join."

When I asked what would help him feel better, he couldn't answer at first. "I'd like to make a real friend," he said at last, so quietly I could barely hear him.

"Is there a place you could go where you might make a friend?" I asked.

He'd seen a poster for an open-mike night hosted by a local music store. "What if I show up to that?" he offered.

"Would that help you feel better?" I asked.

"I'm willing to give it a try," he replied. So there was Dallas's goal: attend an open-mike night.

Another client was a young woman who had felt socially isolated since she was a preteen. "I know I'm sensitive," she said. "I can see right through people. They're hypocrites, users, and liars. Some people can forgive and move on when they get hurt, but not me. I'd rather be alone."

I asked how she was feeling. She blamed herself for her sensitivity, but she also felt disappointed in other people.

PEP TALK: *We achieve big goals, like having a friend we can rely on, one small step at a time.*

"What would help you feel better?" I asked.

"If people weren't such jerks," she said.

I smiled. "I'd like that too," I said. "But it sounds like something that's outside our control. What could *you* do that would help you feel better?"

"I'd like to learn to forgive and forget," she said.

To make her goal SMART, she broke it into smaller, measurable steps. She'd heard that mindfulness helped people be less judgmental toward themselves and others, so as her first step she set a goal to take a mindfulness class.

SMART GOALS FOR LONELINESS AND ISOLATION

Here are the steps to follow to set SMART goals if your problem area is loneliness and isolation:

1. Think of at least one good reason to connect with others.
2. Ask yourself how you're feeling.
3. Identify ways you could connect with others to feel better.
4. Word those ideas as specific, measurable, achievable, relevant, and timely goals.

Kate's Goals

Kate's first task is to name the source of the conflict between her and her husband. That's easy — it's Don's controlling behavior. Yesterday, he went through the department store bag she left in the front hall to find the receipt and then went on and on about how much the shirt she bought cost. Today while she was at work, he texted her every fifteen minutes and asked her to call during lunch, which she couldn't do — her day was so packed with meetings she barely had time to eat.

Next, she asks herself how she's feeling. She's definitely exasperated. She's exhausted. She misses her friends. She feels like a failure, since nothing she does seems good enough for Don. She's not used to feeling outwardly angry like this. She's even a bit worried — is there something wrong with Don? She narrows down her list of feelings to the ones she's experiencing most strongly: exasperation and sadness.

So what would help her feel better? "I wish he would stop watching my every move and texting me all the time," Kate says to herself. That would help with the exasperation. And getting her independence back would definitely make her less sad.

Kate checks to see if her two goals are SMART. The first one — Don stops his overzealous surveillance and check-ins — seems measurable, relevant, and specific, but is it achievable? It doesn't really count as a "small step," Kate admits. So what would a small step be? What if she and Don have a conversation about reducing Don's texting? That becomes her first goal.

Goal number two — getting her independence back — isn't specific enough, since she's not exactly sure what she'd be doing or saying or what Don would be doing or saying if she achieved it. It also seems hard to measure and difficult to achieve in a short span of time. What if she signed up for yoga classes again? That would definitely prove she had some of her independence back. It would reconnect her with her yoga buddies, which would help her feel less sad. The stress management would just be icing on the cake.

Ana's Goals

Peter is working late again. Ruby is down for the night — or at least until she needs feeding — so Ana has some alone time.

Somehow that doesn't make her feel better. She spends too much time alone already — or at least without adult company. So what should she do with her evening? Open a bag of chips? Check Facebook? Watch some TV? Or should she use this time to set some goals?

The chips, time on Facebook, and TV do make her feel better, but only temporarily. She sighs. "Let's set some goals," she says, picking a teddy bear off the floor.

Ana starts listing the many changes that have occurred recently,

PEP TALK: *It's okay to keep doing things the way you always have, but don't expect anything to change if you do.*

including how different her relationship with Peter has become, her anxiety over being a good mom to Ruby, and losing contact with her friends and colleagues.

What's bothering her the most right now? Ana isn't used to being home so much. Taking walks by herself feels really lonely. Going grocery shopping and doing other errands doesn't make her feel better. She's the first of her friends to have children, and she doesn't really know any other women who have babies.

What would help her feel better? Her husband, doctor, and mom have all suggested that Ana connect with other mothers. "Is that my goal, Teddy?" she asks. "To find other moms?" Somehow it doesn't seem specific enough. Where is she going to find these moms? On Facebook? At the park? "How about a moms' group?" she says. So that becomes Ana's first goal: join a moms' group.

Was there anything else that would help her feel better? She's been so resentful of Peter since Ruby was born, and it's only gotten worse since she wrote the letter asking for his help and he basically ignored her request. "It's time to have a conversation about that," she says.

Ana decides that she'll ask Peter to take Ruby when he gets home, so she can have a few minutes to herself, finish (or start) making dinner, and maybe have a shower. Of course, that will require him to come home on time, she sighs. She rewords her goal: ask Peter to take Ruby on those nights when he doesn't have to work late.

She's a little uncomfortable with this second goal. "What's Peter going to say when I ask him?" she says. "I need his support, not a fight." She's still holding the bear. "I know, I know," she says. "It's okay to keep doing things the way I always have, but I can't expect my feelings to change if I do."

She writes both her goals on a piece of paper and slides them into her desk drawer, right on top of the drawing of her social circle.

Over to You

It's important to set goals, especially when we're feeling low, blue, or depressed. The idea isn't to start a revolution. It's to take one or two small, concrete steps that will help you feel better about something that's been bothering you recently. Once you've accomplished those goals, you can set new ones.

It can be rewarding to brainstorm a long list of goals. Go ahead. But working on more than two or three goals simultaneously when you're feeling crappy is going to be daunting. Narrow down your list. Which one will have the biggest impact on how you feel? Which one will be the easiest to accomplish? Which one relates most to how you're feeling right now? Pick the goals that will give you the biggest bang for your buck, and then try your best to make them SMART.

Often, the best goals will connect you with other people. Remember Tiah, the director at the IT firm who was being punished by a sexist VP for her rapid promotion? She set a goal to connect with colleagues outside her company who had similar concerns about sexism in the IT industry and see if they wanted to start a group. Will Tiah end up founding that group? Maybe. And maybe not. What matters more than the end result is the journey she'll take to get there, which will have her sharing her experiences with others, deepening relationships, and finding support. Discovering that you're not alone can be life changing — and you'll feel better for it.

TRY THIS: *Some of the best goals for feeling better are ones that connect you to other people.*

Once you've chosen your goals, write them down and put them somewhere safe — preferably a place you'll see them regularly. (Where did you put your social circle? Could be that's the perfect spot.) You'll need to remind yourself each week about your goals, because they're the focus of the rest of our work together, and it's easy to get distracted.

Even though you've made your goals small enough to be achievable and written them down, you may not believe in them yet. It's hard to do something new. It's frightening to imagine a different future. What will your best friend say if you tell her you feel like she's excluding you? What will happen if you open up to your spouse about the death of your mother? How will you feel if you join a club in your new town? Set a goal or two, and let's find out.

SMALL GOALS ARE BETTER THAN BIG ONES

When my kids were young teens, my life was upside down. Being a parent was challenging. My work as a therapist was stressful. My husband and I were bickering about silly things. My mother was sick. So what did I decide to do? I quit my job and went to teachers college.

I figured that being a teacher would fix everything. I'd have financial security, a regular schedule, and summers off to recharge and focus on my kids.

I finished teachers college and then started teaching at a private school. It was awful, and I only lasted two years. I couldn't wait to return to work as a therapist — and I've never looked back.

When life gets challenging, we look for the Big Fix — the one thing that we think will make all our problems go away — instead of doing small things to make ourselves feel better, issue by issue. I didn't need a new career. I needed to work on communicating more effectively with my husband, coping better with stress at work, and dealing with my feelings about my mother's illness. Heck, a holiday would've been cheaper than teachers college, and probably more effective.

This experience taught me that small steps are better than big ones when dealing with a problem (although I did get a teaching degree in the process!).

GUY TALK: GOAL SETTING IN GUY LAND

Most guys like goals. Goals are concrete. Goals solve problems. But some of us may get preoccupied with whether the goal we choose is "right." We want proof that it will work, that other people have done it, that we won't look like fools. And we want fast results.

One of my clients was a project manager for a commercial construction company. He had been seriously injured on a job site and was having a difficult time with his transition from successful professional to someone living with a traumatic brain injury. He needed a goal that would be achievable over the weeks we'd be working together.

"What would help you feel better?" I asked him.

"I'm too emotional," he said. "I want to stop crying all the time."

I reassured him that crying was normal for someone with a brain injury and would likely go on for a few more months.

"Can't you speed it up, Dr. Frey?" he asked.

Uncontrolled crying isn't in the playbook for most men. Emotional control would help my client feel normal — something that's important when you're going through a transition. But it wasn't achievable in the short term.

"How long does it take to put up an office tower?" I asked.

"Three years," he said.

"If I asked you to do it in one year, what would you say?"

"I'd say it was impossible."

It was the first time I'd compared crying to construction, but he got it. We had to come up with a different goal.

Before the accident, my client had been a social guy, hosting big parties at his house. A more achievable goal, he decided, was to start entertaining again. I encouraged him to start small.

"Invite over one friend," I suggested. "Maybe with his wife."

"Isn't that a bit cozy?" he asked. "And isn't it too easy? Would other guys pick a goal like that? Will it work, Dr. Frey? Do you know someone who's tried that?" He wanted proof that it was the right goal.

In the end, that "cozy" dinner with one couple freed my client up to have a real conversation with his guest — something that wouldn't have been possible if he'd been hosting a big party. He discovered both he and his friend enjoyed the same hobby — fishing — which has led to more life chats while they toss a line over the side of a canoe.

Look for validation of your goal if you need it. Ask your buddies what they think of it. Talk to your spouse. They'll have helpful input, and sharing your goal with them may give them ideas about how to support you. But when it comes to decision time, the right goal is the one that's right for you, nobody else, and the proof will come after you start working on it, when you begin feeling better.

This Week's To-Do List

Come up with a maximum of three goals. Make sure they're goals that will impact how you're feeling now and that you can achieve over a few weeks. Brainstorm a number of goals, if that's helpful; then narrow your list to no more than three.

Check that each goal is SMART. Answer the SMART questions and adjust the goal so you're satisfied with the answers you get. Start the goal with an action word ("write," "list," "play," "ask," "call," "join," etc.), include numbers and time frames so it'll be easy to tell if you're accomplishing the goal, make it realistic, and check that it'll help you resolve the issue you're experiencing right now.

Try rephrasing your goals to include other people. They're your goals, but you'll feel better if you can involve other, potentially supportive people in helping you achieve them.

Put your goals where you'll see them. Your goals will be front and center in everything you do over the next weeks, and you'll want to be able to easily remind yourself of your focus to stay on track.

Mirror, Mirror

This week is all about reflection. We start with a quick recap of everything you've accomplished since Week 1. Then we help you take a closer look at a recent incident that bothered you. By examining what happened and exploring your feelings in a constructive way, you'll be learning a skill that we'll build on in the weeks to come.

After this week, we'll be halfway through our twelve weeks together, which is a perfect opportunity to look back on what you've accomplished so far. I think you'll be impressed.

First, you talked to someone about your depression and gave yourself permission to take some time off from your day-to-day responsibilities in order to focus on getting better. Then you identified and explored the supportive and stressful relationships in your life, started asking yourself the all-important question, "How am I feeling?," chose a problem area to focus on, and set a SMART goal — a small step on the way to something bigger you'd like to accomplish.

TRY THIS: *Start a new habit. Review what you've accomplished and feel good about your efforts — whatever the outcome.*

You've laid a strong foundation for the work to come. Congratulations! How are you feeling? Is there anything that would help you feel better? If so, take the time you need to do the thing that would lift your mood a little. Then we'll get started on this week's work.

Let Off Some Steam

This week we're going to get up close and personal with an incident that really bothered you. We don't want you to try to fix it. We just want you to take it apart, look at it from every angle, and, most important, explore how you feel about it. We offer guidance in the form of ten questions to ask yourself and a detailed recap of how Becky, Kate, Ana, and John answered those same questions for themselves.

Some of us might use the word "venting" to describe this kind of detailed exploration of an event or interaction that made us feel bad. Think of a closed vessel that is continually heated. Eventually the pressure will build up and cause the vessel to explode. If the vessel is vented, however, when the pressure gets too great, steam or gas can escape a little at a time and keep an explosion from happening (we are grateful for the safety vents on our hot-water heaters and pressure cookers!).

Explosions are messy, and sometimes people get hurt. Better to let off some steam in a safe and controlled way than blow your top all at once.

Venting comes naturally to some of us and not to others. If you're a suck-it-up- (or push-it-down-) and-move-on type of person, you might have a harder time with this week's exercise. The same goes if you equate venting with complaining, think of crying as a sign of weakness, don't want to think about something that's very painful for you, would rather fix things than feel them, or are uncomfortable getting angry.

Ron had been helping a social worker whose conflict with her spouse was linked to managing her feelings about her work with children who had been sexually abused. Over the years, she had learned to lock away everything she heard and saw in a part of her that was off-limits to everyone — including herself. It had worked fine until recently. Now her drinking was getting out of hand, and her feelings were coming out at inappropriate times and in inappropriate ways — mostly as anger at her spouse.

She didn't want to open that box of feelings. It was too painful. It was too scary. She'd have to be so careful about who she told and that she didn't share any identifying information about the children or their families. The costs seemed too high. She found it very difficult to explore her feelings about the abuse of children.

"What will happen if I do this?" she asked Ron.

"You'll feel so much better," Ron told her.

"Like magic?" she asked.

"No, not like magic," he said. "When you explore your feelings, you're doing the work. But it'll feel like magic."

What ultimately convinced the social worker that venting her feelings was a more constructive way to handle things than drowning them in a bottle of wine or exploding at her spouse was a question about her own daughter, who was twenty-seven and newly married.

"She'll be starting her own family soon, then," Ron said.

Suddenly, Ron's client recognized that the benefits of exploring her feelings outweighed the costs. It would be better to learn to talk about her feelings now, when she could control the timeline, rather than waiting until she became a grandmother and was forced to deal with her unresolved feelings. Unexpressed feelings could result in unhealthy worry about her grandchildren being harmed.

PEP TALK: *It sucks when things happen that make you feel bad, and it's okay to feel the way you do. Give yourself permission to let it out.*

It can help to remember that feelings aren't things to be ashamed of. You're allowed to feel angry, sad, lonely, disappointed, hurt, and afraid. It's okay to feel that things aren't fair, that life has dealt you a terrible hand, or that people aren't there for you. You're entitled to whatever emotions you're experiencing. Give yourself permission to feel them, in all their raw and powerful glory. They may be very intense, but you won't feel them this strongly forever — because together we're going to work on feeling better.

Mirror, Mirror on the Wall

We called this week "Mirror, Mirror," because we're asking you to reflect on something. The link to the movie *Snow White* is intentional. The analogy isn't perfect — none of us are wicked stepmothers, even if we're going through a transition to a blended family! But we liked the fact that when the queen asked her mirror a question, it answered back truthfully — even when it was an answer the queen didn't want to hear.

Play along with us for a moment and ask yourself this question: "Mirror, mirror, on the wall, what bothered me this week most of all?" Keep your problem area in mind when you answer.

If your problem area is interpersonal conflict, what stressful interaction happened over the last few days? Did your husband forget your anniversary? Did your boss criticize the way you dealt with a customer? The incident you choose should involve, or at least be related to, the primary person you're in conflict with.

If your problem area is complicated grief, what happened recently to remind you of what you lost? Did someone make a comment about your loved one that made you feel sad or angry?

Is your problem area transitions? What happened over the last week to make you miss your old life?

If your problem area is loneliness and isolation, what made you feel cut off from the people around you during the last few days?

TRY THIS: *Keep your focus on the here and now, and pay attention to how you're feeling.*

The event or interaction doesn't have to be monumental; it just has to be the thing that bothered you the most this week. The fact that it happened recently is important. The mirror didn't tell the queen in *Snow White* who was the fairest in the land twelve years ago or even two months ago — it answered in the here and now. Make your answer about what bothered you the most yesterday, two days ago, even a week ago. But that's as far back as you should go.

The incident that bothered me the most last week happened at Friday night dinner at my daughter's house. We're a pretty sarcastic bunch. Get us all in a room, and someone is going to be the butt of a joke — and often it's me. Sometimes I'm okay with it, but other times it goes a little far and I end up feeling hurt.

This past Friday, as soon as the appetizers were served, the "let's make fun of Mom" began. My husband poked fun at the fact that I had brought too much food (I always do!), and then my son joined in. When I said (with my own healthy dose of sarcasm), "Thanks very much for all your love and support," they just kept on kidding with me.

Although I know that none of them meant any harm by their words, I started to feel upset. In the early years I would cry (no surprise there), but now I know it's better if I just give everyone a heads-up if I'm not in the mood. They usually get the hint and lay off, but on Friday they missed my cue.

What bothered Ron the most in the past week was the City of Toronto. "They scheduled a freaking marathon on a main street downtown instead of running it on a pedestrian-only area," he told me over the phone. "I had to drive half an hour out of my way and was late seeing my patient."

Ron lives six hours from Toronto and had agreed to drive to the city and back home in one day to do an assessment for a colleague. He recognized that he felt angry and frustrated, because he was trying to please others instead of keeping himself sane. He drove to Toronto to make his colleague (and the patient) happy. He rushed the trip back home to make his family happy. These were feelings he experienced because he put himself last — the City of Toronto's road race was simply the annoying inconvenience that put him over the edge.

What to Ask the Mirror

We've come up with ten questions you can ask yourself to explore what happened, how you feel about it, and whether it connects to similar situations and feelings you've experienced before.

Make your answers detailed. Write them down, record them on your phone or computer, or tell a friend or family member. The idea is to express yourself, so you can stop carrying around the event and its related feelings.

TEN QUESTIONS TO ASK THE MIRROR

1. What happened?
2. How did I feel?
3. How did I handle those feelings?
4. How do I usually handle those feelings?
5. When else do I feel this way?
6. Why did it bother me so much?
7. What caught me by surprise?
8. What could I have done differently?
9. What stopped me from trying one of those different approaches?
10. What do I wish had been different?

You might feel as though you've seen these questions somewhere before, and that's not an accident — they're similar to the Ten Questions for Emotional Enlightenment that we introduced in Week 3's feelings chapter with two big differences. First, we're asking the questions to explore a specific, highly charged situation that relates to your problem area. Second, we're keeping the focus on you and your feelings, not how others involved might feel. This is your venting session. It's all about you this time around.

Remember, we aren't trying to solve a problem or fix anything. If you gain new awareness about your feelings and behavior, fantastic. The only reason Ron was able to make such concrete connections between his anger at the traffic jam and his tendency to put himself last is because he's been making these connections for a long time. (No matter how many years we've been working on handling our feelings differently and modifying our communication styles, we all fall back into old patterns sometimes, even psychologists.)

PEP TALK: *Venting is where emotional change starts, but it's not about fixing anything. (Of course, if you want to give something new a try, go right ahead. Then ask yourself how you feel!)*

Another thing to keep in mind: don't judge yourself for what happened or your feelings about it. We want you to become aware of and accept your feelings, not hide from them, shove them down, eat or drink them away, pretend they don't exist, or displace them onto something or someone else.

Becky: Five Minutes on Facebook

Becky has no trouble identifying the incident that bothered her the most over the last few days. It happened yesterday when she checked Facebook.

Ever since Brian died, Facebook makes her feel crappy. It's like watching other people move on with their lives in real time. Every post, like, and comment she sees on her friends' pages is a reminder that her life is the opposite of share-worthy. She feels disconnected and sad. But no matter how many times she tells herself she's done with social media, there she is, scrolling through posts.

This wasn't just a regular post, though. This was a photo of Amber, June, Sheree, and some girl Becky hardly knew, all smiles and sunglasses and clinking wineglasses — Amber's bridesmaids and maid of honor on a trendy downtown patio. Becky wasn't in the picture, because although she'd been invited to the big day, she wasn't part of the wedding party.

Becky isn't sure this is the incident she should use for the mirror exercise, because her focal area is complicated grief, and this is not really about Brian. But it *is* about what she lost. And one of her goals is supposed to be to reconnect with people and activities in her life. So she decides it's a good incident to explore. She asks herself the ten questions and records her answers on her phone:

What happened? Against my better judgment, I went on "Fakebook" (that's my new nickname for it) and saw Amber's bridal-party-on-the-town post. I was like a rubbernecker at an accident. I just kept staring at it. When did Sheree start drinking white wine? Why did Amber get her hair cut so short this close to the wedding? What's the name of that girl they're with? I must've looked at that post for half an hour.

How did I feel? Physically sick. So angry and sad and hurt and left out and lonely. Mad at myself for going on Facebook. Mad at myself for letting things get this way. Mad at my friends for having awesome lives while mine sucks. Scared that this is what the rest of my life is going to be like.

How did I handle those feelings? I slammed my bedroom door shut, threw myself on my bed, and cried myself to sleep. When I woke up, I made myself a peanut butter sandwich and watched four episodes of *Gilmore Girls* on my laptop.

How do I usually handle those feelings? That's pretty much textbook for me. Cry, sleep, eat, watch TV, repeat.

When else do I feel this way? All social media is a downer for me, but I even feel bad when I watch a show where people have close relationships. Or when I walk downtown to the market and see friends and couples having a good time together.

Why did it bother me so much? This is beyond FOMO. I don't *fear* missing out — I *know* I'm missing out. I've lost so much — not just Brian, but my friends as well. Amber's getting married, and I don't even have a boyfriend. Everyone is moving forward with their lives. I'm just standing still.

What caught me by surprise? I've had this experience before — maybe not quite so intensely, but feeling jilted after a date with Facebook is nothing new. The paralysis I felt was new, though. I just couldn't stop looking at the post.

What could I have done differently? I guess I could've commented on the post — showed my friends I was still alive by saying something nice. I could've texted Amber or June or Sheree and asked if they wanted to go for coffee. I also could've not gone on Facebook in the first place.

What stopped me from trying one of those different approaches? I worry that it's been so long since I've talked to any of my friends that they've forgotten me or they're mad at me. I'm scared to put myself out there — even doing something as small as commenting on a post. Plus, when Brian was sick and after he died, my friends didn't really understand what I was going through. I remember feeling guilty about having a good time too. One time when I was looking after Brian I went to see a band with my friends, and he made me feel so bad about it when I got home. Oh, God. I shouldn't have said that about Brian. How selfish of me. Anyway, I think I still carry that guilt around with me.

What do I wish had been different? That's so hard to admit. I wish I was Amber's maid of honor or at least in the bridal party. I wish Brian had never gotten sick. I wish I was still doing my art. I wish I still had friends and a social life.

Becky starts crying. She stops recording, puts her phone down, and lets the tears come.

Kate: Walk On By

It's easy for Kate to identify what bothered her the most over the previous few days, but it's not so easy to take the incident apart and explore her feelings. After a negative experience, she'd much rather close the book on her feelings than open it up and write about her anger and frustration. How many hours does she spend every week listening to teachers at her school gripe about their husbands? What good does complaining do? Exploring your feelings just makes you relive painful things.

She's got a choice: do what she always does, which is to lock away her feelings, or try something new. The first approach hasn't been working that well for her lately — isn't that at least partly why she feels sad all the time? Maybe it's time to try something different.

What happened? Last Tuesday was a regular day at school, which meant nonstop texts from Don. He couldn't find anything at the house, including his favorite golf shirt, the gardening knee pads, and one of the pieces of the smoothie blender. Then there were the "I'm bored, what are you doing" check-ins and a couple of texts asking when I'd be home. And a reminder that we were supposed to go to the 7 PM show that night — cheap-night Tuesday, of course — to which I had to reply that I was so sorry, but I'd have to take a rain check; it was report-card time, and we were all working late. He fired back something sarcastic. My colleague noticed I was getting upset and asked if everything was okay, so I laughed it off.

When I got home, Don was parked in front of the TV, well into his third or fourth drink and clearly giving me the cold shoulder. I went to the kitchen (it was a mess), poured myself a vodka soda (he'd taken the last shot of rye and left the empty bottle on the countertop), and walked past him on the way upstairs. "Wow. Not even a hello," he said. I kept walking — he was not going to goad me into a fight.

How did I feel? At work, I felt angry and frustrated about the constant texting. When my coworker asked if I was okay, I felt embarrassed and ashamed. Whose husband does this? When I got home, I was so angry at him for the mess, the drinking, the attitude. But my biggest feeling, sadly, was "Here we go again." It's not like this is new. So what's that feeling? Resignation?

How did I handle those feelings? With my colleague, I handled my shame and embarrassment by closing down the conversation. When I got home, I handled my anger by not saying a word to Don. I went upstairs, ran myself a bath, drank my vodka soda, and went to bed without dinner. I heard Don come to bed hours later, but my back was to him, and I just pretended to be asleep.

How do I usually handle those feelings? I really don't like feeling angry. I hate the flushed face, tightness in my stomach, the choking sensation when I raise my voice. So I push away or ignore those feelings as much as I can. But I'm not usually mean. I think I was mean to Don when I ignored him. We literally didn't say anything to each other until I handed him a coffee the next morning as a peace offering.

When else do I feel this way? I haven't felt this angry and powerless since I watched my mother drink her anger away.

Why did it bother me so much? I'm so tired of this. I thought Don's retirement would be a good thing. I feel like I have to babysit him every day, and I don't have the time or energy. I just know my sister is going to tell me "I told you so" about marrying an older man.

What caught me by surprise? Just how angry I was at Don. I think I'm reaching a breaking point.

What could I have done differently? I could've opened up to my colleague at work and told her how I was really feeling. I could've tried talking to Don when I got home. Okay, scratch that idea. Don was on drink number four — he was in no shape for a heart-to-heart. But I could've at least been a little more respectful of him when I got home.

What stopped me from trying one of those different approaches? Fear, probably. What if my coworker didn't really want to hear about my issues with Don? Or worse, she judged me? What if I ended up exploding at Don instead of saying something respectful?

What do I wish had been different? I wish Don understood that I have a demanding job and sometimes I have to work late. Instead of being so selfish, I wish he'd made dinner for us.

"How am I feeling?" Kate asks herself. She's definitely feeling exhausted. But she's also feeling a little lighter after having vented.

Ana: Girls' Night Out Goes Badly

Ana can barely hold back the sadness and anger as she answers the Ten Questions to Ask the Mirror, her fingers pounding on the keyboard:

What happened? I went out tonight with Amanda and Steph for Amanda's birthday. I almost didn't go. It had been so long since I'd been out with friends and it meant doing a lot of prep to make sure Peter had everything he needed to take care of Ruby — God, do I hate pumping breast milk! — but I made myself go.

We started the evening at a nice restaurant, and then we were going to a club. Things were awkward. There were inside jokes and a closeness between Amanda and Steph that I hadn't noticed before, and the stuff they wanted to talk about I couldn't really relate to anymore. We'd just finished up dinner when my phone rang — it was Peter. Ruby wouldn't take the bottle, she wouldn't stop crying, he was worried something was wrong with her, and would I come home? I said sorry to Amanda and Steph, gave Steph money for the bill, and left.

At home, things were crazy. Ruby was freaking out, Peter was freaking out, and it took everything in me to not freak out. So now it's more than an hour later and finally Ruby is sleeping, Peter's watching TV, and I'm doing this.

How did I feel? When Steph texted me about going out, my first instinct was to say no. I was nervous. Also tired and frustrated with Peter — he was going to be home late from work again, so he couldn't help me get ready. On the way to the restaurant I was actually feeling excited. I missed my friends and started remembering all the great times we'd had together. Which is probably why I was so hurt and disappointed when things felt so different.

When Peter called, I was angry. He couldn't deal with Ruby for three hours? But secretly I was relieved to have an excuse to leave. At home, I felt completely overwhelmed. It took me so long to get Ruby down. Am I that incompetent as a mother?

How did I handle those feelings? I just stuffed them down. I wasn't going to say anything to Amanda or Steph, and when I got home it was all about Ruby.

How do I usually handle those feelings? Usually, I'll talk to my mom or Peter. But it's harder to talk to Peter these days, because I'm mad at him a lot of the time. Even when I'm not mad, he just doesn't know how to help me.

When else do I feel this way? A lot of these feelings are familiar. I get them any time things don't go the way I expect, or I feel inadequate as a mother, or I feel I have no one to rely on, or I'm reminded of the way things used to be.

Why did it bother me so much? I feel like such a bitch saying this, but the simplest task takes so much effort now that I have a baby. I remember the days when it was so easy to go out! Ruby spit up on my first outfit, so I actually had to get dressed twice. Which was hard, because I'm still not fitting into my clothes that well. Dinner was just another reminder of how much things had changed. I didn't even bother talking about my life — spit-up, breast milk, and baby talk. There's no turning back the clock. And of course I wouldn't want to. But there's a lot I miss about my old life.

What caught me by surprise? How different things are with Steph and Amanda. I thought we could pick up where we left off, but apparently that's not the case.

What could I have done differently? I guess I could've told Peter how much going out meant to me and asked him to come home on time if at all possible. I could've shared a little of my life with Steph and Amanda during dinner. I could've called my mom for advice when Ruby wouldn't settle down.

What stopped me from trying one of those different approaches? I want to look like I have it together. I don't want to be the person who can't get ready for a girls' night without backup. I don't want to cry the baby blues to my friends who don't even have kids. I don't want to seem like I can't get my baby to sleep.

What do I wish had been different? I wish the stork would drop off a couple of kids for Steph and Amanda. I wish Peter understood what I needed and was more helpful.

John: Mad at Mom

John thinks back over the previous week for the thing that bothered him the most. Alex had been up to his usual tricks at work, John's boss was demanding and unsympathetic, and his dad had ignored him, but none of that was unusual. Like irritating background noise or a continuous low-level headache, those things affected his mood, but weren't worth commenting on. He did have a big blowout with his mom, though. It was about his brother, Tom. That's probably what he should focus on. But does he really have to write this stuff down? Seems like such a hassle. He decides to answer out loud instead.

What happened? I went to the mall and wandered around for a few hours like I usually do when I'm bored and there's nothing good on TV. When I got back, my brother, sister-in-law, and nephew were all getting ready to leave. What the hell? My brother could tell I was pissed. So he said, "Didn't Mom tell you we were stopping by?" I said, "No, as a matter of fact she didn't." I wanted to say, "Well you could have texted me and told me yourself, but you never do that."

Instead, I waited until they left and yelled at my mom. I said, "Why didn't you tell me Tom was coming over? Didn't you want me here?" She said she had forgotten they were coming, and I was being ridiculous as usual. What the hell was she talking about? She's the one who is ridiculous and rude and disrespectful to me, taking me for granted, not including me in family events, not showing any interest in what I'm doing.

How did I feel? I wanted to explode. I was frustrated, annoyed, really mad at my mom, and tired of the way people treat me. I wondered if anything would ever change, and I started to feel sad and hopeless and really lonely. I don't understand why people don't want me around.

How did I handle those feelings? I yelled at my mom. Then I went to my room. Then I took the car, got a burger at the drive-thru, drove down to the river, and ate my burger sitting in the car.

How do I usually handle those feelings? I get mad and yell. Isn't that what people do when stuff pisses them off?

When else do I feel this way? I get mad whenever someone does something that insults me, takes advantage of me, or disrespects me. If you break the rules or treat me badly, I figure you deserve it.

Why did it bother me so much? It just feels like this always happens. Why didn't my parents tell me my brother and his family were coming for a visit? I would've much rather spent time visiting than wandering the mall. I really like Tom, Greta, and Riley. They're about the only ones who talk to me, and it feels good to have someone pay attention to me occasionally. So then of course I think maybe my parents don't want me around and did it on purpose. Wow, if that was the case, it would really piss me off. I try to help out around the house, and I pay them what I can afford in rent, and they treat me as if I don't even exist.

What caught me by surprise? Nothing surprises me anymore when it comes to my family. They just continue to disappoint me.

What could I have done differently? Why am I the one who's supposed to change? They're the ones that exclude me and make me feel like an outsider in my own family.

What stopped me from trying one of those different approaches? Not relevant. Next?

What do I wish had been different? I wish I'd got a chance to visit with Tom and his family. I wish my mom had told me they were coming or Tom had texted me. Or at the very least that they'd stuck around a little longer when I got home instead of rushing off.

John could keep going, of course, but he decides that's enough for now. He's not used to structuring his venting — if he's honest, the questions cramp his style a bit.

GUY TALK: IT'S NOT ABOUT THE NAIL

There's a funny video on YouTube, called "It's Not about the Nail," that hammers home (pun intended) the challenge that some guys may have with this week's exercise.

The clip is a quick exchange between a young man and woman. She's sharing her feelings about a relentless pressure in her head that she's scared will never end. He gently reminds her that she has a nail sticking out from between her eyes. "Stop trying to fix it," she says, the nail head pointing straight at the camera. "You always do this. You always try to fix things when all I need you to do is listen."

Many men would rather skip past the feelings and jump right to addressing the problem. Who cares about exploring what happened and answering the nine other questions we suggest in this chapter? Instead, how about we just fix it? Pull out the damn nail, already!

It may be hard for you to simply sit with a problem. You may not want to take it apart and examine it from all sides instead of doing something to make the situation better. But exploring why you feel the way you do, how your feelings influence your behavior, and when else you feel that way will help you be a better problem solver in the end. After all, not many problems are as easy to fix as removing a nail to get rid of a headache.

This Week's To-Do List

Complete the Ten Questions to Ask the Mirror exercise. Identify the one thing related to your problem area that bothered you the most over the last few days, and answer the ten questions in as much detail as you can. You're venting — don't hold back! Record your answers on paper, on your computer, or on your phone or simply speak them aloud. You can also do this exercise with a friend or family member. (If you choose to do the exercise with someone else, your job is to answer the questions. Theirs is to listen. Remember, it's not about the nail!)

Take your emotional temperature. After you've done the exercise, take a moment to check how you're feeling. Even if you don't feel better, do you feel different?

WEEK 7

Who Can You Share That With?

This week we help you share your feelings about your problem area and goals with someone in your circle. We offer advice on who to talk to, suggestions for starting the conversation, and tips for getting the most out of the encounter, so you can experience firsthand the mood-boosting power of interpersonal connection.

Sometimes I finish a day of counseling feeling like an owl — and it's not just because I'm wise. It's because I say "who" so much.

We've said it before, but it's worth repeating: the "whos" in our lives are tied very closely to how we feel. When we reach out to others to share what we're going through or ask for advice, we often feel listened to and cared for, and our mood improves. But it isn't just about the ideas or advice. It's about developing relationships with others and realizing we're not alone in the struggles of raising children, dealing with coworkers, coping with the death of a loved one, being married, taking care of aging parents — whatever is contributing to our depression.

Connecting with others also helps us stay healthy. Julianne Holt-Lunstad, a professor of psychology at Brigham Young University, says social connection should be a public-health priority. Holt-Lunstad notes that social connection is associated with a 50 percent reduced risk of early death and that loneliness exacts a grave toll. "It's comparable to the risk of smoking up to fifteen cigarettes a day," she says. "It exceeds the risk of alcohol consumption, . . . physical inactivity, obesity, and . . . air pollution."

PEP TALK: *There's no better time to channel your inner owl. Say it with me now (and every time you're feeling low): "Who? Who? Who?"*

Asking "who" (as in "Who can I share this with?," "Who has gone through something similar?," "Who can I ask?") helps remind you to strategically reach out to people in your circle. Who can you talk to this week? And what will you talk about? Let's find out.

Seek, Don't Hide

It's hard to connect with others when we're feeling low, sad, or depressed. Our tendency to see the glass as half empty means that we come up with sensible-sounding reasons to stay closed off instead of opening up. "They'll think I'm stupid." "I don't know them well enough." "They're too busy." "They have their own problems." "I won't know what to say." "They won't understand." But you never know. That glass could be half full. They might think you're brave. They might offer a unique perspective. If you don't try, you'll never know.

When we avoid picking up the phone, responding to a friend's text, making small talk in the grocery store, or going to a party, it may feel good — in the short term anyway. We avoid feeling socially awkward. We avoid answering that thoroughly annoying question: "How are you?" We avoid the possibility that someone will make us feel worse about our situation. But in the long term, social isolation will make coping with depression that much harder. We're denying ourselves access to people who can help us. It's as bad for us as smoking.

TRY THIS: *If you feel bad, tell someone. Even if you don't feel like it. Even if you think no one wants to see that side of you.*

Remember back in Week 1, when we described depression as a highly treatable medical illness deserving the same kind of care and attention as a broken leg?

This is a good time to remind ourselves that our friends and family don't want us to wait until we're "all better" before reaching out to them. That goes for depression as much as a cracked femur.

If your knee-jerk or autopilot response to an opportunity to engage with your circle is to play ostrich, how's that been working for you? We can guarantee if you continue to do the same thing as you've been doing, you aren't going to feel better. Try a different strategy. What's the best that could happen? What's the worst that could happen? And what's the most likely outcome?

The more you reach out, the better you'll feel. And the better you feel, the more you'll want to reach out. It's the opposite of a vicious circle. It's a virtuous circle. And it works.

PEP TALK: *Reach out, feel better, repeat. It's a virtuous circle!*

Who Are Your "Whos"?

Your "whos" are people you feel you can talk to about your problem area and goals. Usually they're people you consider empathetic and kind, who you think will be open to hearing about your feelings, and who may be willing to share some of their own experiences. It won't be a big group. In fact, you may only have one person you feel comfortable reaching out to.

Your "who" won't be the same for every situation. It can be helpful to ask yourself these questions to determine the best person to help you with what you're going through right now:

Whom do I feel comfortable talking to about this?
Who knows the backstory?
Who has helped me in the past?
Whom do I trust?
Who cares about me?
Whose opinion do I respect?
Who can help me achieve my goal(s)?

Who knows the people involved?

Who has gone through something similar?

Who knows someone who could help me?

If one or two names keep coming up, they're your "whos" this time around.

It can be tempting to think first of people you're close to — your spouse, best friends, adult children, parents, and siblings. They're your high-value relationships. They're also likely to support you.

I was counseling a young woman whose dad had divorced her mom and married a woman he'd had an affair with. My client was very angry — at her dad, at her dad's new wife, at the fact that this had happened to her family. "Maybe you could ask your mom how she learned to deal with her feelings," I suggested.

At our next session she reported back. "Mom reminded me of what I'd told her when *she* was so mad at Dad's new wife," my client said. "I'd completely forgotten, but apparently I suggested she should treat Dad's wife like a stranger, like someone you bumped into at the supermarket. Mom said it worked for her, so maybe I could try it." My client felt supported by her mom, happy that her advice had helped, and willing to try it for herself.

If it feels too soon or too emotionally risky to talk to someone close to you, look at your circle from 30,000 feet up. Are there people farther out — coworkers, your yoga instructor, a neighbor — whom you can try first? Instead of talking to your spouse, can you talk to your sister-in-law? Practice reaching out to people who are in your outer circle to build your confidence and develop your communication skills. By the time you're ready to talk to your inner circle about what you're going through, you'll have some experience under your belt and a whole crew of folks rooting for you.

For Becky, it just feels too scary and hard to reach out to her best friends right now. The only person she feels even remotely comfortable talking to about Brian's death is Lauren, her hairstylist. Lauren knows some of the story already, and if she hasn't gone through something similar, perhaps one of her clients has. Becky makes an appointment to have her hair cut and colored — the first appointment since long before Brian died.

If you're ready to talk about your feelings with someone who's directly involved in the situation that's contributing to your depression, great. Instead of easing into things and borrowing a brain, you'll be jumping right in to talk about the issues with the person or people involved.

One of my clients was passed up for a promotion and was having a hard time imagining staying in the same job. He was feeling ashamed and inadequate ("like a loser" was how he put it), which was affecting his relationships at work and at home.

TRY THIS: *Practice your communication skills and build your confidence with people who are on the outer rings of your social circle.*

His goal was to make a decision about his job: stay or go. Who could help him accomplish his goal? His boss could tell him why he didn't get the promotion, but my client was anxious about asking her. He decided to talk through the pros and cons with his wife, eventually deciding it was worth the short-term discomfort to get an answer from the boss. His boss told him it was a corporate decision to hire from outside rather than promote from within and that it had nothing to do with his skills.

My client felt proud of himself for asking and content knowing the reason wasn't related to his abilities, but he was still feeling awkward with his closest colleagues. "What if they think I'm a loser too?" he wondered. One by one, he told his coworkers how he felt about not being promoted. It wasn't easy, but he had already experienced the benefits of opening up to his wife and his boss.

His coworkers were very supportive. One of them admitted that she'd been overlooked for a management position a couple of years ago. In the end, he decided to stay in his current job.

If you suspect the best person for you to open up to is busy or know

TRY THIS: *Your "who" doesn't have to be a third party. If you feel like addressing something directly with the person involved in your conflict or transition, go for it!*

they have troubles of their own, it doesn't mean they won't want to hear how you're doing. I have a friend whose mother is in the hospital. Yesterday she texted to see what I was up to, and I texted back about how tired I was after hosting a holiday dinner for twenty-six people. "But that's nothing compared to what you're going through," I quickly added.

"Go ahead and vent," she texted back. "I like hearing about it. It's a good distraction."

Finding a New "Who"

If your "who" doesn't immediately come to mind, dig up your social-circle drawing. Still don't have anybody? Is there someone you never considered talking to before?

Liv started coming to appointments with Ron after her husband took his own life during a difficult battle with cancer. When Ron asked her who she could talk to, she had no idea. "Do you know anyone who's been through something similar?" Ron asked.

Yes, as a matter of fact, Liv knew someone at work whose husband had also taken his own life.

"She isn't part of your social circle?" Ron asked.

"No," Liv said. "I never thought of her, even though I always admired how she seemed to cope with everything that happened." It didn't take long for Liv to summon the courage to ask her coworker to go for coffee, and the two women immediately connected. She'd found her "who."

If your problem area is loneliness and isolation, finding someone to talk to may be difficult. Maybe you don't think you have anything interesting to say, or everyone is always talking about their latest accomplishment or their wonderful children and you feel jealous. Maybe you don't feel you have much in common with the people you see. You feel like an outsider. So you keep to yourself.

If you feel you don't have anyone you can share your feelings and experiences with, that's our first task — to help you find that person. It'll take a bit of time and some practice, but you can do it. You just haven't tried yet. Or you haven't found the right person. Or you don't yet see the value in talking to others. We believe there's always someone to talk to if you're brave enough to put yourself out there.

PEP TALK: *Everyone has a "who." It may be you just haven't found yours yet. Or maybe they were under your nose the whole time.*

I often tell the story of two young brothers from across the street who came to our door to ask if they could take the pile of wood that we'd put out with the trash. I asked them how old they were. When they said they were around the same age as my son, I told them they could take the wood if they would take my son with them to play. They've been best friends for over twenty-five years. (Got rid of the wood, and my kid!)

When we're young, Mom (or Dad) arranges the playdates. When we're older, we usually need to do the work ourselves, taking purposeful, planned steps to invite someone into our lives.

Think of the people you see. Is there someone you can connect with that you haven't approached before? Is there someone you've talked to once or twice that you could have a deeper conversation with? Is there someone whose advice you've discounted in the past but who maybe deserves another try?

Is there a place, like a spiritual community, volunteer organization, gym, school, online group, or in-person meetup where you could connect with other people? You can also rely on your professional connections, such as your doctor, a therapist, or members of a support group. Identify a person or a place, and then start a conversation. The risk of rejection will be low, and the payoff in terms of feeling different — and probably better — will be high.

Finding a new "who" can be important if your depression is connected to a transition. If you've moved to a new city or country, for example, your regular supports may not be available to you. If you're going through something that many people misunderstand, you may need to seek out a community of people who "get it" to help you through, at least at the beginning. If you're in recovery, your old circle may be associated with behaviors you want to leave behind.

Sometimes it's just nice to surround yourself with people going through something similar. If you've just had a baby, join a parents' group. First-year college students can attend workshops or social events organized for new students. New grads can get involved with their alumni/ae associations. Just retired? Join a senior center or see if there's a retiree group from your workplace. Research potential groups on the internet. Talk to friends. Ask your family doctor. There's a group for everyone — you just have to find it.

NO KIDS ALLOWED

Not many parents will share deeply personal things with a young child, but they will often turn to their teenage or adult children when they don't have a more appropriate adult relationship to meet their emotional needs. The parent may feel there's no alternative. The child may enjoy the emotional intimacy. But children — of any age — should rarely be their parents' "who" when it comes to personal matters. (They can certainly be a "who" when it comes to technology and pop culture, though!)

When children are a main source of support, comfort, and counsel for a parent, they may feel special and important in the short term, but the responsibility they feel for helping or "fixing" the parent may lead to stress and anxiety, particularly if the issues being shared aren't age appropriate. These children may also start acting like a parent toward their siblings, which hurts the special "we're all in this together" bond between brothers and sisters.

Children who have been a surrogate parent or substitute partner for Mom or Dad often have challenges in later life. They find themselves filling the caretaker role in most of their adult relationships. I speak from personal experience. My mother was a loving, strong, capable, intelligent woman who struggled in her marriage, and I became her confidante. My dad was a good guy, but my mom was stressed by the financial problems that uprooted our happy Arizona family and forced her to move back to live in cold, gray Toronto with her in-laws and work full-time at their convenience store.

My mom and I were very close, but knowing so much about her adult life wasn't good for me. I felt my job was to make her happy. I gave her suggestions, but they were never the right ones. Years later, I realized the special connection I had with my mother made it hard for me to connect with my sister. I was one of the adults, even when I was a child.

Fortunately, for me there was a happy — if bittersweet — ending. My mom and I had a lot of heart-to-hearts when she was in palliative care, and during one conversation I told her I felt sad for her when I was growing up. "All I wanted to do was make you happy," I said. My mother didn't make excuses or apologize to me, but simply said, "That must have been hard for you." She validated my feelings, which was exactly what I needed to hear, and it felt like a special gift.

Starting the Conversation

It might feel awkward and scary to open yourself up to another person. That's okay. Give yourself permission to say what you feel. It's reasonable to have needs, wants, and desires. It's normal to share your feelings with others. No one should fault you for seeking advice or another perspective. Take a deep breath and begin.

Of course, the moment that works for you may not be equally good timing for the person you've chosen to speak to. Check in first by asking, "Is this a good time to talk?" If it's not, make plans to talk another time.

If you've spoken about the subject with this person in the past, you may want to ask if it's okay to talk about it again. Usually they'll say it's fine, but if it's not, respect their wishes and see their response as proof of how strong and honest your relationship is. Then find another person to talk to.

TRY THIS: *If someone asks you how you're doing, tell them. Honestly. And if they don't ask, tell them anyway.*

People will sometimes do the work for you, inviting a more intimate conversation by asking, "How are you?" or saying, "I haven't seen you in a while" or "You haven't seemed yourself lately." Answer honestly. Instead of saying, "Everything's fine," tell the person how you've been feeling and ask if they'd mind if you talked about it a little.

Don't wait for the invitation, though. People aren't mind readers. You can't expect them to know something is bothering you if you don't tell them. Reach out and let them know.

Conversation Starters for Complicated Grief

Starting the conversation can be difficult, especially if your problem area is complicated grief. Yes, it's one of your goals to talk to others about the death of your loved one, but it can be a difficult subject to bring up. Find the right person (Who else knew your loved one? Who else may be feeling the way you do?) and then make a plan to get together. Stay open to unexpected opportunities to connect in a meaningful way with other people too. Maybe you have a few minutes to talk with someone at a memorial or funeral. Or someone you respect starts to talk about their parents — and you've been struggling with the death of your mom. If the conversation door is opened for you, walk through it.

Here are some suggested conversation starters for complicated grief:

"It's my friend's birthday this weekend, and I've been thinking a lot about her death. I was wondering if it would be okay if I talked with you about it?"

"I'm going to visit my husband's grave this weekend for the first
   time in a long time. Would you mind if we talked a little about
   him?"

"I know it's been a while, but I really wanted to talk more about
   what happened when my dad died. Is that okay with you?"

"When I look at other people's family pictures, I feel sad and
   jealous because my sister died so young and she isn't here
   to celebrate special moments with me. Would you mind if I
   talked to you a bit about how I feel?"

"I'm concerned about how the family will handle the upcoming
   holidays. They're the first without Dad. Can we talk about it?
   How are you feeling?"

"My parents died very young. I don't have the experience of dealing with older parents. What's it like for you?"

"I'm very sorry for your loss. I also lost my best friend."

Conversation Starters for Transitions

If your problem area is transitions, your conversation starters will depend
on whether you're reaching out to someone who is directly involved in the
change in your life. If the person you'd like to talk to is directly impacted
by the transition, there may be tension and open disagreements in your relationship related to the changes you're going through
that will make the conversation more challenging.

That's no reason to avoid telling the person how
you feel. In fact, it shows how much the relationship
means to you that you want to share your feelings with
them directly.

TRY THIS: *When
it comes to important
conversations, timing
matters. Always ask, "Is
this a good time to talk?"*

How you approach the conversation can make all the difference.
Choose a time when you're both fed, rested, and in a relatively positive
mood. Speak calmly and directly. Make eye contact. Open up immediately
about your feelings. Acknowledge that your struggles have impacted your
mood and, if relevant, your behavior.

Here are some transition-focused conversation starters you can adapt for your situation:

"I'm really surprised how much time a little one takes, and I'm not sure you understand what I do all day. Let's talk about it. Is now a good time?"

"I really miss our quiet times together. I know I've been bitchy with you lately, and I don't mean to. Let's discuss what's going on."

"I know we both made the decision to move in together, but it's much harder for me than I expected. I really want to tell you how I feel. Is that okay with you?"

"Now that the kids are both in college, you told me I would need to find other things to do, but I just don't know what direction to take. Can we talk about it?"

"I didn't realize the new job would be so demanding. Let's talk about how it has affected both of us."

Conversation Starters for Conflict

If your problem area is conflict, you can choose to share with someone outside the conflict first or go straight to the person you're in conflict with.

If you choose to share with someone outside the conflict, it can still be tricky. Maybe you'd like to share with your mom how you're feeling about your marriage, but you don't want to influence how your mom sees your spouse. Maybe you'd like to get advice from a coworker about a workplace conflict, but you don't want anyone to think you're playing into office politics. Or perhaps you'd like a girlfriend's thoughts on what's happening with your best friend, but don't want her to feel she has to choose sides.

Be up-front about your concerns. You could say to your mom, "I really don't want you to think badly

TRY THIS: *When it comes to difficult conversations, don't assume people will be okay talking with you. This is one time you want to ask for permission, not forgiveness!*

of Sue, but things have been tough for us lately. Do you think you'd be able to talk to me about it without changing your opinion of her?" You could say to your coworker, "Things have been hard lately for me at work. I don't want to put you in a difficult position, but I wondered if you had any advice for me on how to get along better with the team?" To your friend you could say, "You know how much I care about Brittany. I know you care about her too, and I don't want to make you feel uncomfortable. Would it be okay if I talked with you about some problems Brittany and I are having? They're impacting my mood, and I want to start feeling better."

TRY THIS: *When people are honest with you — even when they say something you'd rather not hear — take it as a compliment!*

If the person is comfortable talking with you, keep going. If they're not, respect their wishes and don't take it personally. You were assertive in your communication style when you told them what you needed and asked if they were comfortable giving it to you. They were assertive when they said no.

Even if they say no, it's fantastic that you tried. How do you feel? Do you feel proud of yourself, even though it was difficult and didn't yield the best result? Remember, it was a first shot — and it takes a lot of practice to score. You can even ask the person who wasn't comfortable talking with you for their suggestions about who you *could* talk to.

Kate decides to open up to Mona, one of her closest friends. Mona has survived some rocky rides in her own marriage and took early retirement herself, so she'll probably understand. Problem is, she knows Don too. Kate worries her friend might think less of Don after she hears what Kate has to say.

"I really want to share some difficult stuff with you about what I'm going through with Don," she says quietly on the phone one night, hoping Don doesn't hear her. "But I need you to help me without saying anything bad about Don. I might get mad about him, but it'll be hard for me if you do. Is that okay with you?" Mona reassures Kate that she'll do her best, and they set a lunch date.

Kate wasn't ready to go straight to the person she was in conflict with, but other people are. If that's you, set realistic expectations. At this point, you're not trying to solve the problem or resolve the conflict. You're simply sharing how you feel with someone important to you, who happens to also be the person you're having difficulty with. You don't have to tackle the Big Problem in your relationship — the conversation could simply be about who's doing the dishes, why you weren't invited to a party, or how you feel about the last meeting. This won't be the only time you talk about the issues that are bothering you.

PEP TALK: *If your "who" is also the person you're in conflict with, your first conversation won't likely be your only conversation. Think small!*

If you want to share your feelings with the person you're in conflict with, it could be a difficult conversation. Be open in your approach. Make the person feel that you care about them. Offer to be helpful. Stick to the facts, without embellishment. It may be a harder approach to take in the short term, but the conversation will be more positive than if you act on feelings of anger or frustration — and you'll end up feeling better.

Here are some conversation starters you can adapt for your particular conflict:

"It really bothers me when you stare at your phone when I'm talking. Let's discuss it."

"Dad, I love you a lot, and it worries me when I see you drinking so much. Help me understand what's going on for you."

"Mom, the holidays are so special to all of us, but you seem so frazzled when we do a big dinner. How can I make it easier for you?"

"I wanted to clarify something with you. Sarah said you and she went out last night, and I wondered why you didn't include me."

"I don't really want to argue about that issue again, but I would like to find a solution that we both can live with. Is now a good time to try?"

"It seems we've each committed to a lot of activities today. Maybe
we should set some priorities and see if we can make it work
for both of us, or find a way to compromise."

Conversation Starters for Loneliness and Isolation

If your problem area is loneliness and isolation, starting the conversation
may mean making small talk.

Small talk is where every relationship starts — even a marriage of
forty-three years. I remember being seventeen and sitting through the first
staff meeting of summer camp. Instead of listening to the camp director,
I was scanning the room for good-looking guys. After the meeting was
over, I approached the second-best-looking guy in the room (I didn't see
myself as best-looking-guy material) and said, "Hi, I'm Cindy." He introduced himself and asked if I'd seen the camp. "No," I
said. So he took me on a tour. And the rest is history.

PEP TALK: *Small talk is the key to unlocking meaningful interaction. And you don't have to be smart to do it!*

People who find small talk a challenge often wish
they could skip past the superficial chitchat and get
right to the good stuff. If that's you, think of small talk
as the key to unlocking meaningful interaction.

Other people dread small talk because they think they have to be really smart to do it well. "My life isn't very interesting," they'll say. Guess
what? Other people's lives are just as uninteresting as yours.

Start by role-playing a small-talk scenario with yourself. Where are
you? What topic would be appropriate to talk about? What could you
open the conversation with? What might the other person say back? How
might you feel?

For example, imagine you're waiting at a bus stop with a friendly-
looking stranger. You could ask if he has the app that tells you when the
next bus will arrive. Or you could comment on the weather. Did fares just
go up? Say something. Anything. What's the best that could happen? It's
the start of a long and beautiful relationship. The worst? The guy could

answer rudely or ignore you. The most likely? He answers politely, you talk for a minute or so, get on the bus, and that's the end of it. You won't win the lottery, but the world won't end either. You might feel embarrassed or even a little stupid for a moment, but so what? You also might feel proud that you had the courage to talk to someone and experience the positive feeling that comes with human connection.

Next, take your small-talk experiment out into the real world. Your subjects aren't just at the bus stop — they're at the grocery store ("How can you tell if an avocado is ripe?"), the library ("Do you have a book you could recommend?"), the mall ("I love the way you put that outfit together. What's your secret?"), the yoga studio ("What a great class! Have you tried any other ones here?"), and in the elevator ("I can't wait till it stops snowing. I've had enough of winter!"). A good strategy is to first ask people about themselves and then share something about yourself.

TRY THIS: *A great way to start a conversation with someone new is to ask a question. People love it when you're interested in them!*

Look for opportunities to practice your small-talk skills every day. And pay attention to how you feel after every encounter.

Here are some possible small-talk conversation starters to take inspiration from. (Notice that they're not particularly inspired themselves. Small talk doesn't have to be!)

"Would you like to get a drink after work today?"

"You handled that situation so well! Can we grab lunch so you can give me some tips on how to handle a situation I just had with a client?"

"I'm looking for some activities for my kids who are two and four. Do you know of any?"

"Who do you think is going to win the election?"

"I wanted to introduce myself and welcome you to the building. Have you tried out that new coffee shop around the corner? They have jazz on Friday nights."

WHEN YOUR "WHO" BECOMES A "WHO NOT"

Did your friend brush you off? Did your mother judge you? Did your boyfriend say, "I told you so"? Should you strike them off your "who" list?

Not everyone will be there for you the way you'd like them to. Your friend, your mom, or your boyfriend may help later or for a different situation, but they may not be someone you'll approach this time around.

If you had an exchange with someone that didn't go well, don't give up on the idea of reaching out to others altogether. Go back to your circle and try again. We bet there's a positive, caring person who wants to help you — someone who says, "That's really tough. Call me whenever you need to talk."

Getting to the Heart of the Matter

You're not on a quest to find the single, life-changing answer or solution here. You're simply having a conversation with someone — the first of several probably — to share your feelings about what you're going through, talk about your goal or goals, and receive some support and advice. The conversation itself is usually enough to help you feel better. Even if all you achieve is feeling different from the way you have been feeling, that's success.

PEP TALK: *The definition of success is feeling different from the way you have been feeling because you tried something new. Feel different? Feel proud!*

One of Ana's goals is to join a moms' group, and she's feeling anxious about hanging out with a bunch of strangers. She could share her feelings with her husband, but Peter doesn't really understand how women talk to each other. Her doctor always asks how she's feeling and is a mom herself, but their visits are brief. In the end, Ana decides to talk to her mom. Mamá knows Ana well. Ana trusts her. She might have some good advice. So during one of their frequent FaceTime calls, Ana tells her mom how nervous she feels about connecting with other mothers.

"You go to the park, right?" Ana's mom asks. "Find a new mom and just start talking."

It doesn't feel quite so easy to Ana. "What if she doesn't want to talk, Mamá? What if she thinks I'm strange?"

"We all know you're strange, *mija*," her mom jokes. "Don't let that stop you."

Ana isn't convinced. What if Ruby is fussing and the other babies are sleeping like little angels? What if Ana looks as though she doesn't know what she's doing?

"All babies cry, and all new mothers feel unsure of themselves," Ana's mom says.

Ana is surprised. "You never said you felt that way before, Mamá."

Ana's mom shares some of her experiences from the months after Ana was born. "I was far from my family too, *mija*. I didn't know how to be a mother and didn't have my mamá or aunties to ask. Your father worked long hours and traveled a lot, so I had to make friends so I didn't feel alone. Other mothers understand. They have sleepless nights and hard days, and if you find some nice people, they don't care if you aren't at your best."

After the call, Ana checks her emotional temperature. She's feeling loved and supported, especially now she knows her mom felt some of the same insecurities with a new baby that Ana is feeling with Ruby.

If your problem area is complicated grief, your goal is to speak at length about the person who died. This may take several conversations with different people. You'll cover lots of ground, starting with the relationship you had while they were alive. What kind of person were they? Where did you go together? How often did you see each other? What did you talk about?

Then you'll talk about the death, describing what led up to it, what happened, who you talked to, and what their response was. How did you find out about the death? What did you do? What did others around you do? Are there things you wish you had said or done?

Don't just give the facts — focus on your feelings. It's okay to share sad stories and cry, and to share funny stories and laugh.

When my mother-in-law was in palliative care and could no longer speak, she held court using Post-it notes and her wicked sense of humor. One day her grandchildren were visiting with expensive coffees in hand. She reached for a Post-it note and wrote, "The reason I have such a great jewelry collection is because I didn't waste my money on Starbucks." Another time she wrote, "If you sit around and talk about me now, what will you say at shiva?" Then there was her request that we all put lots of stones on her grave marker when we visited the cemetery (placing a stone on each visit is a Jewish tradition). "I want people to think I'm popular," she wrote. When we tell these stories today, years after my mother-in-law died, we're honoring her memory in a healthy, healing way.

You may not want to talk about your loved one's death because you worry people will think you're whining or tell you to get over it. It could be that you approached someone in the past, and they weren't helpful. They may have been feeling stressed, or the way you approached them may not have made it easy for them to be there for you, or perhaps you expected too much of them — not everyone is a good listener or can express care and concern.

TRY THIS: *Don't wait for someone to offer to help. If you need to talk, ask!*

The person's response may be positive, neutral, or negative, and there's only so much you can do to predict or influence that. The one thing we know for sure is that you won't receive the care from others you desire unless you ask.

Becky is sitting in Lauren's salon chair, staring at her reflection in the mirror. "So what are we doing today?" Lauren asks, pulling Becky's long hair out from under the black cape.

Becky thinks to herself, "You don't know it yet, Lauren, but today we're going to talk about my dead brother."

They decide on a style and color for Becky's hair. Then Becky takes a deep breath and blurts out the conversation starter she's rehearsed. "I hope you don't think this is weird, Lauren, but you're the only person I've really seen since Brian died. I feel like I need to talk about what happened. Would you mind listening?"

Lauren gives Becky's shoulder a squeeze. "Of course I'll listen," she says.

In total they spend about two hours talking — the length of time it takes for Lauren to color, rinse, cut, and style Becky's hair. For Becky, snapshot memories soon give way to vivid recollections, first of her relationship with Brian before he got sick, then of his illness, his death, and her depression. She cries a couple of times, especially when she tells Lauren about Amber's Facebook post and how she feels about not being in her best friend's wedding party.

"Becky, I can't even imagine how hard that must be," Lauren says. "But I would bet a lot of money that Amber misses you as much as you miss her. It's not the same, but I lost touch with a good friend of mine when she moved away. I can tell you what happened if you like." Becky blows her nose, nods her head, and listens to Lauren's ideas for reconnecting with long-lost girlfriends.

When we open up to others, especially those who have been through something similar, they often have advice for us. It's tempting to think that what worked for another person won't work for you, but don't dismiss it immediately. Does it sound reasonable? Ask yourself why you think you're different and why it's not worth trying. What's the best thing that could happen if you tried it? The worst? The most realistic? Then ask yourself if what you've been doing up to now has been working for you. What have you got to lose by keeping an open mind?

TRY THIS: *When your "who" offers you some advice, keep an open mind.*

An open mind has always been a challenge for John. He has a hard time believing that anyone can help him, since no one really listens to what he's saying, and their advice — if the conversation even gets that far — is always stupid. He'd prefer to not speak to anyone about his life, but since he's basically being forced to connect with others, he chooses his brother, Tom.

No matter how encouraging Tom is in their conversation, as soon as he makes a suggestion about how John could handle the situation with Alex, John gets defensive.

"You could talk to him," Tom suggests.

"Talking does nothing," John says. "I just want to punch the guy."

"Yeah, but we know how well that went over at your last job," Tom says kindly. "Why don't you try going for a beer with Alex after a shift? Maybe he's not such a jackass when you get to know him."

John starts listing reasons why inviting Alex for a beer is a dumb idea.

Tom listens. "I get it," he says. "You're probably a little nervous about spending time with Alex, and you want the problem solved immediately. Going for a beer is my advice, and you can take it or leave it. But what if it works?"

John is about to fire something back at his brother and then thinks better of it. What if Tom is right?

When your "who" says something unexpected that you find unsupportive or hard to hear, try not to judge them harshly. One of my clients chose to speak to her sister about a fight she'd had with her boss. Her sister's reaction, which included calling the boss names and threatening to talk to him, upset my client. "It wasn't what I needed," she said. "I just wanted my sister to listen, and she got all 'I'll show *him* who's boss.'"

I encouraged my client to see her sister's reaction as her sister's way of being helpful. "It's different from what you wanted, but she's still showing you support," I said. I also suggested she could give her sister some gentle feedback. "What if you said to her, 'I'm not sure I want you to call my boss, but thanks for your concern'?" Consciously deciding to feel differently about something — in this case, deciding to feel grateful rather than hurt — can lift your mood.

If your problem area is conflict or transitions and you decide to have a conversation with someone who is directly involved in what you're going through, it may take some work on your part to keep the discussion constructive. Flip back to Week 3, where you identified your interpersonal style and we shared some techniques for cooling down your emotional temperature, if you need a reminder of strategies for assertive, calm interactions.

As for conversation enders, here are some specific phrases and approaches to avoid:

"You always..." or "You never..." Generalizing isn't an effective way to communicate. It makes people feel boxed in and that it's not worth trying something new.

"I know you did _____, and it really pisses me off." Accusations are aggressive, and they may be based on misunderstanding. Ask if someone did something, rather than assume they did it. If they did, in fact, do the thing that upset you, ask why. There may be a good explanation. Then try to find an alternate way to handle things in the future that you both can live with.

"I'm not going to tell you what's bothering me. You should know by now." When someone invites you to share how you're feeling, take them up on the offer; don't use it as an opportunity to make them suffer for past wrongs. You may think they should know what's bothering you, but clearly there's some uncertainty — otherwise they wouldn't have asked. Withholding your feelings only hurts your relationship in the long run.

"I give up." This vote of no confidence will most likely bring the conversation to a close — or at least make the other person mad. You're basically saying that the relationship isn't worth working on. (That may ultimately be the case, but this isn't the way to share that feeling.)

"I don't care" (especially when you do). You aren't being honest, and chances are the person you're talking to knows it. You do care, and you're feeling hurt, vulnerable, disappointed, and possibly other feelings. Try saying that instead.

"**Do what you want**" (followed by anger and resentment). Give permission only if you really mean it. Don't test the person to see if they "do the right thing" (the thing that you want them to do), and make them pay later if they don't make that choice. Instead, say what *you* want, directly and respectfully, and see where the conversation goes.

TRY THIS: *Take your emotional temperature after any important conversation. Want to learn even more? Ask yourself the Ten Questions for Emotional Enlightenment!*

Regardless of who you're talking to and the subject matter, don't forget to take your emotional temperature throughout the conversation, and pay particular attention to how you feel when the conversation is over. Different? Better? Worse? How come? Is there something you could do differently? And how would that feel? If things went really well or really badly in your conversation with your "who," go back to Week 3 and ask yourself the Ten Questions for Emotional Enlightenment.

Whatever happens in your conversation, feel good about the steps you took to get there and be willing to change things up next time if you end up wanting a different kind of experience.

GUY TALK: TAKE A HIKE

My friend Joe called up one day and asked what I was doing.

"Nothing," I said.

"Wanna go for a walk?" he said.

Whoa. What? I was totally caught off guard. "Um, yeah, sure," I answered.

I hung up the phone and told my wife, "Joe wants to go for a walk."

"So what?" she said.

"Don't you think that's weird?" I asked. "He's calling me up out of the blue to go for a hike."

"Why is that weird?" she asked. She didn't get it. It was a Mars/Venus moment.

"I don't know," I said. "Maybe he's gonna tell me he's leaving his wife or that he needs money."

Turns out he just wanted to go for a hike. But my reaction was based on the fact that men don't often make special arrangements to talk one-on-one. When it comes to spending time with the guys, we don't want to do anything that feels too emotionally intimate.

We'll organize a round of golf. We'll get together to play cards. We'll help build a deck. We might spontaneously drop by when we're in the neighborhood. Our opportunities to talk with each other are the by-product of other things we're doing. So planning to talk to someone about our feelings may feel awkward and forced.

Take advantage of the small, spontaneous moments with people in your circle: the walk between holes on the golf course, the boring halftime sports commentary, the break you take from hammering nails, the opportunity for a side conversation at the bar.

You don't even have to start with the people closest to you. We *are* talking about feelings after all, and guys don't tend to use their social circle to talk about feelings. We need to. Especially when we're depressed — which, unfortunately, is a time when it's even harder for us to do it. The answer is to take baby steps to get there.

If you drink alcohol, there's always the bartender. Going on a business trip? Try the person sitting next to you on the plane. If you belong to a religious or spiritual community, you could try talking to someone there. If you're in school, try a teacher. Go for a haircut and a shave and talk to your barber. I play soccer, and guys will sometimes come up at halftime and ask if they can talk to me. Now, they know I'm a psychologist. But still, they're taking a swig of Gatorade and laying it out there on the grass.

Once you've tried a peripheral person and practiced talking about how you feel, you can move on to someone a little closer whom you trust, such as a sibling, best friend, cousin, uncle, or parent.

This Week's To-Do List

Choose someone to be your "who." Keep your problem area and goals in mind and choose someone you believe will be kind and understanding, perhaps someone who's gone through something similar. Find a place to connect with new people if no one in your circle fits the bill. Start with more distant relationships if you need to build your confidence.

Get together with your "who." A face-to-face encounter is usually best, but you can chat online, via text, or on the phone if that works better for one or both of you. Adapt one of our conversation-starter suggestions to overcome any feelings of awkwardness or concerns about rejection.

After the get-together, take your emotional temperature. Ask, "How do I feel?" Then compare that feeling to how you felt at the end of last week, after you vented to yourself. Do you feel different? In what ways?

Feel good about your efforts. Give yourself a pat on the back for trying something new, no matter what happened. It takes courage to reach out and be vulnerable. You did it!

Out with the Old, In with the New

This week we help you change things up. We coach you through the steps: choosing what to change, deciding what you want to do instead, coping with the fear of the unknown, trying out your new approach, checking in on your emotions afterward, and sharing your experience with your "who." You can make yourself feel better — and this week proves it.

There's a children's book that I loved reading to my grandkids when they were small. In the story it's autumn, and the book's namesake, Little Yellow Leaf, isn't ready to let go of his big oak tree. The weather gets colder. "Not yet," he says. Apples and pumpkins ripen. "Still not ready," he says. There's a harvest moon. Nope. Winter flurries. He's still holding on. It's only when he discovers a Little Scarlet Leaf on the same tree who asks, "Will you?" that Little Yellow Leaf lets go — and they soar away together.

My grandchildren were enthralled by the illustrations, but what held me was the meaning behind the words. Sometimes we have to leave the comfort of our oak tree and try something new, but the unknown is scary and we don't feel ready — until we hear an encouraging word from a supportive friend, and we're on our way.

Every one of us has something that we're holding on to that's preventing us from moving forward. This week, we'll help you determine what you'd like to let go of — the "old" thing that isn't serving you well anymore — and decide what you'd like to do, say, or feel instead — the "new" way that you're going to try out. First, we help you make the commitment to change. Then we guide you through identifying what to change and what to do instead. We offer examples for each of the problem areas, including a special exercise for those who are coping with a transition. In the process, you'll discover that changing the way you approach a situation helps you feel better.

You don't have to do this on your own. Instead, you'll be finding your Little Scarlet Leaf, the person in your circle who will encourage you to make the leap. It's time to let go, together, and see where it might take you.

Choosing Change

The first step is to decide if you want to give change a try. That's because change is a choice that requires commitment and has consequences. (Of course, not changing is also a choice, with its own set of consequences.)

I can tell you that in more than thirty years as a therapist I've seen people of all ages, shapes, genders, colors, and cultures make small changes in their lives that have had important, positive effects on their relationships and their mood. You can do this — and you won't be doing it alone. So ask yourself, "Am I willing to try something new?"

PEP TALK: *When you choose not to change, that's a choice too.*

If the answer is no, you'll get no judgment from us. This isn't a one-shot deal. If the only choice you make this week is to simply keep reading, that's okay. If you're on the fence, though, don't opt for same old, same old before considering how you've been feeling lately. Has anything you've tried helped you feel better? If so, ask yourself if you want more of those feelings. And if it's been pretty much business as usual — behaving in the same old ways and having the same old feelings — how's that working for you? We hope you'll decide that making a change in your interpersonal world is worth a try.

What to Change

Once you've decided to make a change, the next step is to figure out where to focus your efforts. What old strategies don't seem to be working for you anymore? What interactions or events make you feel anxious, hurt, angry, hopeless, or sad? How do you wish things were different? What small thing could you change to get there? Use your problem area and goals to narrow your options.

> TRY THIS: *Use your problem area and goals to help you decide what small thing to change.*

If you're naturally self-critical — and many people who have depression are — you may be overwhelmed by the lengthy list of things you think you need to do differently. Remember, when we say "change," we don't mean "revolution." We're big fans of the small change, applied to a specific situation. Maybe you have a conversation with your spouse in which you consciously try to listen to what she has to say instead of thinking ahead to your next point. Or you invite a family member to go to the cemetery with you after years of avoiding a visit to your loved one's grave. Or you make an effort to identify a positive aspect of your transition. Or you try sharing one personal thing with a friend or family member to see what happens.

Sometimes the old thing you need to let go of is an emotion that isn't serving you well anymore. One of my clients had just broken up with her boyfriend and came to me feeling very angry and suicidal. After she drew her social circle, it was clear that the boyfriend was just a trigger for rage she still felt toward her ex-husband, fifteen years after their difficult divorce.

> TRY THIS: *Bigger isn't better. Keep your change small, and try it out in a specific situation. Later you can make more changes, or try the change in a different context.*

"If you stopped being angry at your ex, what would be bad about that?" I asked her.

She didn't hesitate to answer. "If I stopped being angry, I'd have to forgive him for what he did to me and my boys."

I asked if there was a new way she could look at things. "What if you separated the two? What if you stopped being angry but didn't forgive him? How might that change things for you and your sons?"

The next week she tried out the new approach, and the change was remarkable. When she came back for her last session, she brought her boys. "What did you do to our mom?" one asked me. "She hasn't spoken to my dad in years, but at my brother's graduation she let my dad buy her a beer, and we even took family photos." The other brother turned to his mother and said quietly, "That was the best graduation gift you could've given me, Mom."

It'll take some self-awareness and self-reflection to come up with your change. If you're having difficulty, ask someone you trust. Set your "who" up for success by giving them some context. For example, you could say, "I'm working on feeling better, and I want to change something small that will help me _____ (for example, 'communicate better with my spouse' or 'talk about my mom's death'). What do you think I could work on? I want you to be honest — I promise I won't get mad!"

Still stuck? You can try the approach of one of my teenage clients when I asked how she was going to solve the problem she was describing. "Cindy," she told me, "I'm just going to google it."

The Bridge over Troubled Water

Does the idea of making your specific, small change make you feel uncomfortable? Good. Then you're on the right track. We don't do things the old way because it's hard for us. We do them the old way because it's easy and familiar, and there's an immediate payoff. Changing those things may result in short-term pain. But the long-term payoff will be worth it.

PEP TALK: *It's easy to do things the old way and hard to change. Sometimes we have to experience short-term discomfort to experience long-term benefits!*

Ron calls the journey from old to new "crossing the bridge over troubled water." Imagine you're standing on one side of a bridge. It's muddy. Your feet are cold. You're uncomfortable, but you've been standing there so long you can't imagine anything else. This side of the bridge represents the old you. On the other side of the bridge is the way you could be. It's far away. You have to cross over a raging river to get there, and you can't really see what it'll be like when you arrive. The mud could be worse over there. Heck, it could be raining. So you stay put.

Giving up an old way of doing things can feel uncomfortable. What if you open up to your friend, and she judges you? What if you give up drinking, and no one wants to hang out with you? What if you say no to your sister's request and she gets mad? What if you recover from your illness, and people don't pay attention to you anymore? What if you stop trying to be right, and everyone takes advantage of you? What if you ask your colleague for help, and he thinks you're weak? What if you tell your wife how you feel, and she leaves you?

When we're feeling depressed, we see things negatively. We think there's only more mud and nasty rain on the other side of the bridge. But when we cross the bridge, we're opening ourselves up to new interpersonal experiences. We don't know what it's going to be like, but chances are it's going to be different. And different can be good.

PEP TALK: *When we try something new, we'll probably have different feelings. Different is good!*

If you're going to make a change, you have to face the unknowns head-on. What could you gain from doing, seeing, or saying things differently? And what could you lose? Can you live with disappointing someone? Having them get mad at you? Hearing them tell you no? What's the best that could happen? What's the worst? And what's the most realistic outcome? Anxiety and worry and fear are simply feelings, and the way to get over them is to do something.

In order to have different — and probably better — feelings, we have to discover what's on the other side of the bridge. We have to cross that troubled water and, in the process, deal with the uncertainty and discomfort that are part of the journey.

The feelings associated with this uncertainty will be intense at the beginning; then they'll get less intense and eventually disappear. If you stop running away from those feelings — shoving them down or trying to drink, smoke, or eat them away — what happens? Why not try it and see?

If you're tired of cold, muddy feet, the only way forward is to cross that bridge — to make that journey from old me to new me — and find out what's on the other side.

Message (Well) Received: New Ways to Handle Conflict

If your problem area is conflict, consider changing something in your communication style that will make it easier to resolve the situation. (Remember, "resolving" a conflict doesn't always mean fixing the problem or getting your way. It may mean having that aspect of the relationship bother you less or choosing to end the relationship.)

If your style leans toward the passive side, how does it feel when you choke down your feelings, give someone the silent treatment, or put the needs of others above your own? If you tend to be aggressive in your approach to others, how do you feel after you control the conversation, yell, or win the argument? How might others feel?

TRY THIS: *If your problem area is interpersonal conflict, try a more assertive communication style on for size.*

Here are some changes that will help you be appropriately assertive in your interpersonal style. For each change, we've included an example of how you could put it into practice — a specific, small scenario where you could try it out. The scenario itself may not apply to you, but it'll give you an idea of how to take that first step.

Old way: I get angry a lot.
New way: I try to express my sadness, hurt, or fear instead of my anger.
Try it out: When my coworker flippantly dismisses my idea, instead of getting mad, I'll tell him how I feel when he dismisses my ideas like that.

Old way: I say yes to things I don't want to do.
New way: I say no when I don't want to do something.
Try it out: When my sister asks me to take her dog for the weekend, I'll tell her that this weekend won't work for me and,

to be helpful, suggest someone else she could ask or another time that would work.

Old way: I get defensive.

New way: I try to understand what's really being said.

Try it out: When my mother-in-law gives me advice about disciplining the kids, I'll ask if she can explain how she sees it working for me.

Old way: I care too much about what other people think.

New way: I act in ways that will strengthen the relationships that matter most to me.

Try it out: When I don't like what my husband wears to the party because I want my friends to like him, I remember that he's a good guy and that he is more important to me than the other people are.

Old way: I need to be right all the time.

New way: I work on being effective, not right.

Try it out: When I disagree with my boss about how to approach a project, I'll consider other ways we could reach consensus instead of trying to convince him that my idea is right.

Old way: I expect the other person to change.

New way: I work on having the other person's behavior bother me less.

Try it out: When my friend doesn't reply to my texts after I've told her that hurts my feelings, I'll remind myself that's the way she is right now, and it's not worth losing a friend over. Then I'll text another friend who is responsive.

Old way: I yell during disagreements.

New way: I take steps to cool down my emotional temperature.

Try it out: When my neighbor gets mad at me because my kids used sidewalk chalk in front of his house, I'll say I can't talk right now, but I'd be happy to come by in fifteen minutes. Later, when I'm talking to him, I'll keep my voice down and try using a more diplomatic style.

Old way: I avoid difficult conversations.

New way: I make an effort to talk about things that feel uncomfortable.

Try it out: When I feel hurt by my friend's behavior, I'll arrange for a time to talk to him about my feelings.

Old way: I resent having to do everything.

New way: I make room for others to carry some of the load.

Try it out: When I'm feeling angry and hurt that my teenager has left all his laundry for me to do, I'll call a friend with a teenage son and ask for ideas to get him to do his own laundry.

Communication Skills

In order to be successful at any of these new approaches, you'll need to work on your communication skills. We've included communication tips throughout the book, mostly in Week 3 (tips to lower your emotional temperature) and Week 7 (suggestions for starting a difficult conversation and conversation enders to avoid). Here are a few more ideas for having a constructive, respectful conversation.

Practice your delivery. People who are experiencing conflict usually say they tried to explain their perspective and listen to the other side, but when we ask them to tell us exactly what they said and did, they weren't as clear in their communication as they thought they were.

Use "I" statements. This is one I make fun of all the time, because it's become such a standard entry in every effective communication guide, but it's still good advice. "I" statements keep the focus on what you feel ("I feel sad when you come home from work late, because I miss our time together and I really need a break from the baby") rather than laying blame ("You never come home on time, so you're never there to help me out"). But simply using the word "I" doesn't magically turn a mean or hostile comment into something you're allowed to say. "I hate it when you act like a jerk," may start with an "I," but it's *not* an effective "I" statement.

Use humor. Whenever you can, disarm with humor. The other day my grandson was using a silly accent to torture his older sister, and she was yelling at him to stop. My daughter told them they were in a power struggle. "What's a power struggle?" my granddaughter asked. "I have zee power, and you have zee struggle," my grandson quipped. They all laughed. Fight over.

Take the high road. You may do your best to fight fairly, but the other person may not follow your lead. Maybe they're stressed or worried about something else. Maybe they're insecure and covering it up with aggression and bravado. Remember, the only behavior you can control is your own. No matter how badly they behave, that's not who you are, or want to be. Take a break. Try again later. If the conversation doesn't improve, decide if you want to seek professional help to manage the conflict, if you want to work on having it bother you less, or if it's time to dissolve the relationship. Whatever your choice, weigh the consequences. Don't pretend that everything will be okay.

PEP TALK: *The way you choose to interact with other people is the greatest gift you can give yourself.*

Consider acceptance. If the other person has to change to achieve the outcome you're looking for, and they decide they aren't willing to, you'll have to decide if it's a deal breaker. Let's say your spouse is overweight. You could say, "Honey, I'm worried about your health because of your weight. Is it something you want to change?" If he says yes, ask if there's anything you can do to help. (Of course, you might not be prepared to do what he wants. If he says he wants to train for a marathon, and you have absolutely no interest in that, lovingly say so.) But if he says he's happy just the way he is, you can choose to accept him as he is or choose to end the relationship.

Hang in there. If the person you're in conflict with starts telling you how they feel, it might not be easy to hear. Resist the urge to get defensive or change the subject. Remember, this is short-term pain for long-term gain. Now that their feelings are out in the open, it's something you can deal with together, so you can hopefully move forward with your relationship.

Kate Talks to Don

Kate needs to have a conversation with her husband, but she knows she's going to avoid it. She decides to ask Mona — the friend she talked to last week — to check in with her every couple of days to ask if she's talked to Don yet.

To prepare, Kate looks on the internet for assertiveness tips and reads a few articles on effective communication. She's supposed to come up with one or two specific things she'd like to address rather than overwhelming Don with all the issues she's stored up over twenty-seven years of marriage. She decides Don's incessant texting is a good place to start. One article suggests something called the "sandwich technique," in which the more challenging part of a hard conversation is "sandwiched" between positive, supportive statements that begin and end the exchange. She incorporates that idea into her plan.

Kate makes herself practice in front of the mirror, trying out different opening lines, anticipating what Don might say, and working to keep her cool, stay focused, and maintain open body language. It feels weird, but there's so much to remember, so it's good to practice.

A few days later, Mona texts to ask if Kate has talked to Don. Kate texts back, "Today's the day." After dinner, she opens with the line she rehearsed so many times. "Honey, I know retirement's been a big change in our lives, and I'd like to talk to you about it. Are you game?"

Don agrees, so Kate begins. "It's been great that you've been at home and taken on some of the things I used to do, but I've been finding it hard to respond to your texts when I'm at work."

Don immediately gets defensive. "I don't text you that much," he says.

Kate clarifies. "Well, you texted me fifteen times the other day, and I found it hard to focus —"

"I didn't text you fifteen times," he says, cutting her off.

Kate wants to show Don her phone as proof, but she doesn't. "Let's not argue about the number, honey. It's the fact that I'm at work that's the issue. I just don't have time to respond properly, even if it's one or two texts. If you could wait to talk to me when I get home, I could give it more attention."

Kate can feel Don getting angry. "You have time for other people when you're at work," he snaps. "It's really crappy that you don't have time to read a lousy text from your husband. You say you'll pay attention to me when you get home, but you're always working late."

Kate's instinct is to retreat and smooth everything over with an apology, but she keeps going. "I want this to work for both of us," she says. "Is there anything I can do to make it easier for you?"

"Yeah," Don yells. "Answer my damn texts!"

Now Kate is getting angry. "I'm trying, here, Don," she says. "It would be great if you could too." She needs to bring her emotional temperature down. She pauses. She takes a deep breath. "If I can't answer the texts, what can we do?"

"I don't know, Katie," Don sighs. "You're the only one who knows where all the pieces of the smoothie blender are."

The conversation doesn't last much longer. "Thanks for talking with me about this, Don," Kate says, remembering she wanted to say something positive at the end of their conversation. Then she checks her emotional temperature. She's feeling disappointed and angry that nothing was re-solved, but she reminds herself that this is just a place to start.

"In with the New" for Transitions

If you're going through a transition, take a look at how you've been han-dling people and situations as you experience this life change. Are you keeping your feelings to yourself? Are you denying yourself the chance to learn from others who have "been there" before you? Are you turning down opportunities to engage in your life the way it is now? Your change may be a shift in perspective, where you gain a more balanced view of your life now. Or it may be a change that helps you learn the skills you need to feel competent again. Here are some suggestions, with examples to show how you could give the new way a try:

Old way: I see my current situation as all bad.

New way: I look for the silver lining.

Try it out: When the morning sun is streaming into my new apartment, I'll sit for a few extra minutes with my coffee be-fore running out the door to work.

Old way: I stay focused on the past.

New way: I keep my focus on the here and now.

Try it out: While I'm out with my friends, I'll try not to compare it to the way it used to be before I had the baby, but will be open to the new experiences I'm having right now.

Old way: I see people and situations as I've always seen them.

New way: I keep an open mind and try to see new interpersonal situations as opportunities.

Try it out: When I can only have one couple over for a drink in-stead of cooking dinner for a whole crowd, as I did before my car accident, I'll try to see the advantages of having a more intimate gathering.

Old way: If I can't do things the old way, I won't do them at all.

New way: I give new experiences a chance.

Try it out: When my married friends invite me over for dinner, I'll go, even though I'll be the only single one, and I may tell my friends how awkward it feels.

Old way: I keep my feelings of incompetence and inadequacy to myself.

New way: I share my feelings with others who may be able to help me.

Try it out: When I'm struggling to understand my new boss's expectations of me, I'll ask a coworker what the boss expected when he started.

When we're having trouble with a transition, we often idealize our old situation or role and see only the downsides of our new role or situation. But the reality is, the past wasn't all good and the present isn't all bad. Seeing the new situation in a balanced, realistic way will help us make the transition and feel better.

PEP TALK: *When you're going through a transition, remember that the past wasn't all good and the present isn't all bad. We'll help you take a more balanced view!*

When Ron was making the transition from his government job to being a self-employed psychologist, all he could think about was the loss — the loss of a steady income, the loss of respect in his parents' eyes, the loss of a career he'd spent years building and had high hopes for. It wasn't until he let himself think more broadly that he started to feel there might be some advantages to his new situation. He didn't have to fight traffic. He didn't have to do the same thing every day. He didn't have to work from 9 to 5.

It was the same for my client Emily, who wanted to leave home, but felt she couldn't because she was her mom's caretaker. Her goals were to encourage her mom to share emotionally with people more appropriate than her daughter, but Emily was having a hard time following through. "If I'm not my mom's go-to person, who am I?" she told me. I helped her identify the aspects of her old role as her mom's confidante that were difficult and the aspects of her new role as an independent adult that would be positive. In the end, she saw that her new role wasn't so much a loss in status as it was a gain in opportunity to have new relationships with her mom, dad, and brother.

Reality Goggles: An Exercise for Transitions

You can achieve a more balanced view of your transition by completing an exercise we call Reality Goggles. Grab a piece of paper and a pen, and let's get started.

Divide the paper into four same-sized quadrants. Label the top left quadrant "Old role: Liked" and the top right quadrant "Old role: Didn't like." Label the bottom left quadrant "New role: Don't like" and the bottom right quadrant "New role: Like."

Next, starting in the top left quadrant, list what you liked about the old situation or role. Think of what you miss, paying attention to your feelings. Here are some ideas:

Old job: I really liked my colleagues. I could walk to work. The salary was pretty good. I knew what was expected of me. I felt competent. Overall, I felt comfortable, confident, and secure. I felt supported by others.

Old city: I felt confident that I knew my way around. I felt loved by my friends and energized by the big-city pace of life. There was always something going on, and I knew great places to hang out. My home made me feel safe and proud and relaxed — I invested a lot of love in it.

Being single: I didn't have to answer to anyone, and I liked the silence sometimes. The dishes were mine, the hairs in the sink were mine, and if something was missing, it was because I misplaced it. I felt free and relaxed and self-sufficient.

Being married: We had great mutual friends. I felt more

relaxed because we shared the responsibilities of home and family. There was always someone to talk to, and I enjoyed the stories he would tell. I felt secure. I felt accepted and included, because everyone was married. I felt things were as they should be.   ·

Here is what Ana writes about in the first quadrant about life before Ruby:

I felt so free — I could pick up and do stuff on my own timetable, with no child care or diaper bag to arrange ahead of time. I had time to myself. I was happy at work — I felt like I knew what I was doing, and I got along well with my coworkers. I liked my prepregnancy body. Peter and I had time together as a couple, and we could be spontaneous about having sex and going out. I felt energetic and even impulsive at times.

Next, fill out the upper right quadrant. What didn't you like so much about your old role or situation? What don't you miss? This one might be harder to complete. Think back to the days before your transition. What did you spend your time doing? Who did you spend your time with? What made you sad? Angry? Frustrated? Can you remember any of your New Year's resolutions from that time? We've included some ideas below, but check in with your circle too. People who know you well will remember things you complained about or experienced during the old days that you may be forgetting now. Ask them.

TRY THIS: *If you can't think of something you didn't like about your old situation, ask someone who knew you back then what you complained about.*

When Ana completes this section she recognizes for the first time how empty her life felt before Ruby:

I really wanted to be pregnant and spent a lot of time wishing I had a baby or worrying I might not be able to conceive. I also had this empty feeling in my stomach, like something was missing.

After a night out with my girlfriends, I wondered sometimes, "Is this all there is?" The girl talk bored me: Steph's new food sensitivity, who was sleeping with whom at the gym, clothes, home renos, vacation photos, yawn.

Next, we'll explore your new situation. We'll start with what you don't like about it. Remember to include how these aspects of the change make you feel. Ana doesn't have any difficulty coming up with the things she doesn't like about being a new mom — and feels guilty about it:

I'm so tired some days I can't keep my eyes open. There's never time to shower, and I feel like I look awful. I'm lonely. The milestones in the baby's development are wonderful, but I'm always by myself when they happen, and telling Peter that Ruby smiled for the first time isn't the same as sharing the experience with someone who was there. I feel like nothing I've ever done prepared me for this, and I'm questioning myself all the time. I never knew one baby could create so much work. I miss adult conversations. There's tension in my relationship with Peter. And I feel guilty that I'm saying all these negative things about my beautiful baby.

Only the bottom right quadrant remains to be filled out: what you like about the new role or situation. This one will be harder. You may have to dig really deep to come up with something positive to write. But every change, no matter how difficult, can have a silver lining. Maybe you've heard a cancer survivor say her life is better for having had the disease. Rationalization? Maybe. But ask her what she means, and she will likely say she has courage she never knew she had, an appreciation of every day as a gift, and a new depth to her relationships. These are all good things

PEP TALK: *An important step to feeling better about your transition is to see the opportunity that lies in the change.*

— and she believes she wouldn't have experienced them if she hadn't had cancer.

If your transition pushes you to do something you wouldn't otherwise do and you grow as a person because of it, that's a good thing. In fact, that's a big part of why you're going to write down what you like about your new situation or role — so you can start seeing the opportunity that lies in the change.

Ana focuses on the joy Ruby has brought to her life:

Really, there are moments when I think my heart will explode with love. I didn't think I could ever feel that way. Peter and I can't stop talking about the baby — I know it's silly but we even talk about how many times she poops every day. Anyway, sharing that experience with someone makes me feel connected and happy. Her milestones are great moments — holding her head up, smiling, cooing. Sometimes I just stare at her while she's sleeping and wonder how I got so lucky.

The last thing you'll do is check in on your feelings, now that you've worn your "reality goggles" for a while. Write down a few sentences that describe how you feel now compared to how you felt before you drew the four squares on the paper and filled them in. Are you able to see your new situation in a more balanced, realistic way?

Here's what Ana writes:

I feel a little lighter. It helps to see that life before Ruby wasn't perfect — there were things I didn't like back then that I don't even have time to think about now. Also, some of the things I don't like now could be improved if I had other moms to talk to. That makes me feel good, because connecting with other moms is one of my goals. I'm on the right track!

LET'S GET REAL

Thanks to Hollywood and Hallmark (and Facebook and Disney), real, everyday human experiences — like friendship, getting married, having a baby, being a family — have been turned into larger-than-life, idealized "moments." Life isn't a fairy tale. But we're told it can be. Not only does that build unrealistic expectations, but it leads to a lot of guilt when we resent wearing baby spit-up as a fashion statement or get mad that Prince Charming doesn't put the toilet seat down. A balanced view of life is a healthy view. If you think you're the only one who feels there are negatives to having a brand-new baby or being newly married, ask around.

"Ask around" is just good advice anyway. When someone at your new job says, "Yeah, I felt exactly the same way when I started," or "If you're having trouble with that software, here's a link to an online tutorial that we all took last year," you're going to feel better about aspects of the new situation that are causing you discomfort, worry, or stress. When another new mom tells you that she has "baby brain" or offers advice to help get junior on a nap schedule, you'll feel less alone and better equipped for your new role.

So next time you find yourself comparing your life to the lives people lead on TV or Facebook, remember to keep it real.

Seeing the Whole Picture:
A New Way to Cope with Grief

If your problem area is complicated grief, what old ways are keeping you from talking about the person who died or making it hard to reconnect with your social circle? Have you been pushing your feelings down? Avoiding situations, people, and conversations that might make you feel sad, guilty, or even happy? Cutting yourself off from the people who care about you? How's that working for you?

To cope with your grief effectively, you need to accept the full range of feelings you have about the person who died and the circumstances of their death and give yourself permission to experience those feelings for as long as you need to, in the company of another person. Here are some ideas for things you could change, with examples of how you could try out the "new you":

Old way: I push down my feelings about the person who died.
New way: I talk about how I feel.
Try it out: When my friend comes back from her cruise with her parents and is talking about what they did, I'll share with her how much I miss my mom.

Old way: I avoid doing things that might bring up feelings about the person who died.
New way: I accept my feelings and do those difficult things anyway.
Try it out: When I need to go through my husband's stuff in the basement, I'll call a friend, tell her how I'm feeling, and ask if she'd mind helping me.

Old way: I hide when I'm feeling guilty or sad about my loved one who died.
New way: I reach out to someone when I'm feeling low.
Try it out: When something reminds me of my best friend who died and I'm feeling upset, I'll tell someone how I'm feeling right away.

Old way: I can't imagine my life without the guilt and sadness I feel.
New way: I realize that I can still remember my loved one without carrying around the guilt or grief.

Try it out: When I'm talking with someone who also loved my mom, I'll ask if they'd like to do something special to remember her.

Old way: I see the relationship with my loved one as having been all good (or all bad).

New way: I see the relationship with my loved one in a balanced way.

Try it out: When my friend is complaining about her brother, I'll tell her how hard it is for me to see anything negative about my relationship with my brother since he died and ask if she'd mind helping me get some perspective.

All relationships have their ups and downs. The "in with the new" for many of us whose depression is linked to complicated grief is to see our loved ones and the relationships we had with them in all their perfect imperfection. Having conversations in which we explore both the beauty and the flaws in these relationships can help us grieve the death and reconnect with our own lives.

PEP TALK: *It's okay to talk honestly about the relationship you had with someone close to you who died. Explore the beauty and the flaws. It'll help you feel better!*

It may feel almost impossible to talk honestly about the relationship you had with the person who died. Your instinct may be to idealize them and share only the positive aspects of the relationship and great times you had together. Saying something negative may seem disrespectful. There may be strong cultural norms that prescribe what is acceptable to say and what is off-limits. But the person who died was human, and the relationship you had was real.

Maybe you were a caretaker during a long and difficult illness. Maybe there's a good reason you weren't at the bedside when the person died — you were estranged or had other priorities because of the kind of relationship you had. Not everyone knows how to die nicely, and maybe the person was difficult during those last days, weeks, or months. It isn't wrong to talk about things as they really were, wholly and completely. It's healthy to acknowledge the good and the bad, to laugh and to cry.

Last week we shared the story of Ron's client Liv, whose husband took his own life, breaking a pact he'd made with his wife to fight his cancer to the very end. Ron asked Liv to fully explore her relationship with her husband.

"Was there anything about him that drove you nuts?" he asked.

"My husband was a very proud man," Liv replied. "He was very stubborn and set in his ways." As hard as it was for her to say that, it was an important moment for her — the moment she realized that his suicide wasn't meant to hurt her; it was simply the act of a proud, stubborn man, the kind of man who wouldn't give up control to cancer or make his wife shoulder the burden of his illness. This realization helped her feel less angry and guilty and helped her grieve her loss.

Stefani, the young woman we met in Week 5 whose mother had died, found it easy to tell me what she liked about her mom. "She was so kind and thoughtful," Stefani said. "She would do anything for me and my brother. I always felt loved." When I asked about aspects of their relationship she hadn't liked, Stefani resisted. "I guess Mom was kind of overprotective," she said finally. We continued to discuss the ups and downs in their relationship in detail, helping Stefani remember her mom as a real person, not an idealized image.

Remember my client Maureen, who had never really felt sad when her mom had died eighteen years earlier? She could speak at length about what she didn't like about her mom, but when I asked about good memories, she had to pause and think. "My mother had a beautiful singing voice," she eventually said. "When she had been particularly mean and maybe felt bad about what she had said, she would gather me and my sisters in her bed and sing us songs before we fell asleep. Those times were special. They made me feel a little better and made me see that she cared in her own way."

When I asked Maureen if she remembered any of the songs, she started to sing one. "You are my sunshine, my only sunshine," she sang, her voice choked with emotion. A few lines in, she stopped and grew thoughtful. "You know, I've sung those songs to my kids and grandkids, but I never really saw the connection between my mom and me and them before," she said. Singing became a positive way for Maureen to remember her mother and to carry a love of music through the generations.

PEP TALK: *Once you've explored both the ups and the downs in the relationship you had with the person who died, you may be able to do other things that will help you feel better.*

When you're able to go through the difficult process of talking with someone you trust about the relationship you had with the person who died, both the ups and the downs, you may find you're able to more easily accomplish other things you've wanted to do (or that loving family and friends have said you should do). Now you have the emotional strength to give away your loved one's clothes. Now you can attend a bereavement group or volunteer in a way that honors your loved one. Now you can go to the cemetery, look at old photos, make your loved one's favorite meal. Now you're ready to go back to work.

Becky Reaches Out

Becky is feeling encouraged after her talk with her hairdresser. According to Lauren, all Becky has to do is text one of her friends.

Amber will be too busy getting ready for the wedding, so Becky decides to text another of their foursome, June. But it's not as easy as Lauren made it sound. What if June doesn't respond? What if she's mad? What if they get together and June doesn't want to hear about Becky's brother?

The best thing that could happen is that June listens to Becky talk about her feelings about Brian's death, Becky feels better, and they're best friends again. The worst thing that could happen is June ignores Becky's text or texts back that she doesn't want to see Becky. The most realistic thing, Becky says to herself, is that she and June will eventually get together, it'll be kind of awkward, they'll talk about Brian but not as much as Becky would like, and Becky will feel a little better.

Becky writes the text ("Hey, it's Becky. I miss you! Can you forgive me for being such a crappy friend? I'd love to see you!"), but it sits on her phone, unsent, for three days. Finally, unable to stand the "should I, shouldn't I" debate any longer, she hits "Send." Her heart is pounding. For the first four hours she checks her phone constantly to see if June has responded. During hour five, the phone vibrates. It's June. "Who is this? LOL" (June always was a joker). Then, "It's so great to hear from you, Bex!"

They go for coffee. Becky apologizes for taking so long to reach out.

"We felt terrible that Brian was sick," June says. "We just didn't know what to do. You seemed to want to handle everything on your own. We wanted to see you, but you said you couldn't go out. I'm so sorry we stopped trying."

For the first time, Becky feels ready to talk about why she turned down all the invitations from her friends. It's okay to say that Brian wasn't perfect, she tells herself. It doesn't mean I don't love him.

Becky tells June how hard it was when Brian was sick, how much of her time his illness took up, how demanding and controlling he had been, and how guilty he made her feel the one time she went out with the girls. "His cancer was horrible," Becky says. "I was his everything. If I went out, he was completely alone. I understand why he acted like he did. And that's why I stopped seeing you guys."

June's response is kind. She tells Becky that she wished she'd known. "We could've come up with some way to help you," she says. "Hell, we all knew what Brian was like. None of what you're saying is really a surprise."

After the coffee they hug and June says, "You've got to come to Amber's bachelorette party. We won't take no for an answer."

Becky takes her emotional temperature. "I feel loved and cared for," she thinks. "I also feel proud of myself for doing this."

"And who can you share that with?" she asks herself. Lauren, of course. Becky pops by the salon on her way back to her apartment, tells Lauren what happened, and gets another hug.

"In with the New" for Loneliness

The way we respond to other people is a big part of why we have friends or don't, have good relationships with family or don't, get along with people at work or don't. If your problem area is loneliness and isolation, you'll need to learn to open up, share your experiences, and show you care if you're going to connect with others in a more meaningful, positive way. Be patient. You're a pro at your old approach and a rookie at your new approach.

Here are some ideas for changes you could make:

Old way: I avoid socializing because I feel people won't like me.

New way: I attend social activities because it's an opportunity to feel different.

Try it out: When everyone is going out for a beer after work, I'll go along and make an effort to talk with my coworkers.

Old way: I judge others based on strict ideas of right and wrong.

New way: I have conversations to understand the reasons people do or believe what they do.

Try it out: When someone says something I don't agree with, I'll ask them why they feel that way before telling them I feel differently.

Old way: I don't trust people because they've hurt me before.

New way: I give people the benefit of the doubt.

Try it out: When my friend tells me that she wants to get together but then doesn't text me, I'll trust that she's telling the truth when she says she just got really busy.

Old way: I don't think people are worth the effort.

New way: I try with others, because I want them to try with me.

Try it out: When I'm having dinner with my extended family,

I'll ask my cousin about something he's interested in, even if it doesn't really interest me.

Old way: I expect other people to initiate contact.
New way: I reach out first sometimes.
Try it out: When I'm feeling lonely, I'll ask someone at church if they'd like to go for a coffee, even though I feel they should've seen that I've been struggling and asked me first.

Old way: I'm always right, and I know best.
New way: I ask other people for their opinions and act sincerely interested in what they say.
Try it out: When my colleague offers a suggestion that he says will make formatting my report easier, I thank him for his input and don't try to convince him that my way is better.

If you're not sure whether you do anything that puts people off or pushes them away — and you're feeling brave — you can ask someone you trust. If the person you ask is feeling brave too and gives you an honest answer, don't argue with them or get defensive. Instead, feel proud that the person you asked sees you as strong enough to handle criticism and that they care about you and the relationship enough to be honest with you.

TRY THIS: *If you ask someone for their advice about what you could change, listen to what they say and feel good that they care enough about you to be honest.*

You don't need to punish yourself for having interpersonal habits that are annoying or irritating. I've been told by my family that I ask too many questions and don't listen to the answers. They're right — my mind wanders and I don't pay close attention to others when they speak. My daughter-in-law has given me permission to ask the same questions over and over about what shows she's watching on TV, which I think is very sweet of her. Sometimes I try to pay attention and remember. I might even write her answers down — but then I'd have to remember where I put the list. I'm wise enough to recognize two things:

first, that I won't be able to change everything, and second, that if I don't change some things, it will have an impact on others.

The thing you need to change could surprise you. Ron was working with Jesse, an engineer who was feeling depressed because his friends were all in serious relationships and getting married. He was desperate for female company and didn't want to look like a loser in front of his buddies, so he started paying escorts to accompany him to parties and dinners out with friends. He knew these weren't real relationships, though, and the evenings out just made him feel worse in the end.

There were no women on Jesse's social circle except his mom, and when he completed the Four Questions exercise from Week 2 with Ron, he couldn't think of a single thing he liked about the relationship with his mother, whom he saw as a controlling and manipulative woman. The "in with the new" for him, then, was to begin thinking of his mom in a more balanced way.

"Start small," Ron suggested. "Think of one thing you like."

Jesse decided to talk to his brother about it. What did his brother like about their mom? What might Jesse be overlooking?

The next week, Jesse gave Ron the nuts and bolts of the conversation with his brother. "My brother thinks that when Mom is overbearing and nosy, it's just her way of showing she loves us," he said. Ron asked how that made him feel. "It helps," Jesse said. "I feel like I can see Mom's side a little bit now. It may not be the way I want her to show she cares, but it's the only way she knows how." This small change was the first step for Jesse to see his mother — and potentially all women — in a kinder, less judgmental way.

TRY THIS: *Appreciate other people for who they are instead of wishing they were different, and you might just feel better!*

Being able to accept your weaknesses and acknowledge your strengths is a good thing. So is taking responsibility for your role in a relationship instead of blaming others. This gives you power and control over your own behavior. It's how you'll learn to relate to others more constructively. And it'll help you feel better.

John Finds a Compromise

John already tried something new when, last week, he decided to stop arguing with Tom over the suggestion that John go for a beer with Alex. John feels pretty good about ending the conversation with Tom on a more positive note, but the thought of actually asking Alex, the "coworker from hell," to go for a beer feels like insanity. If John doesn't actually try Tom's suggestion, is he falling back into his old ways? John decides to text Tom.

"I get that you might not want to go out with Alex," Tom texts back. "But can I say I think it's cool that you even considered my idea?" Then Tom asks John what he feels more comfortable doing.

"I could ask Ben out for a beer," John texts back, referring to another of his coworkers. "We could talk about things at work."

"Ben might have some ideas for you too," Tom texts. "You could ask him how he handles Alex."

John feels better. He hasn't outright dismissed Tom's idea about the beer — which would be his old way — but he isn't going to do something he isn't comfortable with either in the name of trying something new.

There's Always Next Time

The point of this week's work is simply to try something new and see how it feels. If it feels good — even a little bit — resist the urge to dismiss the feeling or say it isn't "good enough." Instead, sit with the good feeling for a while. Then share it with someone. They won't think you're bragging. They'll feel happy for you and possibly relieved that you've had a positive experience.

TRY THIS: *When you try something new, tell someone about it.*

If you set out with the best of intentions and don't follow through, explore what happened. Sometimes when the moment arrives, you feel you aren't ready. Try pushing yourself a little. Ask yourself, "Is this just an excuse? What will I be saying or doing when I'm ready? Is it realistic to think I'll ever get there?" Remember, you don't have to make this change on your own. If you're having trouble letting go of your oak tree, think of who your Little Scarlet Leaf could be.

TRY THIS: *If you can't let go of the old way on your own, ask someone to help you.*

Remember my friend Martine, who was separating from her husband and whose goals got written over a bottle of wine back in Week 5? She had decided to communicate with her lawyer once a week, but three weeks had gone by and she hadn't sent an email or called the lawyer's office.

She didn't feel up to the task. What if she found out she couldn't afford to live on her own? What if her husband's lawyer was a jerk? What if her lawyer thought she was stupid? How much was every email and phone call going to cost her anyway?

Martine decided to tell her sister about her reluctance. "Do you want me to come with you?" her sister asked. No, Martine wanted to do this on her own. "How about if I remind you to call?" her sister asked. Yes, that would be really helpful. The next week, after a loving nudge from sis, Martine emailed her lawyer and made an appointment.

PEP TALK: *It takes time, effort, and practice to get comfortable with the new you. Forgive yourself for the small steps backward and celebrate the small steps forward.*

Every interaction offers a choice: old way or new way? If one time you choose the old way, how does that feel? If it doesn't feel good, next time choose the new way. And when you choose the new way, feel proud of yourself for trying, no matter the outcome. It takes time, effort, and lots of practice to get really good at something new.

GUY TALK: OLD HABITS DIE HARD

One of my clients was a lawyer who was working eighty-hour weeks on his way to becoming a partner. He had three kids, three dogs, three houses, and three cars but no wife — she'd left him months earlier. Turns out she didn't want all those houses and cars. She wanted a husband.

Men, in general, don't make changes until it's almost too late. We don't change our diet until the near-fatal heart attack. We don't spend time with our family until our eldest develops a drug problem. We don't talk about our feelings until our wife threatens to leave us. We need to be open to changing earlier, before all the chips are on the table, to try out a small change when the stakes aren't so high.

My client's problem area was interpersonal conflict with his wife, who had told him she'd like to try again, provided he made some changes. When we were completing his social circle, I asked him about his dad. What was their relationship like?

"I never really saw much of him," he said. "He was working all the time."

A lightbulb went on for me, but not for my client. Eventually I asked him if his behavior reminded him of anyone he knew. Had anyone done the same thing to him? And how did that feel?

"Oh my God," he said. "I've turned into my dad. And I remember it didn't feel good." Suddenly he saw value in investing time and energy in his family instead of sinking it all into his career. He had found the motivation to change.

What if my client had found his motivation earlier? It's exhausting to pretend things are okay when they're not. What would life be like if we weren't wearing that "everything's okay" mask anymore? Let's make a small change, early on, and find out.

This Week's To-Do List

Decide what you'd like to let go of and what you'd like to try instead. Start small, and practice the new approach in a specific situation. If you can't think of something new to try, ask someone in your circle what they think you could change.

Take your new approach for a test drive. What happened? How do you feel? Whatever the outcome, celebrate the fact that you had the courage to try. If the outcome was positive, sit with your good feelings for a while. If the outcome wasn't what you hoped for, try again.

Share your experience with someone in your circle. Tell them what you did and how it felt.

WEEK 9

What Did You Expect?

Our expectations influence our feelings. This week we'll help you re-flect on your own expectations and imagine what another person's expectations might be. Then, if it feels right, we'll coach you through having a discussion to clarify expectations with someone in your life. With your new understanding you can decide what you want to do to feel better.

Buddhist monk Ajahn Brahm once said that his goal in life was to be a loser. (This is coming from a man who has spoken at Google's head-quarters and addressed the United Nations!) His point was that a lot of unhappiness in the world comes from unmet expectations. If we could be losers — lose our expectations and lose our focus on outcomes — we could lead more satisfying and stress-free lives.

Psychologist Dr. Albert Ellis has also linked expectations to hap-piness. He noticed that seriously unhappy people often have three rig-idly held expectations. First, they always expect themselves to do well. Second, they always expect others to treat them well. Third, they always expect life to go well. When these expectations aren't met, it leads to self-loathing, hostility toward others, and an inability to cope with life's inevitable setbacks.

To be happy, Dr. Ellis said, we need to be flexible — to phrase our expectations as desires and preferences rather than demands. We prefer to do well, that others treat us well, and that our life goes well, but we don't expect it to be that way all the time.

Expectations can be reasonable or unreasonable, agreed on or a source of tension. If expectations aren't met, they have the power to make us feel inadequate, confused, sad, angry, disappointed, frustrated, righteous, hostile, ashamed, and more.

TRY THIS: *Be flexible in your expectations, and you'll be happier.*

Every person in a relationship has expectations, but these expectations only become an issue if both people don't agree on them. If both you and your boss are fine with your handing in reports late, or both you and your wife would like to have an open marriage, or both you and your friend are fine if you only get together once a year, there's nothing to be concerned about. But when things don't go smoothly, it isn't that one of you is right and the other is wrong or one of you is good and the other bad — it's just that there's an expectation gap.

Are your expectations of the other person reasonable? How would you feel if you changed them? What does the other person expect of you? How would you feel if you met those expectations? This week we'll help you identify your own expectations, guess at the expectations of another person, and complete an exercise to clarify and negotiate expectations on both sides. Along the way, we'll encourage you to check in with your "whos" for their opinion.

Once you've reflected on the expectations held by all those involved, you can decide what you want to do: negotiate with the other person to see if your expectations can be met, approach the relationship the same way as you always have (and maybe find someone else to meet those unmet expectations), adjust your expectations, or end the relationship.

Expectations and Your Problem Area

Expectations play a role in every problem area. For interpersonal conflict, simmering tension and outright fights often occur because two people are looking for different things from a relationship. Maybe your best friend isn't spending as much time with you since she started dating her new guy, or your wife is too clingy, or your boss isn't satisfied with your working anything less than a sixty-hour week. Your expectations and their expectations are different — and this gap will be filled with unpleasant feelings.

For transitions, if your expectations of your new situation aren't being met, it will affect your mood. Maybe you thought having a baby would bring you and your husband closer together, and instead you're fighting more than ever. Maybe you expected to fast-lane your recovery after your car accident, and instead you're hitting every bump in the road.

PEP TALK: *An expectation gap causes us to feel bad. When we close the gap, we feel better!*

Our transitions are often transitions for others in our lives too. Expectations may change as a result of the new situation. Your postpartum fights with your husband might be connected to differing expectations about who does what for the baby, visits from the in-laws, or sex. If one person in a relationship is struggling in a new job, conflict may arise from differing expectations about the balance between work and home life and who picks up the slack when one person has to work longer hours.

Complicated grief can also involve expectations. How did you expect to deal with your loss? What did you expect others around you to do? And what did other people expect you to do? Remember Garrett, the firefighter who was having a difficult time coping because every conversation he had was about the two men in his department who died? People's expectations of when, how, where, why, and for how long you express your grief can also impact your mood.

If your problem area is loneliness and isolation, do you expect people to meet your expectations all the time? Or do you expect that they'll always fall short? Do you expect more of others than you do of yourself? Or the opposite — do you expect more of yourself and then get resentful because others don't respond with the appreciation you expect or reciprocate with the same level of effort? It could be that your expectations are making it hard for you to connect with other people and modifying them could help you feel better.

Uncovering Expectations

Too often, our expectations go unexamined. But figuring out which expectations are and aren't being met could put us on the path to addressing the problems and feeling better.

The first step is to reflect on your own expectations. Choose an interpersonal situation that took place over the last week that's related to your problem area and has been bothering you. If you can't think of anything more recent, you could use the incident you vented about during Week 6. What were you feeling at the time the interaction took place? Can you link that feeling to an expectation that wasn't met? Think first about your expectations of the other person or people, and then examine your expectations of yourself that might be contributing to your feelings.

PEP TALK: *When you can link your feelings to an unmet expectation, you have a place to start to address the problem and feel better.*

In Week 6, I vented about the Friday night dinner when my family made fun of me. I was feeling hurt and disappointed. My expectations were that they would be appreciative of my efforts — yes, I'd brought too much food, but shouldn't they be saying "Thanks, Mom" anyway? I also expected them to have learned by now that their sarcasm bothers me.

Did I have expectations of myself? Sure, I did. I expected that I would rise above any jokes they told, not feel insecure, and not take myself so seriously.

After you've explored your own expectations, try to imagine what the other person might have expected of you in that situation. Next, see if you can identify what they might have expected of themselves. This requires you to put yourself in the other person's shoes about an issue or exchange that bothered you, which can require some emotional imagination. Have you ever been on the other side of a similar situation in the past? How did you feel? What did you expect of the other person? Of yourself? If you're stuck, ask someone in your social circle for their opinion.

If we use the example of my family dinner that Friday, I'm guessing my family would've expected me to joke around. They would've expected me to know how much they appreciate me and that they weren't trying to make me feel bad. Their expectations for themselves were probably to have a good time.

The last step — you guessed it — is to take your emotional temperature. Often, identifying your expectations and guessing at another person's expectations can reduce the intensity of the emotions you feel, because you have a better understanding of why you feel the way you do and why the other person may have done or not done something.

Back in Week 6, Becky was shocked and saddened to see her friend Amber's Facebook post of the bridal-party photo. Let's say she asks herself what expectations are contributing to her feelings of anger, loneliness, and hurt. Well, she expected Amber to include her, and it's been more than a year since she's had an invite. She expected that Amber would know how difficult things were for Becky and cut her some slack — sure, Becky's been AWOL, but she needed Amber to continue to make an effort. But probably the biggest contributor to Becky's feelings is her expectation that Amber would have asked her to be in the bridal party.

PEP TALK: *When we imagine what another person's expectations might be of us and of themselves, it can help us have a more balanced view.*

Becky also has expectations of herself that are contributing to her feelings. She expected to be at a different place than she is — to be moving forward, as everyone else seems to be — which is causing her to feel disappointed and angry with herself.

Now Becky tries to imagine what Amber might have expected. This is hard. She thinks back to her coffee with June. What did June say? That Becky had seemed as though she didn't need any help. That her friends had wanted to see her, but she turned down the invites. That June had wished she'd known what Becky was going through, so she could have helped.

Would Amber feel the same way? Probably. She would've expected Becky to say yes to going out at least a couple of times. And she would've expected Becky to have opened up about what she was going through.

With the wedding planning in full swing, Amber would've probably expected Becky to make more of an effort to connect too. It's even possible that Amber's expectations of herself would've been to keep her good news to herself rather than risk making Becky feel bad.

How is Becky feeling? She's still hurt about being left out of Amber's wedding party, but the feeling isn't as raw. She can see how Amber would've had expectations of Becky that weren't being met when Brian was sick and after he died. And she can see there are other ways to explain why Amber didn't reach out other than simply not caring about their friendship. It helps Becky take Amber's actions a little less personally.

TRY THIS: *Word your expectations as "I'd like" rather than "I should" or "You should," and you'll feel better. Think like a diplomat!*

Ana and Peter, like all couples who have a new baby, are experiencing changes in their roles, and it's impacting the dynamics of their relationship. Ana runs through her expectations of Peter. She expects him to spend more time at home now and to help out when he's there, especially with Ruby.

Ana has expectations of herself too. She expects to be a confident, capable mother — her feelings of self-worth depend on it. This expectation isn't a preference or a desire; it's a demand she makes of herself every single day. Ana tries wording the expectation more flexibly: "I'd really like to be a confident, capable mother." Suddenly she feels different. When she words her expectation that way, there's room to learn and make mistakes and still be a good mom.

Next, she guesses at Peter's expectations. His behavior is telling Ana that he expects things to be the same as before Ruby was born, when they both worked. Now that Peter is the primary income earner, Peter may expect Ana to be primary caregiver. Could that be why he's working so much? He feels an added financial responsibility, now that he has a daughter?

So how does Ana feel, now that she's named these expectations? She's surprised by the new awareness she's gained. Both she and Peter seem to have high expectations of themselves. But Ana doesn't really care about having more money — she'd rather see more of Peter than have him working lots of overtime. And maybe Peter doesn't expect Ana to be as perfect a mom as Ana expects herself to be. Maybe they're both putting unnecessary pressure on themselves.

Realistic Expectations

If we have realistic expectations — of ourselves, of others in our lives, and of how things are going to turn out — we'll probably feel better. Not euphoric or ecstatic, but better. And often a lot better.

So how can we discover whether our expectations are realistic or not? It can help to try seeing things from a different angle. Do we expect more of the other person than we do of ourselves? Are we forgetting all the other good things that person has done for us? What are that person's limitations? Try to see the relationship in a balanced way. Sometimes when we're feeling down or stressed, our tendency is to look only at the negatives and what we don't like, and that isn't good for us or the other person.

Maybe your friend didn't reach out when she knew you were bummed about work — but what if she's called in the past and you haven't wanted to talk about what's going on in your life, or she's struggling with some of her own issues? Maybe your mom only talks about herself. But what if she's always been self-absorbed — should you expect anything different? You might not like how your boss talks to you, but what if she talks to all the employees like that, and most of your colleagues don't find it disrespectful, just irritating? Seeing the situation or interaction from a different perspective can help you uncover whether your expectations are realistic.

Pay attention to the way you phrase your expectations. Are you "shoulding" all over yourself or the other person? How does it feel to express your expectations as a preference or desire — saying "I'd like it if" rather than "I should" or "They should"? If you want the garbage taken out, try saying, "I'd like you to take out the trash on Wednesdays." Then say, "You should take out the trash on Wednesdays." Which one feels better to say? Which

TRY THIS: *Try seeing your situation like an objective third party to evaluate whether your expectations are realistic.*

one feels better to hear? Expectations that aren't requirements are more realistic.

If we aren't sure if our expectations are reasonable, we can ask one of our "whos" what they think. One day I was complaining to my friend about my husband. "He isn't affectionate enough," I said. "He hardly ever holds my hand in public or kisses me out of the blue. What do you think? Am I expecting too much?"

Now, my friend knows both my husband and me really well. She knows that he has a lot of great qualities, but spontaneously displaying affection isn't one of them. She also knows that she can't simply tell me, "You've been married for how long? More than forty years? And you expect he's going to change now?"

TRY THIS: *If you aren't sure whether your expectations are realistic, ask one of your "whos."*

Instead, she said, "How about you tell him, 'Honey, my life is almost perfect, but if you could take my hand every Thursday at 7 PM and kiss it and tell me how beautiful I am, my life would truly be perfect.' If he doesn't remember, just stick out your hand on Thursday at 7 PM and remind him."

By the time I stopped laughing at what she said — and at myself — I felt a million times better.

Each of us has limitations. Each of us has our own way of doing things. Sometimes life doesn't work out the way we want it to. But maybe that's okay. If we keep our expectations flexible and check that they're realistic, chances are we'll feel happier.

EXPECTING LESS OF OURSELVES

If you see yourself as a giver and other people as takers — and feel resentful, frustrated, angry, and taken advantage of because of it — it may be time to lower your expectations of yourself when it comes to your relationships.

It won't be easy, and you'll have to tolerate the discomfort that comes with a different approach. People in your life may not respond positively at first to this new assertive you. After all, you've probably refused their offers of help and done more than your fair share in the relationships for a while, and now you're changing the rules. You may also worry that if you start saying no, they'll move on to someone who says yes — and they won't need you anymore.

If the way you've been doing things hasn't been working for you, trying something new — like expecting less of yourself — just might help you feel better. If it doesn't, you can always go back to the old way.

The Matrix: A Tool to Explore Expectations

If you're experiencing stress or conflict in a close relationship, as is often the case if your problem area is interpersonal conflict or life transitions, we're going to walk you through an exercise that can help you and another person get on the same page — literally.

Ron invented the Matrix exercise when he was helping a woman whose husband couldn't seem to give her what she wanted, and it was causing her to feel depressed. Ron was having a hard time sorting through the woman's long list of unmet needs.

"Let's write down all the things you expect your husband to do when it comes to your relationship," he suggested.

His client wrote furiously for fifteen minutes. When she was finished, there was an expectation on every line of the page — more than thirty items. The last one was "Learn to play the piano."

Ron asked his client to pick her top five. With this new, narrowed list in hand, Ron and his client were able to have a conversation about where his client's expectations were coming from, the feelings connected to each item, and whether it was realistic for one person (her husband) to be responsible for them. Later, Ron thought about how much better the conversation would've been if her husband had done the same thing — written down his expectations of his wife — and the couple had talked about their lists together. And so the Matrix was born — and it's a tool I love.

The Matrix helps two people in a relationship discuss their needs and wants. It provides the structure we need to clarify what's important, helps us focus the conversation, and encourages us to be empathetic. It's especially helpful when we don't know how to start a conversation about expectations or when hurt, anger, disappointment, or previous failed attempts to talk are standing in the way of a constructive conversation.

PEP TALK: *Getting everyone's expectations out on the table means no one has to assume they know what's going on anymore.*

There are three steps to the exercise. The first step is to examine your own expectations and guess at the expectations of the other person. The second step is to ask the other person to do the same thing. In the third step, the two of you discuss each of the expectations, one by one, and see if you can agree on a single set.

There are no right or wrong answers, no good or bad outcomes to the exercise. The Matrix is simply a way to gather information and start a dialogue in a less heated way than when you're in the throes of an argument. You may find you learn something surprising. Or not. The Matrix will give you the opportunity to share expectations and discover whether you can give, take, and collaborate in order to work things out. If it ends up going sideways, you can try again another time or decide it's time to end the relationship.

The Matrix is a fantastic tool for couples. It's also great for parents to complete with their teenage or adult kids. (You can do a simplified version with your younger kids too.) Best friends, siblings, and even people who work together can use the Matrix.

First, we'll take you step by step through the formal, "official" version of the exercise. Then we'll give you adaptations for different scenarios when you'd rather not go by the book.

If you push through the short-term discomfort of asking someone to do the Matrix with you, there might be some long-term benefit for your relationship. Take one step, see how it feels, and then take another one, even if it feels awkward. Let's get started.

Step 1: Your Matrix

First, grab a sheet of paper and divide it into four quadrants either by folding it or drawing lines with a pencil or pen. Label the top left-hand section "[Your name]'s Expectations of [other person's name]." If I was doing the Matrix with my husband, the title of this first section would be "Cindy's Expectations of Jay." Label the top right-hand section "[Your name]'s Expectations of [your name]." In my case, it would be "Cindy's Expectations of Cindy." The lower left-hand section gets labeled "[Other person's name]'s Expectations of [your name]." For my Matrix, it would be "Jay's Expectations of Cindy." The last section is labeled "[Other person's name]'s Expectations of [other person's name]." In my case, it would be "Jay's Expectations of Jay."

Cindy's Expectations of Jay	Cindy's Expectations of Cindy
Jay's Expectations of Cindy	Jay's Expectations of Jay

Now take another sheet of paper and make a duplicate copy for the other person to fill out. Write the same headings in the same order on the page so that later, after the other person has completed it, it'll be easier for you both to share and compare your lists.

Next, complete all of the sections on your sheet, starting with any section you want. It will help if you focus your expectations on a few key themes, which will vary depending on the nature of the relationship you have with the other person. Here are some possibilities:

Themes with a spouse: money, sex, parenting, time spent together and apart, extended family, roles and responsibilities, religious practices

Themes with a boss: salary, vacation time, hours, professional development, teamwork and independent work, deadlines, what you're responsible for delivering

Themes with an adolescent child: homework, chores, allowance, relationships with extended family, relationships with siblings, relationship with a boyfriend or girlfriend, curfews

Themes with a friend: frequency of contact, the types of things you do together, conversation topics, time spent as a twosome and with larger groups, confidentiality

Themes with a coworker: roles and responsibilities, habits, how conflicts get resolved, your relationship outside work, getting and giving credit

Themes with a sibling: care of elders, finances, shared property, frequency of contact, type of contact, topics of conversation, roles and responsibilities, relationships with children

There are a few important things to keep in mind when writing down your expectations:

Limit the number of expectations in each section to a maximum of five. This will require identifying what's most important to you and what you think is most important to the other person. If you have a list of twenty expectations in one of the squares, it'll be too hard to get through them when it's time to compare lists, and you'll get distracted from what really matters.

TRY THIS: *When you're discussing expectations with someone, limit your list to the most important ones or else you'll get distracted.*

Start expectations of the other person with "I would like" rather than "I expect," "I need," or "I want." If you write down, "I would like my husband to cook Sunday breakfast," it leaves room for your husband to change the expectation a little so it works for him. If you write down, "I expect my husband to cook Sunday breakfast," it gives him only two options: to agree or refuse.

Keep your expectations specific. You may want to be a "faithful Christian" or you may want your husband to be a "devoted dad." But what do those terms actually mean? What would you be saying or doing if you were a faithful Christian? Maybe you'd like to go to church every Sunday or practice your faith every day. What would your husband be saying or doing if he were a devoted dad? Maybe you'd like him to be active in your son's extracurricular activities or be a firm yet fair disciplinarian. It's easier to discuss expectations when they're specific, because we can imagine what it may take to meet them and the potential impact on us and others.

When it comes to expectations of yourself, keep the focus on your relationship. If you're completing the Matrix with your spouse, for example, write down the expectations you have of yourself regarding your work, friends, hobbies, or volunteer activities only if they impact your relationship with your spouse in some way.

Imagine what the other person's expectations would be. You can't ask them, so do your best to put yourself in their shoes. Ask yourself when they seem happy with what you're doing, when they seem disappointed, and what things they just assume you'll do. Uncover their expectations of themselves by asking yourself when they seem happy with themselves, when they seem disappointed in themselves, and what they do without your asking.

Don't worry about what the other person will write. Ron had a client who was reluctant to do the Matrix in case his wife didn't include on her list something that was important to him. Ron reminded him that the point of the exercise was to identify the differences and talk about them, to see if they could get on the same page.

Pay attention to blank spots and imbalances. Can you think of fifteen expectations for yourself but none for the other person? Or is it the other way around? If you're drawing a blank for any section or the expectations are weighted more heavily on one person than another, take notice. An imbalance will affect your relationship — and will be good to discuss when you share your Matrix with the other person.

Include the good stuff. If you have an expectation that's already being met, don't leave it off. It's good to acknowledge that some things in your relationship are working well!

The next page shows what my Matrix might look like.

Step 2: The Other Person's Matrix

The next step is to ask the other person if they're willing to do the exercise with you. Explain that the Matrix is a tool to help two people have a conversation about their expectations. Tell them it's important to you and you hope it'll help make your relationship better. Walk them through the steps. Show them the page you made with the same headings as yours and explain how to complete each of the four sections. (You may even want to give them this chapter of the book to read.) If they say they're willing to participate, give them the sheet to fill out and set a time to get together to talk about what each of you has written — that way there's a deadline to work toward.

If they're reluctant to do the exercise or flat-out refuse, try to discover why. Are they too busy? Are they nervous? Have they misunderstood the purpose? Would they rather do it informally? Are they tired of talking about the problems in your relationship? Try to uncover their objections, so you can

Cindy's Expectations of Jay

I'd like him to be the major financial support for the family.

I'd like him to fix the cars.

I'd like him to watch some of the TV shows I like with me.

I'd like him to speak respectfully to me and the children.

I'd like him to send me flowers on our anniversary.

Cindy's Expectations of Cindy

I expect to contribute financially to the family.

I expect to do the grocery shopping.

I expect to arrange the family celebrations and buy the gifts.

I expect to not bug or criticize my husband.

I expect to be considerate of his needs for independence.

Jay's Expectations of Cindy

He'd like me to not tell him what to do.

He'd like me to do the grocery shopping.

He'd like me to continue to pursue my professional and personal interests.

He'd like me to contribute financially to the family.

Jay's Expectations of Jay

He expects to be the primary financial supporter of the family.

He expects to take the cars in to be fixed where he wants.

He expects to have the independence to make professional/ work decisions.

He expects to play golf with me on Sundays unless there's a tournament he'd like to play in and then he'll discuss it with me.

He expects to be generous in spirit and financially with his family, friends, and colleagues.

clear up misunderstandings, reassure them, or change the exercise so they feel more comfortable with it.

In the end if they say no, or say yes but don't actually do it, or say yes and it takes them a long time (and some nagging on your part) to complete it, how does that make you feel? Do you want to keep trying? Their reaction is telling you something about their commitment to resolving your conflict.

Step 3: The Master Matrix

When it's time to share your Matrices, first check in with each other. Are you both fed? Rested? In a relatively good mood? If you're likely to be interrupted, you've recently had a fight, or are feeling grumpy or stressed, you may want to reschedule. The discussions can be intense. Give yourselves the best start possible.

If you decide it's a good time for you both, grab a blank piece of paper and a pen so you can create a joint list — the "Master Matrix" — which will have five items under each heading that you both agree to. Then exchange the papers you each filled out and read them over silently.

Try not to react if you see something that makes you angry, frustrated, or disappointed. There aren't any right or wrong answers — the pieces of paper are simply a place to start a conversation. Maybe you've misunderstood what the other person wrote. Maybe once they hear your perspective, they'll be willing to adjust their expectation. Try not to jump to conclusions.

PEP TALK: *Expectations can be adjusted. Are you willing to adjust yours? Is the other person willing to adjust theirs? Let the negotiation begin!*

Once you've finished reading each other's Matrix, choose a single section and discuss each item, starting with one person's list and then moving on to the other person's items. We find that there are often one or two issues that are the main source of conflict. Focus your attention on those instead of getting distracted by other, less important expectations.

When you come to an expectation that you don't agree on, talk about it. Why do you each feel the way you do? Can you meet in the middle? If you "give" on this expectation, can you "take" on another? Is there an entirely new way of looking at the issue that you can come up with together?

You may experience some powerful feelings. Try to keep an open mind. Share honestly. Be respectful in your language. Keep taking your emotional temperature. Be patient with the other person (after all, they haven't been coached by us the way you have!). Take breaks if you need them.

In the end, you'll have cocreated your Master Matrix: a single page, divided into four sections, with no more than five expectations in each section that both of you have agreed to live with and live up to. You won't manage to hold up your end of the bargain all the time, and neither will the other person. But you'll both have made a commitment to the relationship and can use the Matrix as an ongoing reminder of your shared expectations.

GUIDELINES FOR THE MATRIX

- Each person fills out their own Matrix independently.
- There are no right or wrong answers.
- List no more than five expectations per section.
- Keep expectations specific.
- Don't avoid the tough topics, like money or sex.
- Ask; don't demand.
- Keep an open mind.
- Don't take what the other person says personally.
- Focus on the most important issue.
- Give, take, and collaborate.
- Remember, you're on the same team.

"Damn, This Is Hard"

Remember my perfectionist friend Leyla, whose boyfriend's "baby steps" mantra helped her get her dishes done? I was telling her about the Matrix one day.

"I want to try it with Dan!" she said.

They decided to complete their Matrices independently but at the same time, sitting side by side in bed, and then go out for dinner to discuss them.

"Damn, Cindy," Leyla told me the next time I saw her. "Doing the Matrix was hard." Turns out they almost packed it in before they started, when labeling the squares triggered Dan's hatred of evaluations. "That's when the yelling started," she said. "I was hurt that he thought I was testing him. He was freaked out about failing and was mad that I wasn't listening to what he was saying."

"So did you guys stop?" I asked.

"No," she said. "Once I acknowledged his feelings instead of being focused on my own, it got better. We decided we both wanted to keep going."

I was curious to know whether they'd learned anything surprising when they discussed their expectations.

"Dan thought I expected him to be a vegetarian, which I totally don't," she said. "And I thought he expected me to do most of the cooking, which he doesn't. He said I expected him to quit smoking. I hadn't even thought of that, but it was true. So those were good discussions."

The conversation got hard when Dan shared what he thought Leyla's expectations were of herself. "At first when he said, 'You expect to have perfect dinner parties,' we laughed — because I do. I get all stressed out days before. I just want people to have a good time. But the more we talked about it, the crappier I felt. Suddenly I was crying into my pizza diavola."

I asked where her feelings were coming from.

"I just felt hurt and like a failure. It was like Dan had said that all my parties sucked because I was stressed. And Dan felt so bad because he never actually said that. It's just what I heard."

"What happened next?" I asked.

"I thought we were going to have to stop. Then he said, 'Beautiful, we're on the same team. What can I do to help you not feel stressed when you have a party?' That turned everything around."

"If you were going to do it again, what do you think would make you both feel better?" I asked.

"We'd definitely limit the number of expectations we put in every square," Leyla said. "I forgot that we were only supposed to have five. I'd also try to remind myself that these aren't criticisms. It's so easy to take things personally. It's just a place to start to make things better." She laughed. "You know, Cindy. Baby steps."

Using the Matrix for Relationship Maintenance

We have Matrix-like conversations quite frequently when we first start a relationship, especially a romantic one. Then real life gets in the way of the late-night, wine-warmed explorations of what we like and don't like, want and don't want, and we stop having the conversations. But relationships aren't static. We have kids, change jobs, or move to another city; the kids move out, our parents require care, or one partner gets sick — our lives change. But we don't have conversations about how our expectations may have changed too. The Matrix gets these conversations started again. And the more conversations we have, the easier they get.

A husband and wife who originally came to Ron for couple's therapy now take a walk in the snow every New Year's Eve and do an informal version of the Matrix, just to keep their relationship on track. It doesn't take them long — after all, it's darn cold in Ottawa on December 31 — and when they get home, they email Ron to let him know how it turned out.

It's like having routine maintenance done on your car or updating an app. Investing a little bit of effort at regular intervals can prevent big issues down the road.

Kate and Don Complete the Matrix

Kate and Don have just exchanged their Matrix worksheets.

As Kate reads through each point on Don's Matrix, she starts to feel frustrated and hurt. Sure, he's recognized that she wants to go to yoga. But where is his understanding that her career matters to her? It irks her that he's only got three expectations of himself — and they're all pretty selfish.

She watches Don read her Matrix. He isn't giving anything away.

"Okay, what section should we start with?" Kate asks.

"I don't know," Don says. "This was your idea."

"We're off to a great start," Kate thinks. Out loud she suggests, "Why don't we start at the top, then, with my expectations of you." She pulls out a blank sheet of paper and writes "Kate's Expectations of Don" in the top left-hand square. "This is our Master Matrix," she explains. "This is where we write the five things we agree on."

They talk through each of Kate's expectations of Don. There's a bit of discussion about just how much is "some" cooking and cleaning.

"Listen, Katie," Don says. "I haven't really cooked before. I can do the dishes. I can make my own lunches when you're at work. But don't expect me to have dinner on the table when you get home. I don't know how."

Hearing Don's honesty about not knowing how to cook helps Kate see things from his point of view. She can imagine that if Don wanted her to, say, fix the leaky tap or the broken basement stair, she'd need some help. It's not really fair for her to want him to make dinner. She can feel herself calming down a little. "Are you okay if I write down that I'd like you to make your own lunches and wash the dishes?" she asks.

He agrees, and she writes it on the Master Matrix.

Don's temper really flares when they discuss the last item on Kate's list of her expectations of him. "What do you mean, 'I'd like Don to understand when I have to work late'?" he snaps. "I hate it when you work late. All you seem to do is work, work, work. You're the one that needs to understand. Do you know how it feels to sit around here waiting for you to come home?"

Kate feels herself getting upset. Don has never understood how important her career is to her. "I didn't ask you to sit around waiting for me," she says. "In fact, if you'd actually read my expectations of you, I'd like you to have an active social life. You used to be busy. I can't entertain you 24/7."

Don is mad. "I don't need someone to entertain me. But I do need a wife. Did you marry me? Or your work?"

Kate takes her emotional temperature. Definitely in the red zone. Time to cool things down a little — otherwise she's going to rip up that Master Matrix with its one lonely item and walk out of the room. "Let's take a break, Don," she says, trying to keep her voice calm. "I want us to be able to talk through these things without hurting each other. I love you. I want to do this because I love you."

Don agrees that things are getting a little heated and says he's willing to try again another day.

"Let's each put our papers somewhere safe and bring them next time," Kate says. Then she takes the dog for a very long walk.

The Matrix Lite

If the highly prescriptive format of the Matrix feels awkward or inappropriate to suggest to a friend, coworker, boss, or elderly parent (especially one whose first language isn't the same as yours), you can take the basic structure of the exercise and use it as a guide to a less formal conversation.

Simply explore your expectations and what you think the other person's expectations might be, and then use that information to start a discussion with the other person to clarify their expectations of you. You might still want to complete your copy of the Matrix, writing down expectations in each of the four sections, but you won't ask the other person to do the same thing. Because you've thought carefully about the expectations on each side, the conversation is more likely to be focused and constructive.

You can also complete your Matrix and, instead of having a conversation with the other person involved, you could share your paper with someone you trust to get their thoughts. Are your expectations of yourself and the other person reasonable? How about your educated guesses at the expectations the other person has of you and themselves?

Remember Tiah, the director whose sexist VP was punishing her for her rapid rise in the IT firm they both worked for? She wasn't prepared to have a conversation with him, but she did share her sheet with two colleagues at a different IT firm.

Both colleagues felt she had accurately portrayed the unreasonable expectations of the VP and confirmed that her expectations were reasonable. This validation helped her feel better and resulted in a very supportive discussion about sexism in IT.

John Borrows a Brain

John decides he's not up to having a conversation with Alex yet, but he is willing to complete his Matrix and then show it to Tom.

He gets out a sheet of paper and starts writing. It's easy for John to list his expectations of Alex. Alex shouldn't steal John's deliveries, he shouldn't pick on John, and he shouldn't bad-mouth John to other co-workers or the boss. John's expectations of himself are to show up at work on time, to mind his own business, to take only the deliveries that are supposed to be his, to do what his boss says as long as John agrees with it, and to control his anger as much as he can.

Now comes the tough part. What does Alex expect of John? Alex expects John to be the butt of his bad jokes, to be a sucker he can pick on and take advantage of, and to shut up and take it when he steals John's deliveries. And what does Alex expect of himself? To be the alpha dog, to get ahead by hurting other people, and to get more tips than he deserves.

John emails his Matrix to Tom, explaining that he wants Tom to tell him if the stuff he's written down seems reasonable.

They discuss John's expectations of Alex first. "There's a lot of 'shouldn'ts,'" says Tom. "What if you worded your expectations of Alex more positively? Would that help you feel better?"

John wants to tell Tom that's a stupid idea, that there's nothing positive about Alex, but instead asks, "Like what could I say?"

"How about, 'I'd like it if Alex only took the deliveries that were his.' And 'I'd like it if Alex treated me with respect.' And 'I'd like it if Alex spoke respectfully about me to my coworkers and the boss.'"

Putting the statements that way makes John feel less mad at Alex.

Tom is curious about what John means when John says he expects to do what the boss says, "as long as John agrees with it."

"Well, sometimes my boss sides with Alex," John tells Tom. "He wants me to ignore Alex. He doesn't think this stuff is a big deal. But it is."

Tom pauses, then says, "What if you did ignore Alex?"

"I can't," John says. "What he's doing is wrong. I can't let him win."

"Okay," Tom says. "But sometimes when you win, you actually lose."

John is getting exasperated.

Tom explains. "I mean that by paying attention to Alex, he's getting a rise out of you. If you ignore him, yes, you may not be arguing for what's right, but in the long run you'll enjoy work more and probably get along with your coworkers better."

"So I'm just supposed to let Alex steal my tips?" John snaps.

"How much would you lose if you did that?" Tom asks.

John guesses about twenty bucks a shift. "But it's not just about losing money," John says. "It's about losing face too."

"Just play along with me for a second," Tom says. "While Alex is out doing your deliveries, what do you do?"

John says he just sits around at the restaurant.

"That doesn't sound so bad," Tom laughs. "And if you stopped caring about Alex taking your deliveries, he may stop taking them. He's doing more work while you take it easy — and he isn't getting a rise out of you anymore, so he isn't getting that rush. Plus, your boss may start asking questions. How come you're getting paid by the hour to do nothing? How come Alex is out doing all the deliveries? Your boss may decide to do something about it."

John grumbles a little, but he can sort of see Tom's point. Could he ignore Alex? It's kind of fun to think about Alex working his ass off while John takes it easy at the restaurant.

When Someone Can't Meet Your Expectations

Whether you complete the Matrix formally or have an informal conversation about your expectations, things may not turn out exactly as you'd hoped. What if your expectations of each other are so different that you can't imagine meeting them? Or they're not that far apart, but you just don't want to make any kind of change? Or you decided something together that you can live with, but you don't feel great about it? That's okay. At least the cards are on the table. You aren't shoving your feelings down, getting angry at something unrelated, or holding on to bitterness and resentment. That, in itself, is something to feel proud of.

With this new awareness you can decide what you want to do. One option is to stop expecting those things from one another and accept what is, focusing on the aspects of the relationship that do work. Another is to stop expecting the other person to fulfill those expectations and agree to get them met elsewhere. A third option is to do nothing and stay angry or resentful. The last option is to dissolve the relationship.

TRY THIS: *If the other person can't meet your expectations, you can accept things as they are or dissolve the relationship.*

One of my colleagues was counseling a fifty-year-old woman whose husband had an emotional affair with a coworker. Months after he'd realized his hurtful mistake and cut all ties to the coworker, his wife was still angry, hurt, and frustrated. She was sick of feeling like the only one working on the marriage. She wanted her husband to relate to her in an open and emotional way and to initiate difficult conversations — things he'd never done in the past.

No matter what her husband did to apologize and show he loved her, it wasn't good enough. She wanted him to feel the hurt the way she had felt it. My colleague helped the woman understand that no two people experience things exactly the same way, and it's unrealistic to expect they can. "It doesn't mean your husband doesn't care or doesn't feel badly that he hurt you," my colleague said. "Imagine two seeds. Inside you is a sunflower seed and it grows into a beautiful yellow sunflower. Inside him is a tomato seed, and it becomes a juicy red tomato. You can't turn a tomato into a sunflower. But they're both beautiful in their own way, if you let yourself experience them on their own terms."

The woman ended up accepting her husband for the tomato he was — and found her emotional connection with her women friends, who were sunflowers just like she was.

If you've examined your expectations and neither of you is willing to change, you can also decide to end the relationship. Ending a relationship is difficult. It's painful and sad to admit things are over and frightening to think about what the future might bring. What would it feel like if you didn't have a relationship with that person anymore? What would you miss? What opportunities might it present? Ask someone in your circle — especially someone who has gone through something similar — what they think too.

TRY THIS: *If your relationship isn't going to change, your attitude is going to have to.*

If, in the end, you choose not to end the relationship, maybe it's time to stop talking about how much it bothers you. Something has to change, if you're going to feel better. If it isn't going to be the relationship, it has to be your attitude toward it.

GUY TALK: MIXED MESSAGES

I'm responsible for buying the cars in our family, but every car I've bought my wife hasn't liked. Take our current ride, the Honda Element. She hates cars with uncomfortable headrests and clamshell doors. The Element has both.

We're in the midst of car shopping again, and it's down to two options: the Prius (uncomfortable headrests and normal doors) or the BMW i3 (comfortable headrests and clamshell doors). I've told her that, this time, the decision is hers.

"I guess the Prius," she said, reluctantly.

"Okay," I said. "I'm going to buy it today."

"But don't you think you'll regret it?" she said.

"No," I said.

But she wasn't convinced. "You'd like the BMW."

I wanted her to make the decision, and she was refusing to send me a clear message.

Many women have a hard time saying, "This is what I want, and I don't care if you're not happy about it." (Guys don't tend to have the same problem.) For many women, speaking directly about their needs and desires isn't culturally acceptable. Instead, they use phrases like "Don't you think...," "Maybe...," "What if we...," and "I believe..." Or they give their decision-making power away by asking, "What do you think?"

This kind of diplomacy can be a strength in close interpersonal relationships, but it's frustrating when you're looking for clarity. It's confusing when you're asking for direction. It's hell when you need to know which car to buy.

Men need to be patient and encourage their wives and girlfriends to state their needs with confidence. Women need to recognize that their husbands and boyfriends aren't mind readers — if you don't say what you want, you might not get it. It's worth the short-term pain of a difficult conversation to have years of peace behind the wheel.

This Week's To-Do List

Choose a situation or interaction that bothered you and examine the expectations on all sides. What did you expect of the other person? What did you expect of yourself? What do you think the other person expected of you? Of themselves? Pay attention to your feelings.

Check in with your circle about your expectations. Ask a friend, family member, or coworker what they think. Are your expectations reasonable? Have you missed seeing something from the other person's perspective?

If you're experiencing conflict in an important relationship, complete the Matrix. You can do the full exercise with another person or use it as a guide for an informal conversation. If you like, you can also just complete the expectations sheet on your own and share it with someone you trust. How do you feel?

If a number of your expectations can't be met, consider your options. You can choose to keep the relationship as it is, change your expectations, or end the relationship. Be sure to check in with one or two of your "whos" to see what they think.

The Rehearsal

Practice doesn't make perfect, but it can help us feel more prepared. This week we give you some strategies for practicing an important conversation or interaction, so, come showtime, you can choose an approach you've rehearsed and be ready for what might happen.

If you've ever been involved with theater or other performance productions, you know the value of rehearsals for helping everyone get it right on opening night. A friend of mine has told me some good stories.

One time she was rehearsing for a charity event and decided to ad lib between songs. "What do you call a man who has lost his intelligence?" she joked. Pause. "A widower!" Turns out many of the people watching the actual show would have lost loved ones. Oops. The cast, who liked the idea of some improv, revised the banter to be more sensitive.

Another time, my friend was watching a rehearsal and realized the male lead's costume, illuminated by the stage lights, was a little too revealing in important places. Time to talk to wardrobe!

Then there was the rehearsal for *Les Mis*, when my friend and her fellow actor muffed the lines to their big song. After they stopped laughing (how could they forget something they'd practiced a million times?), they came up with some cues to help if it happened during the performance.

Practicing a significant conversation gives you the chance to try out new skills and run through your lines ahead of time. You get to experience how things feel, try out different approaches, and put yourself in another person's shoes. In the end, you'll think more clearly, communicate more effectively, and feel more confident in your beliefs and position. You'll stay focused. You'll be able to manage your emotions. And you'll be a better listener, because you won't be so concerned about what you're going to say or do next. Rehearsing is especially important if you feel anxious.

PEP TALK: *Rehearsing something helps you focus, listen, empathize, experiment, and be brave. No wonder we recommend it!*

That's because the way to reduce anxiety isn't to avoid doing things, but to do them over and over.

This week, we'll help you rehearse something that's important to achieving the goal or goals you set back in Week 5. We'll coach you to explore different outcomes and identify the feelings you experience with each. Which rehearsal approach should you use? Who can you ask to help you? How do you feel during and after your rehearsal? What did you learn — and what will you do with this new awareness? What did John, Kate, Becky, and Ana do? Let's find out.

Three Different Endings

We've asked you more than a few times in the previous pages to imagine the best, worst, and most realistic thing that could happen in a particular situation. We're building these three scenarios right into your rehearsal by suggesting that you rehearse three different endings — the best outcome, the worst outcome, and the most realistic outcome — in that order.

Remember Ron's client Liv, whose husband took his own life during a difficult battle with cancer? Liv's depression was linked to complicated grief, and one of her goals was to speak about her husband's death with the coworker whose husband had also taken his own life. She was having a hard time initiating the conversation, so Ron suggested they rehearse what might happen. The setting was a coffee shop near work, where the two women often ran into each other.

"Let's start with the best-case scenario," Ron said. They role-played a conversation in which Liv (who played herself) and the coworker (played by Ron) started with their usual small talk. Then Liv said, "I was wondering if I could talk to you about something else for a second. Do you have time?"

Ron, as the coworker, said, "Sure."

They went to a cozy corner of the café. Liv opened up about how she'd been struggling with the loss of her husband.

"Oh my God, I know what you must be going through," Ron said in his role as the coworker. "I've wanted to talk with you about it. I just wasn't sure if you were ready."

After rehearsing that outcome, Liv checked her emotional temperature. She was feeling relieved and optimistic, but also a little panicky. What if the conversation didn't go so well?

Next, they role-played the worst outcome. "The worst thing would be if I invited my coworker to talk about our husbands, and she looked at me like she'd seen a ghost and just walked away," she told Ron.

They rehearsed that scenario. Afterward, Ron asked Liv how she was feeling. "Hurt and insulted," she told him. "It makes me not want to take the risk."

Ron reassured her that the worst outcome rarely happens, but that it's good to be prepared for it.

"I don't think my coworker would do that anyway," Liv said. "It's not her style."

PEP TALK: *Worst-case scenarios very rarely come true. If they ever do, it's not the end of the world.*

What was the most realistic scenario? "She's probably going to stop, look at me, and think to herself, 'Did I hear that right?' then we'll continue to talk."

They practiced that outcome. How did that feel?

The moment of silence was pure torture, Liv said, but it was worth it to finally make a more meaningful connection.

Rehearsals can be very helpful for people experiencing loneliness and social isolation. Remember Jesse, the engineer whose difficulty maintaining relationships with women meant he was paying escorts to go with him to parties? Ron had suggested that a way to gain confidence with women was to volunteer at a hospital and make small talk with the female nurses. Eventually, they invited Jesse out for coffee.

Ron asked him what happened.

"Nothing," Jesse said. "I just sat there."

Then Ron asked how that made him feel.

"Well, I didn't feel like I made a fool of myself." That was the immediate payoff, but the long-term cost was that he continued to feel disconnected from the people around him.

Ron asked what the best-case scenario would be.

"That instead of waiting for them to invite me for coffee, I invited them," Jesse replied.

They role-played a scene in which Jesse said to the nurses, "Anyone up for coffee today? I'm buying!" He felt very uncomfortable with this possibility, but the nurses — played with great enthusiasm by Ron — liked it a lot.

What was the worst-case scenario? That the nurses went for coffee and didn't invite him.

The most realistic outcome was that the next time the nurses issued the invitation and Jesse went along, he was quiet for most of the coffee break, but thanked them as they were all getting up to leave.

How did that make him feel?

PEP TALK: *Rehearsing different outcomes lets you experience the feelings associated with each, so you can make choices that will help you feel better.*

"A bit better," he admitted. "At least I was acknowledging that I was glad I was included, so maybe they'll keep asking me."

Role-playing the scenarios allowed him to experience the positive feelings associated with making small talk and the negative feelings of being left out — which was likely to happen if he didn't make an effort when the nurses invited him.

If your problem area is life transitions, you'll want to rehearse an interaction that will help you see the upside of your new situation and develop the skills to manage in your new role. Years ago, I helped a friend's teenage daughter who was feeling anxious about starting at a new high school. We practiced how to start a conversation with a complete stranger, going through the when, where, how, and what of the conversation for the best, worst, and most realistic outcomes. Practicing the scenarios convinced her that the actual risks of starting the conversation were small and the potential benefits were large.

When there's conflict in a relationship, it's always a good idea to rehearse a conversation ahead of time. It'll help you plan what you want to say, practice controlling your emotions, and imagine ahead of time how your words will be received by the other person, so you can adjust them to optimize the response.

Remember Oscar, the aggressive finance director who wanted to be seen as a team player but didn't know how team players at his new job were supposed to act? His goal was to have a conversation with each of his four fellow executives to explore their expectations of him.

PEP TALK: *If you're in conflict with someone, rehearsing a conversation ahead of time helps you practice controlling your emotions.*

Ron asked if there was anyone he could rehearse with. Oscar suggested his wife would be a good practice partner. She agreed, and they talked through each conversation, imagining the best, worst, and most realistic outcomes. It was a two-week process. Ron asked how the rehearsals were going.

"They're definitely helping me prepare," Oscar said. "Especially practicing the meeting with the marketing director. She's actually a lot like my wife, so my wife helped me understand how she might respond to what I was saying — stuff I could never have gotten on my own."

A rehearsal can also give you important awareness about possible outcomes, so you can decide if you want to have a conversation at all. One of my clients was an art teacher who was feeling depressed because of conflict in her relationship with her husband. She wasn't ready to acknowledge that her husband's controlling behavior and unrealistic demands were hurting her emotionally, and she stopped coming to therapy after a few weeks.

Six months later, she made another appointment. She had decided she wanted to have a Matrix conversation with her husband, so they could talk about their expectations of the relationship, and we role-played three possible outcomes.

"He's never going to let me do extracurricular activities with my students," she told me. "He's never going to help out at home. I can hear him right now: 'Dinner is your responsibility. I want you home at 4 PM.' But that's not what I want."

Something had changed for my client during the six months she hadn't been to see me — she was no longer willing to accept a life dictated by her husband's expectations. The rehearsal helped her realize that if she tried to talk about expectations with her husband, nothing would change, including her feelings. If she wanted to have different feelings, she needed to take a different approach — so instead of having the worst-case scenario discussion, she decided she was ready to take steps to end the relationship.

Some Rehearsal Approaches

Step 1 to any rehearsal is to identify the conversation you want to practice. This will probably be obvious. If it's not, ask yourself what interpersonal experience will get you closer to the goal or goals you set in Week 5. Why haven't you had that conversation or experience yet? If the answer is fear about initiating it or anxiety about the outcome, a rehearsal could help you.

The next step is to figure out how and with whom you want to practice the interpersonal experience you've chosen. There's no right or wrong approach — simply choose the person you're most comfortable with and get to it.

TRY THIS: *Some people need to practice more than others, but don't overplay your rehearsal or look for perfection.*

Whether you're comfortable talking through what might happen on the fly or think you'll need a full dress rehearsal, the important thing is to try out a new interpersonal skill and, hopefully, experience some of the emotions you may feel during the actual conversation or event. Don't look for perfection. You can refine your approach once you use it in the real world.

Asking someone to help you practice is a chance to connect with your social circle in a new way too. It can be fun to rehearse together. If you do an actual role-play rather than simply talking through the scenarios, you may experience emotions as if you were actually having the conversation. You may laugh together. Or cry. Or both. Simply going through the exercise, regardless of the outcome, will help you feel supported and may deepen your relationship with your "who."

PEP TALK: *It's best to rehearse with someone in your circle. It can even be fun!*

Choose someone you feel is trustworthy, will keep your confidence if you ask them to, and can be relatively objective. A judgy friend or someone who's likely to be biased toward you or the other person probably isn't the best choice. If your "who" knows the person you'll be talking with and has things in common with them, they'll be better able to help you understand where the other person is coming from and how the conversation may play out — just reassure them that you aren't asking them to choose sides.

If you're feeling vulnerable, sensitive, or anxious, you can ask them to be kind, not critical. If you're concerned they're going to tell you what you want to hear, not what they honestly believe, ask them outright to tell you the truth, and tell them that you won't hold their honesty against them.

TRY THIS: *Be assertive with your "who" by directly talking about any hopes or fears you have when you ask if they'll rehearse with you.*

Once you've found someone willing to practice with you, decide how you want to rehearse: in person, over the phone, by email, or by text or instant message. Together, you can decide if you want to do a full-blown role-play or something a little less formal. You can also write out different scenarios ahead of time and read them to your "who."

Pay attention to your feelings as you're talking through or acting out the different scenarios. Ask your "who" for feedback during and after the rehearsal. How are you coming across? What could you change to make the outcome better? Are you expecting too much or too little from yourself, the other person, or the situation? Use the feedback to adjust the setting, content, or style of delivery for the actual conversation.

If you're uncomfortable asking someone else to rehearse with you, you can always practice on your own. You can rehearse a one-person role-play by using two chairs. Play yourself when you sit in one chair and assume the role of the other person when you sit in the other. You can also practice in front of a mirror or record yourself on your phone to see how your body language and words come across. If you like to write, you can explore the best, worst, and most realistic scenarios as stories and then read them over. Draw, paint, videotape, or journal — your solitary rehearsal can take many forms. Just like when you rehearse with someone else, pay attention to how you're feeling as you explore the scenarios and debrief with yourself afterward.

TRY THIS: *You can rehearse on your own too. Write the scenario down, videotape yourself, or act it out in front of a mirror.*

Whether you're rehearsing on your own or with someone you trust, it's a good idea to start by considering what you want to have happen and what you want to avoid when it's showtime. Here are some questions to ask yourself.

QUESTIONS TO SET THE SCENE

What do I want to talk about?

What do I hope to achieve?

When and where is the interaction going to take place?

How do I want to feel during the interaction? After it's over?

How do I want the other person to feel during the interaction? After it's over?

Are there things I want to make sure I say or do?

Are there things I want to make sure I don't say or do?

What are the best, worst, and most realistic outcomes?

What can I do or say to increase the likelihood of a positive outcome?

What can I do or say to help prevent the worst possible outcome?

Then ask these questions of yourself or the person who's helping you practice during or after your rehearsal to get feedback on your communication style.

QUESTIONS FOR DEBRIEFING

Was my approach respectful of the other person? .
Was it respectful of myself?
Was I being too judgmental toward the other person?
Did I take the other person's feelings into consideration?
Was I too passive?
Was I being clear?
Did I talk too much?
Did I interrupt?
Was I being too negative about what might happen?
Are there other scenarios that I didn't consider?
How did I feel before, during, and after the interaction for each of
    the best, worst, and most realistic outcomes?

Seeing the Other Side

It's easy to get caught up in one way of seeing things — my way or the highway — but as another old adage goes, there are two sides to every story, and imagining what it's like to be on the other side can actually help us feel better.

This kind of emotional imagination is called *empathy*. It involves understanding what another person is experiencing, feeling what they're feeling, and then responding appropriately using this new awareness.

This week's rehearsal exercise is an excellent opportunity for some empathetic learning — put yourself in another person's shoes and use this experience to guide what you say and do.

If you're role-playing, try playing the role of the other person instead of yourself. How does it feel to hear what's being said? Is there anything you wish had been said but wasn't? What do you feel like saying back?

You may be surprised to learn that something you thought would go badly didn't feel so awful when you put yourself in the other person's shoes. Or you may learn that what you thought would be no big deal actually hurt when you were on the receiving end. You may discover that some words or ways of speaking don't deliver the message the way you'd intended.

TRY THIS: *Put yourself in the other person's shoes — almost literally — by taking their part in your role-play. You may be surprised at what you'll learn!*

If you don't feel comfortable role-playing and have chosen a less formal approach, such as talking through a dry run of your interaction with someone, you can try asking specific questions to achieve your empathetic learning. Here are some examples:

If I were watching this unfold instead of being involved in it, what would I say was behind the other person's behavior?

What might I be saying or doing that is contributing to the problem?

How would I feel if someone said or did to me what I'm saying or doing in this conversation?

If I'm feeling hurt, angry, ignored, lonely, stressed out, or rejected by the other person, is it possible that they're feeling the same way as a result of my words or actions?

Can I use a time when I was in the other person's situation to help me say and do things that will be positively received?

Use your empathetic learning to adjust your delivery, your expectations of the outcome, or both.

John Invites Ben for a Beer

John is at the restaurant, waiting for his next delivery, when he gets a text from Tom. "How have things been at work?" Tom asks. Then, "Have you gone for that beer with Ben yet?"

Crap. John totally forgot he'd told his brother he was going to invite his coworker for a drink. Ben wasn't a jerk like Alex, but John was still procrastinating.

"No," John texts back.

"Nervous?" Tom texts.

"I guess," John writes.

Tom asks what John could do to increase the odds that Ben would agree to the beer.

"If I say I'm buying, he'll say yes," John texts. "He'll probably drink up fast and get the hell out of there."

"So when are you gonna ask him?"

Geez. Tom just won't drop it. John gives it some thought. It's Ben's first shift back after being off sick, so not today. John checks the schedule. On Monday they're both working until close, and Alex isn't in. "Monday," John texts.

Monday arrives, and John asks Ben during their first break together. "Wanna grab a beer after work today?" he blurts out. "I'm buying."

Ben looks surprised, but not in a bad way. "Sorry, man," he says. "I've got plans. How about tomorrow? I finish at 8 PM."

"Sure," John says. John isn't working tomorrow, but Alex is, so he suggests they meet at the bar next door.

"You better still be buying," Ben says with a grin, as he heads to the kitchen to check on his delivery.

John wipes his sweaty palms on his jeans. Could Ben tell how nervous he was? Maybe. But whatever. He said yes! John feels a huge sense of relief. He decides to text Tom the news — and it feels good to share something positive with his brother.

"Congratulations!!" Tom replies. Tom's enthusiasm makes John feel good — again. Then, "Any idea what you'll talk about?"

John hasn't thought that far ahead. Well, he wants to get Ben's take on Alex. Maybe ask him for some advice on what John could do so the tips were fair.

"Probably good to keep things light the first time you go out," Tom advises.

"I'm pretty sure this is a one-shot deal," John thinks. "I'm not wasting time with meaningless chitchat." But he resists the urge to disagree.

The next evening, John is waiting at the bar for Ben, compulsively checking the time on his phone and nursing his beer. Ben arrives around 8:15. They make some small talk. Then John cuts to the chase. "What do you think of Alex?" he asks.

Ben pauses. "He's a pretty good guy."

This was a mistake. Ben's on Alex's side. Everyone's on Alex's side. Ben looks at John. John looks down at his beer. This is awkward. What should John say?

Ben speaks first. "I mean, he can be a bit of a knob sometimes. Just don't let it bug you."

"Don't let it bug me?" John thinks, feeling his anger rising. "Easy for you to say," he mutters into his beer. "Alex doesn't steal your tips."

"Do you want some advice?" Ben asks.

"No," John thinks. "Sure," he says.

"Ignore him," Ben says, taking a sip of his drink. "Alex is one of those guys who thinks it's fun to bug people. When you make a big deal out of things, he likes it."

"So I'm just supposed to let him steal my tips?" Last time John asked that question, he was talking with Tom, and Tom basically said yes.

"Listen," Ben says. "Alex doesn't want the money. He wants the reaction. What's a couple of bucks? Let it go."

John can't believe he's hearing this crap again. "Would you let him steal *your* tips?" he asks, trying to keep his voice down.

Ben tells him he would. He says he'd rather have a good time and get along with people than be in a bad mood and get into pointless arguments. "You're not getting the tips, regardless," Ben reasons. "So isn't it better to be chill about it?"

John has a choice. His old way would be to get mad at Ben for saying something so stupid. But he could also try a new approach. People always seem to like Ben. Why not ask his advice? "I just don't know what to say to Alex when he takes a delivery that's supposed to be mine," John admits. "What would you say?"

Ben considers the question. "A joke is usually good," he says. "I remember one time Alex told you he was taking your delivery because the customer was really hot. I probably would've said something like, 'She's all yours, man. Hot girls are terrible tippers.'"

John laughs and raises his glass in a beer salute. "Nice one," he says. "Don't know if I could pull it off, but it's an awesome idea." For the first time in forever, he's feeling like maybe this thing with Alex isn't worth all the attention he's been giving it.

Becky: Should I Go?

When Becky gets the text from June reminding her of Amber's bachelorette party, Becky's instinct is to ignore it. She's been feeling awful lately. The anniversary of Brian's death is coming up, which makes her feel bad for so many reasons, not the least of which is that she expected to be feeling a bit better by now. Amber's party just isn't on her to-do list.

The party is an old-school sleepover at Sheree's place. What did the invite say? "PJs mandatory. Teddy bears and booze stolen from your parents' liquor cabinet optional." Why couldn't it have been something a little less intimate? Becky can't think of anything she'd like to do less than stay up all night talking with girls she hasn't seen in ages. If she hadn't promised June, she wouldn't even consider it.

What should she do? "Maybe the answer will come to me in a dream," she says sarcastically.

Becky pulls the curtains closed and climbs into bed, but she can't sleep. Her head is full of thoughts of the party. "Apparently this answer is coming the hard way," she says, turning on her lamp and grabbing a sketch pad and some colored pencils.

She opens to a blank page, writes "Best Outcome" at the top, and starts drawing. It's Sheree's living room, and four girls in pajamas — Amber,

June, Sheree, and Becky — are dancing together, hands in the air, holding drinks, laughing, and smiling. The colors are warm and bright. It's like there's a spotlight on Becky and her three friends — other girls sit nearby on the floor or Sheree's small couch, talking and watching, but their colors are muted. Becky feels happy as she draws. Her hand moves effortlessly across the page. She's drawing the old days, when the four of them were inseparable.

Becky flips the page, writes "Worst Outcome" at the top, and thinks for a second. What's the worst-case scenario? Going to the party and being ignored? Or not going at all? She grabs the black pencil and sketches her bed, complete with a small, sad lump under the covers who Becky knows is Becky but no one else would recognize, and then colors everything else in her bedroom solid black. Her strokes are short and angry. She feels sad, lost, alone, forgotten. "This is how I'll feel if I don't go," she says. "I know this feeling all too well, and it's definitely the worst."

Page three is for the most likely scenario. Not what Becky expects will happen — because, let's face it, she expects the worst — but the most realistic outcome.

Becky draws Sheree's living room again. There are three girls on the couch — Amber, Sheree, and the girl in the bridal party whose name Becky can't remember — sharing a bowl of popcorn and laughing. There isn't room for four on Sheree's small couch, or else June would probably be there too. Instead, June is sitting on the floor beside the couch with Becky and some other girls, and they're all listening to what the girls on the couch are saying. The colors are still warm, but not as bright. The focus is on the couch, not on the rest of the room. Becky's strokes are more thoughtful than exuberant. As she draws, she feels a little sad, but not lonely or forgotten.

Drawing the three scenarios has given Becky the answer. She should go to the bachelorette party. It won't feel like the old days, but it'll feel better than shutting herself away in her dark bedroom and crying herself to sleep.

Ana Pretends to Be Peter

Ana is on a video call with her mom. "Mamá," she says a little shyly. "I need your help with something." She explains that she wants to ask Peter to help more with Ruby. "I want to practice what I'm going to say to him," she tells her mom. "We could act it out. You play me, and I'll play Peter."

Her mom loves the idea, but admits to being a little confused. "Why don't you play yourself, *mijita*? I can be Peter. It will be easier." Ana says that she wants to put herself in Peter's shoes — to try to feel what he might feel and guess what he might say during the conversation — and a good way to do this is to pretend to be him.

Ana sets the scene. "I think it would be good to talk to Peter on the weekend. So let's say it's Saturday. Ruby is napping. You'll have to start, Mamá."

"*Un momento*," Ana's mom says, stepping away and returning wearing sunglasses — the pair that Ana left last time she visited her parents in Texas. "Now I feel like Ana," she laughs.

"Great idea!" Ana says. "Wait a sec." When she rejoins her mom on the call, she's wearing one of Peter's baseball caps. They both giggle.

"Now I'm ready. You start, Mamá."

"Peter, I'd like to talk to you about something," Ana's mom says. "Are you busy?"

Ana grabs a newspaper off the floor beside the bed and lays it open in front of her. "Hmmm?" she says, imitating her husband when he's absorbed in reading. "What did you say?" Ana's mom repeats herself. Ana doesn't look up from the paper. "I just want to finish this article, hon, and then we can talk."

"That's just like him," Ana's mom laughs. Then she pauses, gets back in character, and says, "Okay, but don't take too long. Ruby is sleeping now. We never know how long we've got before she wakes up."

Pretending to be Peter, Ana folds up the newspaper. "I'm done now," she says. "What's this big talk we need to have?"

It isn't hard for Ana's mom to imagine what Ana would say, considering all the discussions they've had recently. "I have needs as a mother," Ana's mom says. "You aren't helping me enough with them. I need you to help me more."

Ana, in her role as Peter, feels caught off guard. What her mom has said makes her feel defensive. The word "needs" sounds very demanding. The phrase "you aren't helping me enough" sounds accusatory. "Let's try that again, Mamá. Be a little softer. I think Peter would get mad if I said that to him."

"Okay, *mija*," her mom says. "How's this?" She pauses. "Peter, you know I love you very much, and I love our baby."

"Yes, of course I know you love us," Ana says, playing Peter.

"I have been feeling very tired, and I'm not sure whether I'm doing a good job as a mother, plus I feel lonely," Ana's mom continues. "I need your help while I get used to our new life."

"Oh, so much better," Ana says. "By saying it that way, I think Peter will feel like we're both on the same side."

Ana returns to playing Peter. "You're a great mom, Ana," she says. "I don't understand why you don't see it."

As an aside, Ana says, "He always says that, Mamá. He thinks a little compliment will make it all better. It bothers me so much. It feels like he's trying to get out of helping me."

"*Mija*, you *are* a great mom," Ana's mother says, no longer roleplaying. "But, that doesn't mean you don't need help from your husband. But maybe he isn't trying to get out of helping you by complimenting you. Maybe Peter just wants you to be less hard on yourself. He doesn't understand why you don't see what he sees — what we all see — a beautiful, capable new mother."

"I never thought of it that way," Ana admits. It feels good to accept what Peter says at face value, instead of assuming he has an ulterior motive. "So what should I say when he says that?"

As Ana, her mom says thank you for the kind words, says that she's working on being more confident as a parent, but gently repeats her request for help with the baby.

"I want to help with Ruby, hon," Ana says in her role as Peter. "But I don't know how."

A look of shock crosses Ana's face. "Oh my gosh!" she says, covering her mouth with a hand. "I suddenly felt what Peter might be feeling. If it's hard for me to manage as a new mom, why wouldn't it be hard for him as a new dad? Especially since I'm the one who sets up all the routines and knows where everything is. It would be hard for him to just step in."

Ana's mom smiles. "Sure, it can be hard for dads too. Maybe you'll need to help him a little before he can help you."

Ana takes her emotional temperature. She's feeling grateful for her mom's wisdom and better prepared for her conversation with Peter, especially now she's had the opportunity to experience the conversation from his side. Plus, acting was fun — Ana and her mom have never done something like that before.

Ana decides to share how she's feeling with her mom. "Thank you, Mamá," she says. "Practicing with you helped so much. I feel ready to talk with Peter."

"It was fun, *mija*," her mom laughs. "If I'd practiced some of my conversations with your papa ahead of time, well, maybe you would have heard less fighting growing up."

Kate: Advice from Mona, Take Two

After the unsuccessful first attempt to complete the Matrix, Kate takes a day or two to calm down and then considers what to do next. She feels frustrated and bewildered. What is going on with her husband? Why is he acting this way? How is she supposed to respond? She has no idea. Who could she ask?

The answer comes to her right away: Mona. Mona was so helpful the first time Kate opened up about her issues with Don. Kate texts her ("Loved our lunch. Things still aren't great with Don. Drinks this week?") and immediately feels better.

They meet at a café. Kate arrives late. She's flustered and upset — Don dumped a steaming load of guilt on her as she went out the door, and she almost canceled.

"I'm glad you didn't," Mona says kindly. "White wine?"

Kate tells her friend about the Matrix exercise and Don's inability to see how important her career is to her. "It's like he's jealous," Kate says. "He actually asked me if I married him or my job." She asks Mona for help understanding where Don is coming from. "He's not an irrational man — quite the opposite actually. But he's acting so weird. What do you think is going on?"

"I bet it has to do with his retirement," Mona says. "Think about it. For more than forty years he was a cop — and you know what kind of job that is. Then there's this big retirement party where all they talk about is how great his career was and the next day he wakes up as a regular guy."

Huh. Kate hadn't thought of things quite that way. She can see how being a cop one day and a civilian the next would be a big adjustment. But she isn't willing to let Don off the hook for his behavior. "He's got so much time now," she says. "Why doesn't he figure out what to do with it instead of expecting me to babysit him? I have a life. I have friends. I have a job. I have a hobby. Heck, if I could spend all day every day doing yoga, I'd love it."

Mona laughs. "Ha! Who's jealous of who now?" Then her face turns thoughtful. "I don't know why Don's not jumping into his new life. Maybe he's scared. Maybe he's confused. Does he have any friends that aren't from work? Does he have hobbies?"

"He likes to tinker in the garage, but he's never had time to get really good at anything or start a big project," Kate says. "His friends are all from the force. He went a couple of times to the club the officers all belong to, but he hasn't been for a while. I thought that would be perfect — the retired guys hang out there — but I don't think he liked it."

"I wonder if this retirement thing has been harder for him than he expected," Mona says. "Have you guys ever talked about it? Has he ever told you what he's going through?"

Kate chuckles. "You know Don, Mona. Can you imagine him talking about his *feelings?* There's no way he's going to admit he doesn't have everything under control." She pauses. "But I never asked him either. I could try." Kate tries to imagine how that conversation would go. What would she say? What would he say?

"Can you help me practice what to say to him?" she asks her friend.

Together, Mona and Kate run through different scenarios. Kate realizes that if she just drops hints that she wants to talk about Don's feelings about his retirement, he won't pick up on them. But she also can't be too bold in her approach, or he may feel defensive. The worst practice conversation happens when they try the Matrix again. The best conversation between her and Mona happens when she is caring and open and asks questions, keeping the focus on what retirement is like for him.

"I feel like his therapist, not his wife," Kate jokes.

Mona agrees. "If you think of it that way, it'll probably be easier to focus on his feelings and not take things personally."

Over to You

Now it's your turn. Whether you're going to rehearse your conversation like a three-time Oscar winner or simply talk through a plan with someone you trust, first set the scene and then explore the best, worst, and most realistic outcomes. Try to imagine what the other person in the situation will be feeling too. Take your emotional temperature throughout the rehearsal and ask questions of yourself or your practice buddy at the end. Use what you've learned through the whole experience to decide what you'll do next.

You may not think anything other than the worst outcome will happen. You may be feeling frustrated ("Why do I have to deal with this crap anyway?"), disheartened ("I've had this conversation before and nothing changes"), or fatalistic ("Nothing I do turns out the way I want it to. Why bother?"), but that could be your depression talking. Rehearse with another person whose take on life isn't so negative, and when they tell you they don't think it'll be so bad, listen to what they have to say!

PEP TALK: *If you don't think any good can come of a rehearsal, that's probably your depression talking. Don't listen!*

No matter the outcome of your rehearsal, just the fact that you were willing to try something out of the ordinary makes it a success. Plus, as Ron likes to say, people are pretty predictable. By rehearsing the best, worst, and most realistic scenarios, paying attention to your feelings, and putting yourself in the other person's shoes, you're as prepared as you can be for the conversation that's going to get you one step closer to your goal.

GUY TALK: REHEARSING FOR THE REHEARSAL

Men typically have conversations about subjects we consider safe — sports, politics, money, work, and sex come to mind — and we deliberately keep things light, or at least impersonal. Jokes are welcome. Heated debate is acceptable. But heartfelt confessions, emotional vulnerability, and requests to role-play? Not so much. That's why this week's task is particularly tough for a lot of men.

Of course, you can forgo the awkward conversation and simply do your rehearsal on your own. But you'll get more out of your practice session — a different perspective and different feelings — if you involve another person. Here are some ideas to help you ask a friend, romantic partner, or family member to help out.

First, is there a woman in your life you could ask? Most women don't mind talking about emotional topics, and they usually respect men who are comfortable broaching these subjects too. Ask your wife, your sister, your female coworker, your friend's wife, even your mom. On second thought, maybe not your mom.

Second, no matter who you're asking to help you, think of a way to ease into the conversation. Is a related topic in the news right now? Do you always talk about a certain subject together — your kids, for example — and could you use that as a conversation starter? During another conversation did the person offer some practical help — a lawyer referral for your divorce, let's say — which you could use as a safe topic to open with? A subtle segue can help both of you feel more comfortable.

Then think of how you want to ask your "who" for their help. Does an email, a text, or an online chat feel more like "you"? Are you more comfortable with a spontaneous conversation than a scheduled get-together? Is there a time when you're likely to casually encounter the person with enough time to talk? Figure out the "how" ahead of time.

Next, practice your request. What will you say to the other person to ask them to help you with your rehearsal? What do you think they'll say back? How do you think that will feel? Make sure you aren't focusing just on the worst-case scenario.

I've recently started playing on a new indoor soccer team, and one day one of my team members sat down beside me while I was tying my shoes and said, "Hey, Ron. I heard you're a psychologist." We chatted a little about my practice and then headed out onto the pitch. The next week, he sat beside me again. "Ron, since you're a psychologist, I was wondering if I could ask you a question." Then he told me a little about his son's anxiety.

I'm imagining that my new teammate had it all mapped out ahead of time: pick a good time to sit near Ron, ask some general questions about psychology, and see if he's a snobby doctor. Then he probably based his next week's approach on how the first week went. Like most people, I was pretty easy to talk to, and I didn't mind him asking me questions, so it was probably safe to ask me for some advice. Now, he didn't ask me to help him role-play a conversation with his ex-wife about, say, getting their son professional help to deal with his anxiety. But that could always come later.

Every conversation we have presents a choice: keep things superficial or go a little deeper. When we go deeper, we'll feel different — and usually better.

This Week's To-Do List

Identify a suitable conversation or interaction to rehearse. Good candidates are conversations that you suspect will be difficult, that you've been putting off, or that you've tried to have unsuccessfully in the past. Make sure your conversation is tied to accomplishing your goal.

Decide on the rehearsal format. Do you want to involve someone you trust in your rehearsal or do it on your own? Do you want to act it out or simply talk it through? Do you want to write it out or otherwise record what you think will happen?

Rehearse it. Imagine the best, worst, and most realistic scenarios, so that you can be prepared for all three. Use a strategy, such as role-playing the other person or recording what you're going to say and playing it back to yourself, to allow you to put yourself in the other person's shoes.

Take your emotional temperature. How were you feeling during the rehearsal of the different outcomes? How are you feeling now? Is it different from how you usually feel about the situation? Based on your feelings, decide what you'd like to do next.

Feel good about your efforts. When you went ahead with your rehearsal, you chose to do something different and experience different feelings. No matter the outcome, that's worth celebrating!

Tell someone about your rehearsal. Share your experience with someone in your circle. The more people you tell, the more ideas and encouragement you'll receive and the more fans you'll have sitting in the audience come opening night.

Just Do It

You've done what you can to prepare, and now it's showtime. This week, we help you set realistic expectations for the interpersonal event that's going to get you to your goal, give you some examples for inspiration, and cheer you on from the sidelines. You've got this!

My granddaughter, who is ten, is a hardworking, intelligent, responsible kid who, no matter how much she prepares for a presentation, gets anxious. She recently had to speak in front of her religious school class. Forty pairs of eyes were on her, some belonging to her fellow students and others to their parents, and it wasn't long before she forgot what she had practiced. She started to sweat and stammer. Her face got flushed.

Her teacher came and stood beside her. Her mom could see something was wrong and was perched on the edge of her chair. "The room was spinning, Bubbe," she told me. "But I thought it would be more embarrassing to faint than keep going!"

She saw the presentation through to the finish, even though her teacher had whispered to her that she could go back to her seat if she needed to. She even returned to the front with the other presenters to take questions from the audience at the end.

I share my granddaughter's story for a few reasons. First, because she told me I could — which I think is very cool of her. Second, because it shows that when you try something that people know you struggle with, many times they'll be there to support you. And third, no matter how much we'd all like to get a standing ovation, sometimes we just need to power through and be happy we didn't faint.

PEP TALK: *When you try something that's hard for you and you've let others know, chances are they'll support you.*

This week you'll do the thing you rehearsed last week. It's an important step, but no more important than any other step you've taken over the previous ten weeks. You've practiced, paid attention to your feelings, and now you're ready. Just do it — then see how you feel!

When All Is Said and Done

Most of the time when people go through with an interpersonal experience that's important to achieving their goal, it goes pretty well. They'll say, "That wasn't as hard as I thought," or "I don't know why I put that off for so long," or "It wasn't perfect, but it was good enough." When they take their emotional temperature, they're feeling much better.

It's important to have realistic expectations. This conversation isn't going to fix every problem in your relationship, make you love your post-transition life, magically resolve your grief, or suddenly turn an acquaintance into a best friend. It's one step in the right direction. If you think of it as anything more, you may be disappointed. But if you look for a small but meaningful improvement, you'll probably see it — and you'll feel better.

PEP TALK: *Most people who "just do it" find it goes better than they expected — if their expectations were realistic, that is.*

Every interpersonal experience is a learning opportunity. Once your conversation or event is over, do an Instant Replay. Ask yourself these questions so you can learn from what happened and feel good about what you did.

THE INSTANT REPLAY

How did I feel before? During? Afterward?

What went well?

What could I do differently next time?

What's my next step?

What can I feel proud of?

Who can I tell?

If things didn't go as well as you expected; take the experience apart, moment by moment. What did you say? What did you do? What did the other person say? What did they do? It can help to review what happened with someone else. What do they think happened? What do they think you could do differently next time?

Whatever happens, take a moment to feel good that you tried something different. Remember Dallas, my client whose goal was to go to an open-mike night in his new town? The first time he went, he didn't get up and play, but he had a short chat with the person behind the bar. Next time he goes he might congratulate one of the performers or actually get up on stage with his guitar. Each is a baby step worth celebrating. No matter what you try, there's a value to trying something different!

John: Not Just Another Friday Night

It's the first night John's worked since the beer with Ben, and he hasn't given much thought to how he wants to approach things with Alex. He considers his options as he gets ready for his shift.

Both Tom and Ben have told John to ignore Alex. Let him take your deliveries, they say. What's a couple of bucks? "But it's not the money," John thinks. "It's the principle." Ben wouldn't care about a principle, John reminds himself. Ben would rather get along with people than be right.

Could John set aside being right to get along with his coworkers? Would it make things better? Tom and Ben think so.

John imagines the best-case scenario. John ignores Alex, and Alex gets bored and leaves John alone. Forever. How does that make John feel? Awesome — John sacrifices a few dollars in tips for a lifetime of peace.

In the worst-case scenario, John ignores Alex, it makes Alex mad, Alex picks on John even more, they get into a fight, and John gets fired. That scenario feels terrible. This is the longest job John has had, and he'd like to keep it.

Then there's the most realistic outcome. John ignores Alex, Alex keeps stealing John's deliveries for a while, and then he gets bored and leaves John alone, at least most of the time. How does that feel? Pretty good, John admits. Better than he feels right now, at any rate.

John heads to work and is waiting for his first delivery when Alex sits down beside him.

"John!" Alex bellows, giving John a resounding thump on the back.

"Don't take his bait," John reminds himself.

"Alex!" he yells back. It sounds awkward and squeaky. Not what he intended, but whatever.

"Gone on any hot dates lately?" Alex asks him.

"He's trying to upset me," John says to himself. "Don't fall for it."

"Naw. I've been too busy playing *Donkey Kong*," John says. "I'd rather save a damsel in distress from a gorilla."

Alex looks at John with mock disbelief. "Johnny boy," he says. "Was that a joke? Did you just make a joke? Look everybody!" Alex says to no one in particular. "John just made a joke!"

John doesn't know what to say next. Is Alex making fun of him? Or is he genuinely surprised? Who cares? John did make a joke. How does he feel? Actually pretty good. Like maybe he can handle what might go down tonight.

A delivery gets called. "I'll take it," Alex says lazily. It's supposed to be John's.

"First one to the kitchen gets it," John says, pushing back his chair and making a run for it.

Alex just watches him. "Johnny boy is two for two," he says. Then under his breath he mutters, "Next one is mine."

Later that night, Ben, Alex, and John are waiting out a lull together, takeout containers of chow mein, chicken balls, and fried rice open on the table in front of them. A delivery is called. It's supposed to be John's.

"Be my guest," John says to Alex, patting his stomach. "I need some time to digest."

Alex shrugs and gets up from the table.

Ben smiles at John. "That was sweet," he says when Alex is out of earshot.

John feels good. Somehow it's better to sacrifice his own delivery than to have Alex steal it. John's actually having a little fun tonight. He chats with Ben until the next delivery gets called.

"It's all yours," Ben says. "You deserve it."

After the shift is over, John decides to text Tom. "Work was good tonight," is all he says.

Becky: Pajama-rama

Becky pulls on her pink T-shirt and flannel PJ pants — the ones with flamingos on them — and then takes a long, hard look at herself in the mirror. "God, I look awful," she thinks to herself. "This is going to be the hardest thing I've done in a long time."

"I don't want to go," she says out loud to her reflection in the mirror. "You have to go," she answers herself sternly. "Remember that black bedroom of despair you drew?"

Becky packs her bag. There's something she's forgetting. Right. Teddy bear. Becky's apartment is pretty much a stuffed animal–free zone — except for that silly floppy cat with big eyes that she gave to Brian when he was begging her for a pet. He joked about it being a cheap way for Becky to get out of cleaning a litter box. Becky feels the sob coming — a wave that starts in her gut and crests at the top of her throat.

The apartment buzzer cuts through her impending tears. It's June. What should she do? Tell June she's sick and she can't go? Head down and pretend everything's okay? Invite June up and tell her how she's feeling? "Hey June," Becky says over the intercom. "I'm having a bit of a moment. Can you come up for a sec?" She buzzes June in.

"What's up, Bex?" she asks.

Becky tells June about Brian's stuffed cat. "I know it's stupid," Becky says. "I just miss him so much."

June tells her it's not stupid. She gets Becky a glass of water. "Want to talk about it?"

Becky feels awkward, but she knows she's supposed to talk about Brian if she wants to eventually feel better. She starts with her guilt over not getting Brian a real cat. Fifteen minutes later, she and June are laughing about the time Brian showed up at one of Becky's art openings with a bunch of tipsy engineers. It feels good to be remembering something about Brian from before he was sick.

"Okay," Becky says, taking a deep breath. "I think I'm ready to go." They grab their bags and head down to get a cab.

They hear the music from Sheree's apartment as soon as they step off the elevator. Becky links arms with June. "Be my wingman?" she asks.

"I'd be honored," June replies.

There are more girls at the party than Becky expected. Some she knows. Some she's seen before, but she's not sure of their names. Some of them are brand-new. Everyone is wearing pajamas. Becky hangs back at the door.

"C'mon, Bex," June says. "Let's go find Amber and Sheree. They'll be so happy to see you."

They find Sheree in the kitchen refilling snacks. "Bex!" she shrieks, dropping the bag of chips she was holding and giving Becky a big hug. She grabs Becky's hand and leads her straight to Amber, who's in the living room talking.

Becky's feeling overwhelmed. She hasn't even had a chance to put her bag down or mix herself a drink. "Look who's here!" Sheree says to

Amber, interrupting Amber's conversation. Becky recognizes two of the girls, and a third she knows from college.

Amber immediately gives Becky a hug. "I'm so glad you came," she says. Then she introduces Becky to the girls. Sheree heads back to the kitchen.

"Just gonna grab myself a drink," Becky says to the group, and then follows Sheree.

It's quieter in the kitchen. Becky asks Sheree what she's been up to. Sheree asks Becky the same question. The conversation is a little stiff — they're both feeling awkward. "I'm sorry I kinda disappeared," Becky says. "Things have been hard."

Sheree nods. She tells Becky that it's okay, that she understands, that she's missed Becky. Then Sheree says that things haven't been so easy for her lately either. "I don't know if you heard, but my mom was diagnosed with breast cancer a few months back." They spend a minute or two talking about Sheree's mom and how Sheree is feeling, but it's not the best time for a heart-to-heart.

"I really want to talk more with you about it," Sheree says. "Let's get together soon. Just the two of us." She picks up the snack bowls. "Now let's put on our happy faces. It's party time!"

The rest of the night is pretty uneventful. Becky's conversation with the third bridesmaid — the one whose name she can never remember — is hard at first. Becky has thought of this girl as her replacement, but she's nice, and she lets Becky in on some of the wedding gossip. Amber's been a bit of a bridezilla. The dresses are a hideous orange. It's costing a fortune. The fiancé's family is crazy. There's only one good-looking groomsman, and he's got a girlfriend.

June and Becky yack as they head home together.

"Did you have a good time?" June asks.

"I did," Becky says. "It was weird, but I'm glad I went."

They're quiet for a moment. Becky sits with her feelings. She would never wish cancer on anyone, but it's reassuring to know that she's not the only person in her circle with direct experience of that horrible disease.

Talking with Amber's third bridesmaid showed that being in the wedding party isn't just about clinking wineglasses on a sunny patio, which makes Becky feel a little less resentful about being left out. She would've liked to have talked more with Amber at the party, but that's okay. Overall, she feels good. She's surprised how easy it turned out to be. And she's a little disappointed that it took her so long to reconnect with her friends — what was she so afraid of anyway?

Kate: No Quick Fix

Kate feels as if she's been riding an emotional roller coaster. The Matrix discussion with Don was discouraging, but her most recent get-together with Mona — especially when they rehearsed the conversation between Kate and Don about Don's retirement — helped Kate feel a little more in control of her emotions. She decides that she needs to have realistic expectations. Resolving the conflict with Don is going to be a process, not just one amazing conversation in which Don sees the light.

Kate has decided to make a nice dinner and not bring up the retirement topic until after they're done eating. She's going to give the sandwich technique a go again, saying something encouraging or positive to Don at the beginning and end of the conversation and saving the more challenging stuff for the middle.

He's probably not going to talk about his feelings, she reminds herself, but he's a good guy. This has been hard on both of them. Plus, most women would love their husbands to want to spend more time with them. It's a different way to look at things, and it makes Kate feel a little better.

Don does the dishes after dinner. (Kate has to give him credit. Don's doing the dishes was the only expectation they wrote down on their shared Matrix, and he hasn't missed a day of dish duty since.)

Kate picks up a dish towel and starts to dry. "I know we didn't do a lot of planning before you retired, Don," she says. "We looked at things from the money end, so we knew we could do it financially, but we didn't think about what it would be like when it happened. The changes have probably been hard for both of us."

Don doesn't say anything. It's as though he's waiting for her to keep going. Instead of talking about herself or saying what she thinks he's feeling, she asks him a question. "What's it been like for you since you left work?"

Don is clearly uncomfortable. "I don't know," he says. "It's been okay."

There's a long pause. Kate decides to ask another question. "What do you like about retirement?" she asks.

Don says he likes the freedom and not having a schedule.

"What don't you like?" she asks.

"Sometimes it's hard to fill my day," he admits. "Some days I feel pretty unproductive."

Kate continues to focus on Don. "You put in a lot of long hours and hard work over the years," she says. "You've earned this time to yourself, to be able to do what you want, when you want."

Now it's time for the more challenging part of the conversation — the middle of the sandwich. Don's empty day is hard for Kate too, when Don expects her to be the one to fill it up on top of a demanding job. But how can she put it so the conversation stays positive? "I want things to be good for both of us," Kate says. "I know it must be a big adjustment, having all this free time, especially when I'm still working and sometimes have to stay late at the school. I want to find a way for it to work for both of us."

Don doesn't say anything. But that's better than if he said something snippy or sarcastic.

"Okay," Kate thinks to herself. "We've taken one step forward. I should quit while I'm ahead." She suggests that over the next few weeks they continue to talk about the adjustments both of them are making and find a way to manage as a team. Don nods in agreement, lets the water out of the sink, and heads to the living room to watch TV.

They're watching football, a game Kate doesn't really follow, so it gives her some time to explore how things went. She runs through the Instant Replay questions. The first one — no surprise — is about her feelings. Before the conversation, Kate felt nervous. What if Don reacted badly? What if he yelled? Once the conversation started, she felt more relaxed. Now that it's all over, she feels a bit better. It's nice to be spending time with Don — even if it's football — instead of hiding in her bedroom feeling angry and resentful.

The next question is about what worked well. Kate thinks for a few seconds. It helped to ask Don questions instead of filling in his silence with assumptions. The sandwich method was also a good approach.

What would she do differently next time? She'd practice asking questions beforehand, so she didn't have to think so fast on her feet. What's the next step? Another small conversation with Don. What is she proud of? The fact that she went into the conversation with realistic expectations and didn't try to get everything fixed in one go. Time for the last question: Who can she tell? Mona, of course.

Ana: A Walk in the Park

It's a warm Sunday afternoon and a perfect time to pop Ruby into her stroller and take a walk. Ana tells Peter she'd love to spend time with him and invites him along. Peter, who's had his head buried in a client's file all day, asks if she can give him half an hour.

"Sure," she says, hoping he didn't hear her sigh.

Forty minutes later, they're walking on the sidewalk in the sunshine. "I love you and Ruby so much," Ana says. "But I'm having trouble adjusting to being a new mom, and I think I need your help."

"You're a great mom, Ana," Peter says.

Ana resists the urge to laugh. It's just the way Ana and her mom rehearsed. She decides to see Peter's statement as simply a vote of confidence, as her mom advised, not as an effort to get out of helping her.

"Your confidence in me means a lot," she says. "I'm trying to see myself as more capable, but the reality is, this is a huge adjustment for me. I miss you. I miss our old life. I miss going to work. And I'm just so tired all the time."

Peter looks at Ana kindly. "We tried for a baby for so long, Ana, but I don't think we realized what it would be like when she was born. Just the other day some of the guys at work were talking about how tiring it is to have a new baby and how none of us could have the patience our partners have. I don't know how you do it, Ana."

Ana starts to get teary-eyed. Peter does recognize some of the stresses of motherhood, even if he doesn't get the full picture. She says, "It would be so great if you'd take Ruby when you get home from work. Or if you'd get up with her at night once in a while on the weekend. Or if you'd just change her."

Peter reminds Ana that he doesn't have experience with babies — he didn't have younger siblings or nieces or nephews, and there's no babysitting on his résumé. "I don't know how often you're supposed to change a baby. When she's crying, I don't know if it's because she's hungry, tired, wet, or gassy," he admits. "How do you know?"

"You just know," Ana replies. Then she laughs. How do you teach someone the skill of just knowing?

Peter tells Ana he's happy to change Ruby if she asks him, but she needs to be patient with him. Ruby is so tiny and fragile, and he doesn't want to do anything wrong, so sometimes he hesitates. "There have been times when you've criticized me and said I'm being too rough with her," Peter says. "Or Ruby will cry when she's with me, and you'll ask, 'Is everything okay in there?' It makes me feel like you don't trust me."

As if on cue, Ruby breaks the tension with an adorable coo. Ana is overcome with gratitude for this moment with her husband and her baby. She thanks Peter for sharing his feelings with her and suggests they keep the lines of communication open. "It's a big change for both of us," she says. "And we need to help each other."

That evening, Ana calls her mom and gives her the play-by-play of the conversation. "I feel so much better," Ana says. "I know one conversation can't fix everything, but now that we've started talking about it, we can tell each other what we need and be there for each other."

GUY TALK: GIRL TALK

My eighteen-year-old daughter had some friends over last weekend. My son and I were finishing dinner, and in the background was the constant buzz of their conversation from the next room.

Everything they said was about relationships — how the girls they knew had changed, what things used to be like, what they were like now, who was getting along with whom, who was fighting with whom, who said what to whom. It was all shared in great detail, with an abundance of feeling and an overwhelming amount of interpretation.

I turned to my son and said, "Thank God you don't have more sisters. Can you imagine listening to this stuff every night?" My son sighed, nodded his head, and went up to his room.

For many guys, it's hard enough to talk about things once. We figure out how to make the conversation happen, and it's all we can do to get through it the first time, let alone rehash it afterward. We might ruminate or complain to a friend if we didn't get what we wanted. But if things went okay — if our goal was achieved — we're not about to do a full review.

The Instant Replay is a great learning opportunity, though. If you can answer a few questions about what happened and how it felt, you'll be ahead of the game next time around. It's like a sports broadcast. The analysis — whether we agree with it or not — helps us understand what's going on in the game. It gives us something to think about, and we may learn something we can apply the next time we're watching.

You might say my son and I were simply eavesdropping on my daughter and her friends as they offered their color commentary on the game of life. It was helping my daughter and her friends make sense of their interpersonal world — and it's an approach many guys could benefit from.

As an aside, after my son left the room, the girls stormed the kitchen and picked my brain about the psychological makeup of all their friends until 1 AM. I eventually threatened them with an early morning psych exam if they didn't let me go to bed!

This Week's To-Do List

Do some last-minute prep for your important interpersonal experience. Review what you rehearsed. Give yourself a pep talk. Set realistic expectations.

Just do it. Remember to use the tips for effective communication we've offered throughout the book. Work on being assertive in your communication style. Don't feel as though you have to fix everything in the relationship or check every box on your conversation topic checklist — it's better to end the conversation early when everyone is feeling positive than for things to fall apart because everyone is getting tired.

Do an Instant Replay. How did you feel before, during, and after the conversation or event? What went well? What could you do differently next time? What's your next step? What do you feel proud of? And, finally, who can you tell?

Tell someone what happened. You can do your Instant Replay with that person or simply share your feelings. Don't forget to mention what went well!

Do Your
Happy Dance

It's our last week together, and time to celebrate what you've accomplished. We'll help you reflect on what you've learned, recall who you can rely on, and plan for future moments that may be stressful for you. If you tried anything new over the last twelve weeks, you'll be feeling better — and that's worth getting out your dancing shoes for (and inviting someone to dance)!

Clients will sometimes give me a token of their appreciation at our last session. I've received cards, journals, flowers, and homemade jam, but one of the more memorable gifts I opened was a charming children's board book called *Do Your Happy Dance!: Celebrate Wonderful You*.

The book stars Charlie Brown, Snoopy, and other characters from the *Peanuts* cartoons. The format may be for kids, but the message is inspirational for all ages. "You tried your best. You gave it your all. You went for that kick, when you knew you might fall," Charles M. Schulz writes. "So take a deep breath, then jump at the chance: This day is your day, and this dance is your dance!"

This week, we help you review everything you tried during our time together and encourage you to seize the day and do your happy dance. What helped you feel better? What new skills do you want to work on?

What do you want to celebrate — and who do you want to invite to the party? We want to make sure your new skills will carry you through the days, months, and years ahead. Let's get started!

Looking Backward — and Forward

Your first task is to think about some of the things you've done over the last eleven weeks that have helped you feel better. This is not a make-work project. It's a what-works project. We want to remind you of what's been working for you, so you can continue to use those strategies in the future.

Did you ask a friend for ideas about your transition? Did you invite someone to go to the cemetery with you? Did you try a new interpersonal style in a conversation with your spouse? Did you talk to a stranger at the grocery store? Did you recognize the tie between shoving down your feelings and hitting the bottle or the chip bag? Did you complete the Matrix with a loved one? Volunteer with a nonprofit? Join a support group? Give someone the benefit of the doubt? Work on having more realistic expectations? Think of what you tried and who you learned from.

It may be easy to think of one or two things that you did. To help you think of some more — plus identify some of the other things you learned during our time together — we've put together these questions to ask yourself.

TEN WRAP-UP QUESTIONS
1. What makes me feel bad?
2. What makes me feel better?
3. What did I learn about myself?
4. What did I learn about other people?
5. Who can I go to?
6. What's the old me?
7. What's the new me?
8. What skills do I want to work on?
9. How do I want to celebrate what I've accomplished?

10. What might be a challenge for me in the future, and how will
    I handle it?

The last question, "What might be a challenge for me in the future?"
is about being prepared for times you know will be hard for you. Major
holidays, such as Christmas, Ramadan, and Passover, can be difficult. So
can the anniversary of a loved one's death, the approach of winter, an
exam period, or a performance review at work.

Look ahead in your calendar. When are your trigger times? And
what's your plan for handling them? Can you establish a code word with
your husband for when to leave your cousin's wedding reception? Who
will you sit beside at Christmas dinner? What's your plan for when your
baby is born? Write it down in your calendar and
share the plan with one of your "whos," and you'll
feel better about being able to make it through the
tough times ahead.

TRY THIS: *Think
ahead to your trigger times
and make a plan to handle
them using your new skills.*

You may also want to revisit the book, paying
closer attention to a secondary problem area you had. For example, you
may have chosen interpersonal conflict as your problem area, because
you've been fighting with your spouse and it's affecting your mood, but
you're also going through a transition at work. Or you may have chosen
loneliness and social isolation as your problem area, but you'd like to set
some goals and work on some strategies related to managing conflict better. The skills you've learned are transferable. Use the book as a refresher
and work on your second problem area.

As a result of the baby steps you've taken, you
may feel ready to tackle some other significant issues
in your life, such as trauma or abuse. If you're not
sure how to do it on your own, a family doctor or
therapist can be a valuable "who" for you. Ask if they
know interpersonal psychotherapy (IPT), which is the therapeutic model
that underpins all of the work we've done together. IPT can be used with
PTSD, anxiety, eating disorders, borderline personality disorder, bipolar

TRY THIS: *If there's
another problem area you'd
like to work on, head back
to Week 5 and set some
new goals!*

disorder, and more. If you can find a professional familiar with IPT, you can continue using the skills we've been working on together with your in-person practitioner.

Celebrate the Little Things

The next thing you'll do is take a moment to recognize the things you've accomplished, no matter how small or inconsequential those accomplishments may seem to you.

My grandson was telling me the other day about the great mark he got on his science test. Being the proud grandmother, I started to gush.

"It's no big deal," he said, cutting me off. "It was just really easy."

"Don't put yourself down," I said. "Maybe it wasn't as easy as you think. Maybe you knew the material so well it felt easy to you."

"Bubbe," he said, with the sigh of a six-year-old who is wise beyond his years. "If they ask you to circle the things that are living and not the things that aren't, it's an easy test."

Okay. I had to give him that. But still, I wanted him to feel good about doing well, because we can always find reasons to dismiss our accomplishments. Instead, why not enjoy the moment?

In order to celebrate your accomplishments, you'll need to take credit for what you've done. I saw a client today who said, "Cindy, my mother and I aren't fighting nearly as much now. She must've made so many changes!" Humility is a wonderful character trait, but there are times when the back we need to pat is our own. The improvements in my client's relationship with her mother weren't primarily due to her mom's efforts; they were the result of the new communication style my client was using and the work she was doing to have her mom's words and behavior bother her less. Ask yourself, "What did I do that made me feel better?" and, "What did they do to make me feel better?" Then celebrate both.

PEP TALK: *Celebrate your efforts, no matter how insignificant they might seem to you.*

Back in Week 5, you set goals to work on during the book. If you accomplished one or more of those, that's worth celebrating. But what if you didn't achieve your goal? If you feel better, that's all that matters. Your goal might not have ended up being important or relevant, but the other things you did were key to lifting your mood.

Progress is simply making an effort to try something new and having a different feeling. Are you sleeping better? Is your appetite back? Are you less irritable? Are you feeling more positive? Did you accomplish these things through making changes in who you spend time with and how you spend that time? Then pop that cork!

PEP TALK: *If you're feeling better because you're trying something different, that's all that matters. Goal, schmoal!*

It won't come as any surprise, given everything we've said over the past few weeks, but your celebration can't be solitary. It's important to share what you accomplished and what you learned with at least one person from your circle.

Your celebration can be as simple as coffee with a friend or as complex as organizing an event for two hundred. Ron tells the story of a female police officer who worked really hard to overcome depression related to an on-the-job injury. She decided to celebrate her accomplishment by putting on a workshop for her colleagues. She asked the police chief — her boss — and he loved the idea, since the organization wanted to reduce the stigma of job-related stress. For her, celebrating with her circle meant staging an event to help people in the same situation. But such an undertaking isn't for everyone.

TRY THIS: *Celebrations are meant to be shared!*

Have realistic expectations. Your celebration should feel easy, not hard.

TWENTY-SIX SIGNS TO CELEBRATE

Back in Week 1, we shared "Thirteen Signs You May Be Depressed." Eleven weeks later, it's time for a new list — one that includes many of the approaches you'll have tried during our time together. Whether you can check off one, a few, or a bunch of the items, feel good about your progress!

1. I ask others for advice and listen to what they tell me.
2. I'm seeing my situation in a more balanced way.
3. I share my small victories with others.
4. I try to imagine how others might feel.
5. I can see the connection between my feelings and my behavior.
6. I've told at least one person what I'm going through.
7. I ask myself how I'm feeling.
8. I know what my go-to interpersonal style is.
9. I try to let things bother me less if it's not realistic to think they'll change.
10. I trust what others tell me.
11. When I'm feeling bad, I don't hide.
12. I have different feelings now than I did back in Week 1.
13. I recognize that relationships have value to me.
14. I'm reengaging with activities I used to enjoy.
15. I'm giving myself a break.
16. I'm practicing being more assertive with others.
17. I rehearse interpersonal scenarios with someone I trust.
18. I'm considering dissolving a relationship that's hurting me.
19. I know how to set a SMART goal.
20. I'm working on having realistic expectations of myself and others.
21. I ask myself what the best, worst, and most realistic outcomes might be if I'm anxious about trying something new.
22. I ask for help.
23. I use techniques to cool down and warm up my emotional temperature.
24. I try new approaches even though they may feel uncomfortable at first.
25. I feel good when I try something new, no matter the outcome.
26. I don't give up if I slip back into the "old me."

Keep It Up

Over the last few weeks, you've "tried on" some new ways of doing things to see how they fit. The more you practice, the more comfortable you'll get with them. Here are some skills to work on if you want to keep feeling better:

Reach out. Use your circle of friends, coworkers, family members, neighbors, and even hair-care professionals as sounding boards and sources of advice. Start with your more peripheral relationships if you need to build your confidence before reaching out to your inner circle.

Check in. Make it a regular habit after any interpersonal exchange to pause, hit rewind, and ask yourself, "How am I feeling?" Always take time to figure out what you did that made you feel better, so you can try it again. Reflect on what didn't feel so good, so you can take a different approach next time. If you can do your check-in with someone else, that's even better!

Stay open. The old way you approached things hasn't been making you feel better, so why not be open to trying something new? Listen to what others tell you. If you can't think of a really good reason to trash their advice, try it instead. Stay open to new ways of communicating with people and experiment with more constructive ways of asking for what you need. Be open in your expectations too. It's not "You should," or "I should"; it's "I'd like." Remember that the best way to get over anxiety about trying something new is to just do it — cross that bridge over troubled water, and see what's on the other side!

Rehearse important interpersonal exchanges. If you can, rehearse three different possible outcomes: the best thing that could happen, the worst, and the most realistic. Rehearse with someone in your circle for maximum benefit.

Nurture your circle. Our social circles are constantly changing. That flux is normal, but a move to a new city, the death of someone close to you, separation from a spouse, the kids moving out, or the end of a friendship can throw the circle off balance. Review your circle regularly. Invest in your ongoing relationships. Make new ones when you need to. I decided to do it systematically at one point, making a list of all my friends and relatives and connecting with at least two of them every week. You don't have to be so formal in your effort, but make sure you're nurturing your circle, not neglecting it.

TRY THIS: *Here are seven skills to practice: reaching out, checking in, staying open, rehearsing important moments, nurturing your circle, taking baby steps, and talking positively to yourself.*

Take baby steps. Remind yourself that it takes time and practice to make a lasting change. Every small step forward is a step closer to what you want to achieve. And any small step backward isn't the end of the world. Have realistic expectations. Are you feeling better overall? That's what matters.

Talk to yourself positively. Give your inner critic the day off and be kind to yourself — you deserve it just as much as anyone else. You'll be happier if you're less negative with yourself. Always celebrate your successes, no matter how inconsequential you may think they are.

If You're Not Feeling Better

A few people may make it to Week 12 and still have many of the symptoms of depression they had in Week 1. If that's you, here are some possible explanations.

It could be that your expectations of "feeling better" are too high. The techniques we've shared aren't a magic pill. You won't one day wake up and feel you can conquer the world. It'll take time to become familiar with the interpersonal way of doing things and to realize the full benefits of connecting — or reconnecting — with your social circle. You'll still have the odd down or sad day. That's only normal.

Maybe you need to dissolve a relationship that's holding you back. Or maybe you have dissolved a relationship, and right now it's really hard.

You won't feel great if either of those is your situation. If you've recently ended a relationship, it'll take time to get used to your new life and recognize the advantages of your decision. This would be a good time to switch your focus from interpersonal conflict to life transitions. Reread the book, paying closer attention to the transition exercises and examples.

TRY THIS: *If you aren't feeling better because you've dissolved a relationship (or you know you need to), your problem area is now transitions.*

Could your lingering depression have a physical cause, such as a thyroid condition or a medication side effect? How are you sleeping? It's common to equate a lack of motivation and inability to concentrate with depression, when it could actually be caused by sleep apnea, chronic pain, or another condition that's interfering with your sleep. Back in Week 1, we encouraged you to make an appointment with your doctor to rule out any physiological problem. If you didn't do it then, it's a good idea to do it now.

Are you exercising? A number of studies have linked moderate exercise with helping to alleviate the symptoms of depression and prevent its return. Make your exercise routine even more effective by doing your workout (or your walk around the block) with at least one other person.

It could also be time to seek professional help. A different therapeutic method may work better for you. Or it could be that IPT is a valid approach for you, but it's hard for you to stay motivated and on track without an in-person therapist to keep you focused, offer encouragement, and hold you accountable week by week. Definitely seek professional help if your symptoms of depression are getting worse.

Ana: The Present Is a Gift

Ana is sitting at her desk with her laptop open and the Ten Wrap-up Questions she's supposed to answer typed up and staring back at her.

All she can think of is the paper in her desk drawer — the paper with her two goals written on it. Two goals, but she only achieved one. "I didn't join a moms' group," she sighs. The all-too-familiar feelings of inadequacy and failure start to surface.

Who could she talk to? Peter is in the next room playing with Ruby. It probably isn't a good time to share how she's feeling with him. She tries calling her mom. No answer. Should she text one of her other friends? Maybe she'll just wait until after she and Peter have put Ruby to bed to talk to her husband.

Knowing she'll be talking with Peter later helps her focus, so she returns to the questions and starts typing.

What makes me feel bad? When I miss my life before Ruby was born, and when I don't feel like I'm doing a good job as a mom. I also feel bad when there's stress in my relationship with Peter.

What makes me feel better? I feel better when I talk to my mom. Also when Peter and I have a good conversation.

What did I learn about myself? Loneliness is really hard on me! I don't make new friends easily, but I do need some women who are also new moms in my life. I tend to think I'm the only person who feels a certain way, but that's not actually true.

What did I learn about other people? It's common to lack confidence as a new parent. Even Mamá felt that way, and she was a fantastic mom. Peter questions his ability with Ruby too. I need to help him rather than criticize him. I also learned that my mom is a great actress! I can go to her whenever I need to rehearse an important conversation.

Who can I go to? My mom. Peter. I could probably go to Steph and Amanda, my old friends; I just haven't yet. Eventually I'll be able to go to my new mom friends.

What's the old me? The old me was stuck in the past.

What's the new me? The new me enjoys what life has to offer right now. The new me doesn't look for what's wrong; she looks for what's right.

What skills do I want to work on? I'd like to be a little less hard on myself. I'm working on seeing the positive side to the changes in my life since Ruby was born. I'm also working on putting myself in Peter's shoes, so I can understand why he does and says certain things.

How do I want to celebrate what I've accomplished? Peter and I haven't been on a date since Ruby was born. What if I asked Steph or Amanda to babysit for us? (I may have to rehearse that conversation with my mom first!)

What might be a challenge for me in the future, and how will I handle it? Going back to work will be another transition — and it'll be here before I know it. I'll need to keep reaching out to people, especially working mothers. Maybe I'll meet some in my moms' group. I'll also talk to women at work who have young kids to see how they manage juggling work and family life. Going for lunch or coffee with my work friends before my first day back would help me feel less anxious about returning to work.

Ana saves the file, closes her computer, and goes to join Peter and Ruby. Peter is sitting on the floor beside his daughter, giving her tummy a tickle from her teddy bear every time she rolls from her belly to her back. The giggles are infectious. Ana sits beside her husband and rests her head on his shoulder with a big smile.

How is she feeling? At this precise moment, like the luckiest woman in the world.

Becky and the Roll of Life Savers

Becky resists the temptation to watch one more episode of *Gilmore Girls* and closes her laptop. It's time to look back on what she's accomplished over the last weeks and plan for tough times ahead. She grabs her phone and starts recording, answering each of the Ten Wrap-up Questions in turn.

What makes me feel bad? When I shut myself away. It's a really vicious circle. Feel bad. Hide. Feel worse. Hide more. Ugh.

What makes me feel better? Seeing humans. And talking about Brian, especially when I remember the good times with him.

What did I learn about myself? That I'm not an island.

What did I learn about other people? That they can help me. That they don't mind listening to me talk about Brian. And that bad things happen to them too — like Sheree's mom getting cancer.

Who can I go to? Lauren, June, and Sheree for sure. Probably Amber.

What's the old me? The old me took care of Brian but didn't take care of myself. The old me punished myself for being the one still alive.

What's the new me? The new me can talk with different people in my life about my brother, his illness, his death, and the impact it had on me. The new me doesn't feel guilty talking about Brian as an imperfectly perfect person.

What skills do I want to work on? Seeing Brian as real, not an ideal. He was my brother, and I loved him, but he was human. It was hard being his caretaker. He wasn't always nice to me. I know why, and I don't blame him for it, but I can't pretend it didn't happen. It's part of why I lost touch with my friends in the first place. The pattern started when Brian was alive and just got worse after he died.

How do I want to celebrate what I've accomplished? I could wait until after the wedding and plan a get-together with the girls. But I think that's too soon — I'm not ready to plan a party yet. It's also too late — Amber's wedding isn't for a couple of weeks, and I want to celebrate now. It's been five weeks since Lauren did my hair. I think I'll make an appointment for a cut and tell her what's been going on for me and how much it meant to me that she listened and offered her advice.

What might be a challenge for me in the future, and how will I handle it? The anniversary of Brian's death is in ten days. There is no other day that is harder for me. Other tough times will be Amber's wedding — who knows who I'll be sitting with — and Brian's birthday. Maybe I can talk to Lauren about how I'm feeling about the anniversary of Brian's death. And I should get together with Sheree before Amber's big day. We can talk about her mom, yes, but I can also talk to her about how I'm feeling about the wedding. Maybe she knows about the seating arrangements! Brian's birthday isn't for a couple of months. By then I'll be ready to remember him in a formal way. Like maybe I'll invite the girls over and serve his favorite meal, and we can share Brian stories.

Becky stops recording and decides to give the salon a call before she loses her momentum. When she hears Lauren's voice on the other end of the phone, she's caught off guard. "Hey Lauren! I wasn't expecting you to pick up. It's Becky."

"We're all on phone duty because the receptionist is out sick today," Lauren laughs. "How are you?"

Becky resists the urge to say, "Fine." "I'm actually doing a lot better. My chat with you was so helpful, I'd like to schedule another one." She smiles, and Lauren can hear it in her voice. "Oh, yeah. You can cut my hair too." They set Becky's appointment for three days later.

Haircut day arrives, and Becky heads downstairs to the salon. Lauren greets her with a big hug.

"Lookin' fine, lady," Lauren says. "I can tell you're feeling better."

Suddenly Becky feels a little shy. Should she renege on her last-minute and probably corny plan to thank Lauren? No. The worst that could happen is Lauren thinks it's silly. More likely, though, it'll make her laugh.

"I am feeling better, and you're the one who got me started," Becky says, taking Lauren's hand and placing a roll of Life Savers candy in it. "All the colors of the rainbow," she says with tears in her eyes. "Just like you used to do my hair."

John: The Wise Uncle

It's Saturday — the day after John made the joke with his coworker Alex — and Tom has dropped by.

"Mom's gone to the store," John tells him.

"I came to see you," Tom says with a laugh. "I want to hear all about what happened at work last night!"

"It was no big deal," John says.

"I still want to hear about it," Tom says.

"I tried what you and Ben said to do," John tells his brother. "I ignored Alex." Tom is impressed. John describes what happened in detail: the jokes he told, how he gave up a delivery to Alex voluntarily, and then how Ben did the same thing for John. "It felt good. I had fun. Like not a lot of fun, but a bit. And it wasn't as hard as I thought it would be."

Tom tells John he thinks that's a great way to handle Alex. "You really had to think on your feet, and that's not easy," Tom says with admiration. "So what's next?"

"I guess I'll try the same thing next shift," John says. "What's the worst that could happen? I'm learning that life isn't always fair, but maybe it's better to make the best of it." He's pleased that Tom is showing so much interest in him. The encouragement feels good. So does reviewing last night's shift with someone supportive.

Tom has some errands to run, but before he leaves, he invites John for dinner. "Just you," he says with a sly smile. "Mom and Dad don't always have to tag along."

That afternoon, John decides he'll answer Week 12's questions. His goals seem like a good place to start. Where did he put them? They aren't in his night-table drawer, under his mattress, or on the bookshelf. He tries to remember them on his own. One of them was about figuring out a fair tip system at work. The other was about handling Alex better — coming up with three responses and using them half the time. He remembers that, because at the time he thought being so specific was pretty hilarious. Half the time. "Guess that means I don't have to try so hard next shift," John says to himself.

So how did he do in the goal department? The first goal didn't end up mattering, since in the end John decided to not care so much about whether things were fair. As for the second goal, time would tell. He kind of hit a home run his first time up to bat. Next time might not be so great. But, as his goal says, he can expect to swing and miss sometimes.

Now on to the questions. John's not much of a writer, so he answers in his head.

What makes me feel bad? When other people don't meet my expectations or follow the rules.

What makes me feel better? When I stop caring so much about who's right.

What did I learn about myself? I can cool situations down with a joke. Also, that if I don't have to prove I'm right, I get along better with people.

What did I learn about other people? They're worth listening to sometimes. And they care about me. I'm still a little shocked that Ben gave me his delivery last night, and Tom has been really supportive all the way along.

Who can I go to? Tom and Ben.

What's the old me? Angry and set in my ways.

What's the new me? I'm trying for easygoing.

What skills do I want to work on? I need to work on cooling my emotional temperature, because I get angry really easily. I need to work on letting go of things that I can't change.

How do I want to celebrate what I've accomplished? I think I'll do it tonight, at Tom's. It's time for a toast!

What might be a challenge for me in the future, and how will I handle it? Every shift with Alex will be a challenge. I need to keep my cool, which means practicing strategies to lower my emotional temperature. I can also go to Ben and Tom for advice if things don't go well.

Later, at Tom's house, everyone is finishing up dinner. Tom turns to his son, Riley. "Uncle John came up with a great way to solve a problem with someone at work," he says. "John, why don't you tell us what happened?"

John takes a second to check in on how he's feeling. Wow. This is the first time in his entire life that someone has asked him to share a life lesson. He's feeling surprised and excited.

"Well," he says to Riley, "let's just say it started with a jackass and ended with a joke." Then John tells his nephew about how Alex was bullying him, how John handled the situation at first, the advice he received from Tom and Ben, and finally how his shift went last night. "I'm trying to be realistic," John says. "It won't always go that well. But I'll keep trying. And asking your dad what he thinks I should do."

John raises his glass. The family joins in. "To Tom and Ben," John says, "for their great advice. And to me, for taking it!"

Kate's Highlight Reel

It's early morning on a weekday, and Kate has a few minutes before she has to leave for work. Don is still sleeping. The house is peaceful. She's got a full mug of fresh coffee. It's a perfect time to do her Week 12 wrap-up. She grabs her journal, flips to a blank page, and starts writing.

What makes me feel bad? I'm still getting used to expressing my anger, but I think I feel worse when I keep my anger bottled up inside.

What makes me feel better? Rehearsing a conversation with a friend gives me confidence. I also feel better when I address issues directly with Don. It may not always end perfectly, but at least we're starting the dialogue.

What did I learn about myself? I can stay calm during difficult conversations. Also, if I get mad or someone else gets mad, it's not the end of the world.

What did I learn about other people? Don has a temper. I guess I always knew that, but I never poked the bear before. Also, he's trying. He does the dinner dishes all the time now!

Who can I go to? Mona, definitely. I'm sure I can go to my other girlfriends as well; I just haven't asked them yet. I can also go to Don.

What's the old me? The old me avoids conflict.

What's the new me? The new me uses my new communication strategies to face conflict and work through it. The new me can handle the short-term discomfort of the conversation, so I feel better about our relationship over the long term.

What skills do I want to work on? Putting myself in Don's shoes. He won't talk about his feelings very often, but I can ask other people who know him what they think he may be feeling. I also want to work on seeing the positive side of things, like he wants to know where the smoothie blender is because he wants to eat healthy. He texts me all the time because I'm an important part of his life.

How do I want to celebrate what I've accomplished? Isn't it about time I went back to yoga? It was one of my goals after all. Maybe I'll invite my yoga friends out for a tea afterward, and hopefully one of them will be free. Then I'll tell them what's been going on in my life, and all about the new me!

What might be a challenge for me in the future, and how will I handle it? Don and I aren't done talking about our life now he's retired. We haven't even resolved the texting issue, let alone that elephant in the room — that he doesn't understand how important my career is to me. We've got some tough conversations ahead of us, and I know I'll put them off. I'll ask Mona to check in with me to make sure Don and I have talked, just like she did before. I'll also rehearse with my friends and debrief with them afterward.

Kate closes her journal and smiles. It's cheap-movie Tuesday, and there isn't any reason why she would have to work late tonight. In fact, she'll tell her coworkers first thing that getting home for date night might just be a marriage saver. "I bet they'll make sure I leave on time," she says to herself. "They'll probably push me out the door."

She opens her scrapbooking tote and finds a blank card. There's no time for anything fancy, so she grabs three markers — black, red, and yellow — and draws two hands reaching into a bucket of popcorn. "Dinner and a movie" she writes in bold block letters above her drawing. Then on the inside she writes, "I'll be home at 5. Be ready. I love you." She puts the card on the kitchen table where Don will see it, grabs her briefcase, and heads to work feeling lighter than she has in a long time.

Let's Not Say Goodbye

You know that feeling you get when you're on the last few pages of a really good book? It's hard to say goodbye to the characters. And sometimes you aren't so happy with the ending! This book is a little different, because the ending is whatever you make it. Plus, I like to think of endings the way the English poet T. S. Eliot does; he wrote, "The end is where we start from."

It's natural to feel a little anxious about making that start on your own, though. What if you feel low again? What if you can't manage? What if the approaches you've been using stop working? What if something catastrophic happens in your life? What then?

The first thing we'll say to reassure you is that there's a difference between a bad day and depression. We all have moments when we feel sad, low, anxious, self-critical, angry, frustrated, disappointed, jealous, left out, and more. These are feelings, and they're normal. They only become depression if they interfere with our functioning for two weeks or more. We need to be able to tolerate these feelings moment by moment and not worry that we're going to spiral down into a dark pit of despair and have to start all over again.

The other thing we'll say is to pay attention to those feelings. Treat them like a friendly reminder: "Hey! It's time to try something different!" Ask yourself what made you feel better in the past and who you could ask to help you. Research has shown that if you continue to use the strategies we've taught you, your mood will keep improving, and you'll be better equipped to deal with the inevitable down days. You'll even be able to handle a catastrophe or two.

We'll always be here on these pages, ready to offer advice and support like an old friend. Reread specific sections of the book for a refresher. Skim the "Pep Talk" and "Try This" messages for quick encouragement. Refer to the strategies and advice we give for a problem area different from the one you worked on the first time through, if circumstances in your life change. Redo a specific exercise, such as the Matrix. Or redo them all to see what's changed.

We've reached the end of the book, but not the end of the journey. The training wheels are off, and you're free to go where you want. If you ever feel wobbly, just ask someone to help steady your bike. And always invite someone along for the ride.

GUY TALK: LIVE LONG AND PROSPER

Ron here. It's my last Guy Talk, and I've got to admit I'm experiencing some strong emotions — which is fitting, since so much of what I've tried to do in these Guy Talks is help guys learn the language of feelings.

Guys, you've come a long way. First, you recognized that the way you're feeling isn't something you should just ignore or power through. Then you explored your feelings in connection to four or five of your relationships. You made the most of the small moments that guys have with each other — moving a couch, building a deck, having a beer after work, or taking halftime on the soccer pitch — to explore how you're feeling about your situation, ask for advice, or try a new interpersonal style. You set a goal. You asked yourself questions. You made a change. You practiced with a buddy. And you did a postconversation analysis, so you could learn from an important interpersonal exchange.

Along the way, I hope that you've come to value your feelings and your relationships and understand the connection between the two. Most of all, I hope that when you're spending time with someone and you're faced with that inevitable choice to stay superficial or go deep, you'll choose to talk about personally meaningful topics that will help you feel better.

I can guarantee that your new interpersonal skills will be appreciated by your spouse, children, coworkers, friends, and extended family. A guy who speaks the language of feelings — a guy who can listen, be open, ask for advice, put himself in another person's shoes, be assertive, and connect his feelings to his behavior — is a guy who will more successfully navigate a world where what it means to be a man and what it means to be a woman are getting more complex and fuzzy with every passing year.

A guy who can do all that is probably going to live longer too. Ever wondered why, across the developed world, women live an average of six to eight years longer than men? According to researcher and TED Talk presenter Susan Pinker, all that guys need to do to catch up is have stronger relationships and interact with more people every day.

I opened by saying I'm experiencing some strong emotions. So how am I feeling? Proud of what you've tried. Excited to think of what worked — and what you learned along the way. And a little sad that our time together is almost over.

I think I'll give Cindy a call, so we can talk about it. Of course, I'll probably have to listen to some "cute" story about her grandkids first. But it's worth it.

This Week's To-Do List

Answer the Ten Wrap-up Questions. They'll help you review what helped you feel better and what you want to work on. If you aren't feeling better, who could help you find out why?

Plan for challenges ahead. What will you do when the going gets tough? Mark the challenging times on your calendar or create another reminder system and share your plan with one of your "whos."

Plan your happy dance. If your celebration will take a significant amount of energy, time, or money, think about whether it will be worth the effort. Remember, small is beautiful. Make sure your celebration includes at least one other person.

Do your dance. Don't put it off or get sidetracked. Life gets busy, yes, but this is important. If you find yourself procrastinating, is there another smaller celebration that you could do right away? Take your emotional temperature after it's over. Then share what happened at your celebration with someone in your circle.

Practice your new skills. Keep your interpersonal mojo humming by using your new skills whenever you can. (One of the skills is positive self-talk — if you slip back into the "old you," just try again with the "new you" next time. No judgment!)

Work on another problem area. Is there something else that's contributing to your sad, down, and depressed feelings? Head back to Week 4 to pick another problem area or Week 5 to set some goals if you already know what you want to work on; then do the exercises specific to that area. The skills you've already learned will give you a head start!

Acknowledgments

From Cindy Stulberg: This book would not have been possible except for what I have learned from the important relationships I have had in my life. Thank you to my parents; my husband, Jay, who taught me more about relationships than anyone else; and my precious children and grandchildren, Jen and Johnny, David and Ronit, Hannah, Noah, Benjamin, Elia, and Sasha. Jennifer Dawson, you are a writing genius and a great person. Thank you, Trena White and Transatlantic Agency and New World Library, especially editor Georgia Hughes and publicist Kim Corbin. Thanks to all my colleagues, teachers, and clients, Dr. Laurie Gillies, Dr. Jennifer Steadman, Dr. Leora Pinhas, and Dr. Myrna Weissman, who started it all. Last but not least, thank you, Ron Frey, especially for calling me "the boss."

From Ron Frey: As with "the boss," my foray into the world of interpersonal psychotherapy would not have been possible without Dr. Laurie Gillies, who gave me the opportunity to learn and practice interpersonal psychotherapy; or Cindy Stulberg, who was (and still is) so enthusiastic to share IPT with the world! Family and friends are really what make life worth living, and I am forever thankful to my parents; my sister (who had to tolerate her older brother); my wife, Sonia; and my two teens, Xavier and Claudelle, for being part of my journey. I would also like to thank some great champions of IPT, including Cicatelli Associates, Joanne Jones, Laura Leong, and Michela McConnell, who have helped us promote and share this model with a wide population. I would also like to express my gratitude to Irwin Altrows and Jack Adams Webber, both of whom, despite not being IPT therapists, have had a significant impact on my career as a psychologist. And finally, special thanks to Jennifer Dawson, an artist with words; of course our agent, Trena White; and the New World Library team.

Notes

Page 3, *Eighty percent of those who've had two episodes*: American Psychiatric Association, "What Is Depression?," accessed July 9, 2018, https://www.psychiatry.org/patients-families/depression/what-is-depression.

Page 130, *"It's comparable to the risk of smoking"*: Julianne Holt-Lunstad, Theodore F. Robles, and David A. Sbarra, "Advancing Social Connection as a Public Health Priority in the United States," *Close Family Relationships and Health*, special issue of *American Psychologist* 72, no. 6 (September 2017).

Page 185, *Buddhist monk Ajahn Brahm once said*: Anne Wisman, "Happiness, Expectations, and Learning to Be Losers: An Interview with Ajahn Brahm," *Buddhistdoor Global*, June 2, 2017, https://www.buddhistdoor.net/features/happiness-expectations-and-learning-to-be-losers-an-interview-with-ajahn-brahm.

Page 185, *Psychologist Dr. Albert Ellis has also linked*: Albert Ellis, quoted in Clifford Lazarus, "Three Expectations Typical of Unhappy People," *Psychology Today*, December 16, 2016, https://www.psychologytoday.com/ca/blog/think-well/201612/three-expectations-typical-unhappy-people.

Page 269, *According to researcher and TED Talk presenter Susan Pinker*: Susan Pinker, "The Secret to Living Longer May Be Your Social

Life," *TED* 2017, accessed July 9, 2018, https://www.ted.com
/talks/susan_pinker_the_secret_to_living_longer_may_be_your
_social_life/transcript?language=en.

Index

SMART goals (*continued*)
102–4; for complicated grief,
94–97; Guy Talk, 107–8; for
interpersonal conflict, 92–94; for
loneliness and isolation, 100–102;
setting, in action, 89–91; SMART
questions in, 91; specific, 89;
starting small, 105–6; to-do list,
108–9; for transitions, 97–99. *See
also* just do it
SMART questions in SMART
goals, 91
social-circle project: adding names
to, 25–27; completing for yourself, 37–38; death of a loved one,
33–35; drawing, 21–23; family
in, 30–32; Guy Talk, 38–39; new
awareness gained from, 36–37;
spouse in, 28–30; to-do list, 40
social media, 9, 23, 117, 118
surprise, 43, 45; expectations linked
to, 190; in Ten Questions to Ask
the Mirror, 118, 121, 123, 126; in
transition-focused conversation
starters, 140

Ten Questions for Emotional Enlightenment, 56–58, 63, 116, 151
transitions, 166–72; change in
coping with, 166–68; conversation starters for, 139–40;
exercise for (Reality Goggles),
168–72; interpersonal conflict
and, 71–75; as problem area,
71–75; questionnaire for, 73–74;
SMART goals for, 97–99. *See
also* change

unspecified depressive disorder, 3

venting, 112–13, 116, 126, 127

Weissman, Myrna, x
"whos": children as, 136–37; finding a new, 134–36; when your
"who" becomes a "who not,"
145; your, 131–34
World Health Organization, xi, 4
wrap-up questions, 250–51

About the Authors

Cindy Goodman Stulberg, DCS, CPsych, is a psychologist, teacher, wife, mother, mother-in-law, and grandmother. With Dr. Ronald Frey, Cindy cofounded the Institute for Interpersonal Psychotherapy, which trains, supervises, and certifies mental health clinicians in interpersonal psychotherapy. She trained with one of the early practitioners of interpersonal psychotherapy, Dr. Laurie Gillies, who was trained by Klerman and Weissman, in New York City and has successfully used the model to help hundreds of children, youths, and adults — including couples and families — deal with a broad range of psychological challenges. She helped develop a hospital-based eating-disorder therapy program that is now considered best practice in Ontario; was part of a New York City–based consultation to develop the go-to book on using IPT with groups; trained staff at the Child Mind Institute who transform the lives of children and families struggling with mental health; and helped conduct research comparing the efficacy of group IPT with that of cognitive behavioral therapy for adolescents. She lives in Ontario with her husband of forty-five years.

Ronald J. Frey, PhD, CPsych, is a former acting chief psychologist for the Royal Canadian Mounted Police and a registered forensic and clinical psychologist. In addition to teaching interpersonal psychotherapy, Ron conducts risk assessments for governmental and private industrial organizations and disability assessments for independent medical-examination purposes. Ron is a subject-matter expert for the Canadian Police College, family law courts, and Department of National Defence. He has been recognized by the Senate of Canada for his efforts in the prevention, assessment, and treatment of occupationally related stress injuries. He lives in Quebec with his spouse, Sonia; his two children; and a dog who thinks he is a cat and a cat who thinks he is a dog. What is up with the pets? It's complicated, and no, Cindy would never understand.

www.interpersonalpsychotherapy.com